Shareholder Cities

THE CITY IN THE TWENTY-FIRST CENTURY

Eugenie L. Birch and Susan M. Wachter, Series Editors

A complete list of books in the series is
available from the publisher.

Shareholder Cities

Land Transformations Along
Urban Corridors in India

Sai Balakrishnan

PENN

UNIVERSITY OF PENNSYLVANIA PRESS

PHILADELPHIA

Published by
University of Pennsylvania Press
Philadelphia, Pennsylvania 19104-4112
www.upenn.edu/pennpress

Printed in the United States of America on acid-free paper
1 3 5 7 9 10 8 6 4 2

A Cataloging-in-Publication record is available from the Library of Congress
ISBN 978-0-8122-5146-3

To my parents

CONTENTS

ABBREVIATIONS

Institutions

CAG	Comptroller and Auditor General
DC	district collector (Revenue Department)
HCC	Hindustan Construction Company
ITI	Industrial Training Institute
KEIPL	Khed Economic Infrastructure Private Limited
LCL	Lavasa Corporation Limited
MIDC	Maharashtra Industrial Development Corporation
MKVDC	Maharashtra Krishna Valley Development Corporation
MoEF	Ministry of Environment and Forests
MSRAC	Maharashtra Remote Sensing Applications Center
MSRDC	Maharashtra State Road Development Corporation
MTDCCL	Magarpatta Township Development and Construction Company Limited
NAPM	National Alliance for People's Movements
SDO	sub-divisional officer (Revenue Department)
WRD	Water Resources Department

Central Government Programs

LARRA	Right to Fair Compensation and Transparency in Land Acquisition, Rehabilitation and Resettlement Act
MGNREGS	Mahatma Gandhi National Rural Employment Guarantee Scheme
PMGSY	Pradhan Mantri Gram Sadak Yojana
RTI	Right to Information
ULCRA	Urban Land Ceiling and Regulation Act

Corridor Regions

In 2001, the newly liberalized Indian state[1] launched one of the most ambitious development programs the country has ever seen, comparable in scale only to the massive railway-building enterprises of colonial India: economic corridors. To fill in the "infrastructure gap," the Central Government started the construction of the Golden Quadrilateral highway-building program to connect the four major cities of Delhi, Mumbai, Chennai, and Kolkata. World Bank studies estimate that these upgraded highways will translate into significant annual savings, because faster travel times will translate into lower freight costs and economic gain. Some of these highways were also designated as economic corridors: a bundled spine of high-speed roads and internet, water, and power networks, along which will develop new globally competitive industrial nodes and "smart cities." The scale and accelerated pace of change along these new transportation networks have captivated the popular press. In a series of stunning photo essays, various journals have shown rural women covering their heads with their saris as they anachronistically make their way across an expressway that could easily be mistaken for a U.S. highway; bullocks calmly seated in the middle of roads designed for the fastest cars and heaviest trucks; and sacred cows, holy men riding elephants, and other religious travelers sharing the asphalted strip with speeding vehicles. Popular narratives interpret the changes along the new economic corridors as collisions between two Indias: the modern, urban, westernized India, and the primitive, rural, superstitious India.

These popular narratives recall older modernization tropes from the 1950s, created by development economists like Walt Whitman Rostow as part of their "take-off" theories. But, contrary to these urban/rural and traditional/modern binaries, a brief survey of some of India's most contentious land conflicts of the past decade reveals that the new economic corridors are not anachronistic but instead accrete on former agricultural modernization programs. Take, for instance, the land conflicts over the 160-kilometer Yamuna Expressway that connects the cities of Delhi and Agra. The "dream project" of the country's first female Dalit chief minister, Mayawati, the expressway sparked violent protests by farmers and clashes between farmers and the police, resulting in casualties on both sides. These "farmer" protestors belonged to the powerful agrarian constituency of the Jats, and public officials have since resolved the conflict by paying the aggrieved landowners an additional compensation of 64.7 percent.[2]

Likewise, the Bangalore-Mysore Infrastructure Corridor in the state of Karnataka in south India has been mired in opposition both on the streets and in the courtroom. This corridor is also known as the NICE corridor, named after the acronym of the concessionaire consortium, the Nandi Infrastructure Corridor Enterprises. During the height of the protests, protestors hung banners and posters around the unfinished corridor that dubbed it the "not so NICE corridor." Eventually this fracas entered popular culture, inspiring the making of regional movies like *Puttakkana Highway*, which follows the travails of Puttakka, a marginal agrarian landowner, after the state government coercively acquires her agricultural land for the building of a highway. But, crucially, the resistance to the Bangalore-Mysore Infrastructure Corridor received this level of publicity and political visibility primarily because it was led by a specific caste/class constituency of Vokkaliga agrarian landowners, who form the backbone of the region's electorate.[3]

As the South Asian scholarship on agrarian studies has shown, from the 1960s to the 1980s the Indian government launched the Green Revolution program with the aim of modernizing agriculture and food production. The state-subsidized provision of water, seeds, and fertilizers was captured by regional caste groups, and by the 1980s the Green Revolution had helped transform these agrarian propertied classes into one of the most formidable electoral constituencies. Some of the most publicized land conflicts of the past decade have been in these former Green Revolution regions, where the economic corridors are encountering organized agrarian propertied constituents who own the land now getting recommodified and reallocated for the corridors and corridor cities.

A locational lens, then, allows for a new reading of India's contemporary land conflicts. Once freed of the silos of urban studies and agrarian studies, which rarely converse with one another,[4] the economic corridors offer new empirical and analytical entryways into a political economy of land that cuts across the urban-rural divide. I argue that some of India's most decisive conflicts over its urban future will unfold along the new economic corridors, where the electorally strong, agrarian propertied classes are coming into direct contact with financially powerful urban firms. By moving the narrative of urbanization out of cities into the economic-corridor regions, new protagonists come into view. One that has hitherto been eclipsed in the analyses of urban real-estate markets is this agrarian propertied class. Much of the scholarship on urban real-estate markets, derived as it is from the experiences of western cities, focuses on the urban fractions of capital, such as developers and mortgage companies. How does the entry of agrarian elites into real estate force us to rethink conventional theories on urban property relations? More broadly, what new narratives of urbanization arise when older histories of agrarian capitalism and caste/class formation collide, collude, and recombine with the new economic corridors and corridor cities?

To answer these questions, I focus on the Mumbai-Pune Expressway, India's first economic corridor, which was completed in 2000. The region around the Mumbai-Pune Expressway is an ideal site for excavating the politics of land across the urban-rural divide, as it is home to three antagonistic groups: an indigenous, urban capitalist class that controls Mumbai; the agrarian propertied class of sugar elites, one of the strongest agrarian lobbies in the country; and Dalit and Adivasi groups who earlier worked on the lands of the agrarian elites but are now becoming more enfranchised with democratic reforms. Structured around three cases of diverse agrarian property regimes—fertile sugarcane fields, forest lands, and waste land—this book uses a natural experiment within the Mumbai-Pune corridor region to show how diverse agrarian property regimes, shaped by histories of colonial and postcolonial agrarian capitalism, are now intersecting with the urban governance structures of a liberalizing economy to produce new geographies of land commodification and uneven development.

Corridor Regions

India's new economic corridors are part of the wider "Make in India" campaign of the current Modi government. The Central Government has proposed five major industrial corridors: the Delhi-Mumbai Industrial Corridor, the Chennai-Bengaluru Industrial Corridor, the Bengaluru-Mumbai Economic Corridor, the Vizag-Chennai Industrial Corridor, and the Amritsar-Kolkata

Industrial Corridor. Alongside these corridors are planned "21 new nodal Industrial Cities," which will have such advantages as "large land parcels, planned communities, ICT [information and communications techology] enabled infrastructure, sustainable living, excellent connectivity by road, rail, etc." The economic-corridor policy took its inspiration from the Mumbai-Pune Expressway. In their intent, the new expressways—including the NICE Expressway that connects Bengaluru and Mysore, as well as the Yamuna Expressway between Delhi and Agra—fit the description of economic corridors; these are not just highway constructions but are envisioned as spines along which "new nodal Industrial Cities" will be built. The most publicized of these corridors, the Delhi-Mumbai Industrial Corridor, is advertised on the website as "a mega infra-structure project of USD 100 billion with financial and technical aids from Japan, covering an overall length of 1,483 km. . . . [The corridor] will intersect 7 states namely Delhi, Uttar Pradesh, Haryana, Rajasthan, Madhya Pradesh, Gujarat and Maharashtra."[5]

These new economic corridors resonate with a renewed interest in megaprojects around the world, with national and subnational governments pouring huge capital and resources into the building of high-speed rail networks, cross-national motorway systems, signature international airports, freight-container harbors, telecommunications networks, cross-border oil and gas pipelines, and energy networks. Variously called "splintering urbanism,"[6] "infrastructure space,"[7] and "logistics networks,"[8] these megaprojects are creating a new geography of post-1970s globalization that seamlessly connects certain valorized nodes within the global economy while simultaneously disconnecting others. The megaprojects create a new sense of capitalist space, in which distance is measured not in miles or kilometers but in minutes and seconds. Nation-states are giddily rushing to build these megaprojects because "power, wealth and status increasingly belong to those who know how to shrink space."[9] They embrace new technologies of governance through indicators like the World Bank's Logistics Performance Index, which ranks the trade competitiveness of different countries based on the quality of these megaprojects.[10]

However, the desire to "annihilate space by time"[11] is hardly new within capitalist societies. Recall, for instance, the critique by nationalist leaders in colonial India in the late nineteenth century that the railways served colonial capitalism and were a "pitiless drain [of India's wealth] to Europe."[12] By manipulating tariffs and selectively routing the railways, the colonial state simultaneously disconnected the cotton-growing hinterland from its physically adjacent domestic textile mills and connected it to the textile mills in physically distant Lancashire, via port cities like Bombay.[13] The current arguments of "splintering urbanism" find precursors in the colonial megaprojects that dramatically changed the economics and experience of distance.

The current infrastructure projects, emerging out of a global supply-chain revolution, open new fields of critical inquiry as the "site[s] of multiple, overlapping or nested forms of sovereignty, where domestic and transnational jurisdictions collide." They give rise to new forms of private authorities that are often enabled by, but displace, the nation-states as governance actors.[14] Even if not displacing India's nation-state, the new authorities that govern the Delhi-Mumbai Industrial Corridor lean much further toward the private side of the public-private spectrum than earlier, hybrid organizations. The Delhi-Mumbai Industrial Corridor Development Corporation is a newer-generation parastatal "whose main offices occupy a hotel suite rather than a government building."[15] The development corporation is governed by a CEO, an odd but growingly ubiquitous title for someone who manages not a firm but a public agency. The former CEO, Amitabh Kant, rose to fame with the successful entrepreneurial strategies of "Incredible India" and "God's own country—Kerala," which branded India and Kerala as tourist destinations. These branding strategies are part of the wider governance shift of the economic corridors, which aim to signal the nation's transformation from a red-tape bureaucracy to a business-friendly state that rolls out the "red carpet for investors."

The new economic corridors cast a spotlight on a vast new geography that, though not categorized as urban by the Indian census, nonetheless exhibits characteristics of the urban. The proliferation of census towns,[16] statutory towns, and other liminal categories that lie somewhere between the megacity and the village has been referred to as "subaltern urbanization"[17] and "unacknowledged urbanization."[18] Scholars have argued for the need to move away from metro-centricity[19] in order to grasp the scale and nature of urban growth in contemporary India. The development program of the economic corridors allows me to string these vast, seemingly fragmented urbanizing settlements into a new unit of analysis that I call "corridor regions."

A corridor region resembles what Terry McGee in the 1970s termed a *desakota*—a neologism that combined the Baha Indonesian words *desa* (city) and *kota* (village)—to make sense of the "transactive urban-rural environment around Java."[20] McGee was clear that the desakota was not a universal, invariant form of urbanization "in the Asian context." Instead, the desakota was actively produced by the "uneven incorporation of Asian countries" into a colonial economic system. McGee's formulation is a powerful reminder that "the existence of [prior] agroeconomic systems provides the possibility for the emergence of certain urban systems and regions."[21] Similarly, in this book I trace the evolving relationship between landed property and various forms of colonial/postcolonial and agrarian/urban capitalism by focusing on two moments of postcolonial development: the Green Revolution and the new economic corridors.

The transformation of land from a resource into property is inherently conflictual because of the various meanings attached to land.[22] Recent scholarship extends these contested debates on the public/private, resource/commodity attributes of land to various "new" resources—including the air,[23] oceans,[24] outer space[25]—all of which are being reframed as forms of private property. The commodification of agricultural land in contemporary India takes us back to an old debate about landed property but in the new context of a country that is attempting an experiment that few other countries have tried: introducing market relations in land in the context of an electoral democracy. The focus on land transformation in the corridor regions fundamentally concerns the changing role of landed property within different forms of earlier agrarian and now urban capitalism.

My main argument is as follows. In the former, state-controlled agrarian society, agricultural land was privately owned, but it was so tightly regulated by the state that real estate as a sector did not exist. During this period, a key determinant of the economic value of agricultural land was its fertility: the more fertile the land, the more food commodities it could produce and the higher the agricultural profits were for the landowner. Fertility, however, is not a natural attribute of land: it is sociotechnically produced by infrastructural networks. Because India achieved universal suffrage when it was still a predominantly agrarian society,[26] many agrarian landowners who had been part of the anticolonial nationalist struggle became powerful state-level politicians. In the federal structure of Indian democracy, "subjects," including land and water, were under the jurisdiction of state legislatures. The agrarian elites who controlled the state legislature helped shape a geography of uneven agrarian development through their control of the water infrastructure. In Maharashtra, for example, these political elites were of the regionally specific caste of Marathas, and the most influential Maratha elites in the 1960s, including the first chief minister of the state, Y. B. Chavan, came from western Maharashtra. In the early decades after Independence, and especially during the Green Revolution, political negotiations ensured that irrigation canals were routed through certain lands but not through others. The unevenly routed canals consolidated the power of the

Maratha elites by securing their control over well-irrigated and high-priced land. The lands bypassed by irrigation were relegated to marginalized groups; as a result, the Adivasis in western Maharashtra are disproportionately concentrated on uncultivable waste land. If one wanted to map social power within the Maharashtra state, one could effectively do so by mapping the routing of irrigation canals to see whose lands they passed through and whose got left out.

Now, with liberalization reforms, agricultural lands that were earlier the least fungible commodities in the economy are being transformed into transnational real-estate assets. Location now trumps fertility as the main calibrator of land price. And as land markets in the corridor region are recalibrated, plots of land that were undesirable and unproductive in an agrarian economy are now becoming coveted market assets, provided they are located near the economic corridors. The surprise finding in western Maharashtra is that certain advantageously located waste lands in the corridor region are now fetching a higher market price than even the most well-irrigated but disadvantageously located sugarcane fields. The re-valuation of former waste land is unsettling historically produced, land-based forms of social control, with some Adivasi households now finding themselves owners of a commodity that is more desirable than even the most thoroughly irrigated Maratha-owned land.

How does this conflicted process of postliberalization land commodification in contemporary India speak to general theories on land markets? How do agrarian propertied classes fit within theories of urban real estate? How do general theories of urbanization, largely if not exclusively derived from the experiences of western cities, explain the linkages between agricultural and urban land markets? And how adequate are these urban theories for making sense of India's twenty-first-century corridor regions? I will now introduce the three-pronged analytic of caste/class/space as a key device in understanding the agrarian-urban entanglements in the corridor regions, and I will situate India's contemporary land commodification within three dominant schools of thought: the economic view of location theory, the various strands within Marxist thought, and the Polanyian school.

Economic Views: Waste Land as Frontier

The field of economic geography has long pondered the questions of why cities look the way they do and how land markets shape the structure of cities. An early canonical work in economic geography comes from a nineteenth-century Prussian farmer, Johann Heinrich von Thünen.[27] Both von Thünen and later land economists were intrigued by the influence of the "invisible hand" of the market in structuring land use. Von Thünen noted that, even though the farmers in Prussia did not know one another and there was no coordinating planning agency that regulated land use, the farmers arranged themselves around market towns in a pattern that was strikingly similar not just across Prussia but across all the industrializing societies of the West (which formed the sole empirical basis for his work). Von Thünen eventually systematized his observations into a mathematical model that predicted the spatial ordering of land use. This was before the time of refrigeration, when it was imperative for farmers of intensive agriculture (dairy, orchards, market gardens) to transport their commodities to the marketplace as soon as possible. These farmers were sensitive to distance, and they would bid vast sums for the land closest to the central marketplace. Farmers growing less perishable commodities were outbid by the intensive agriculturalists, with the result that agricultural land use sorts itself out in space in a pattern of concentric circles: closest to the market town is the zone of intensive agriculture; then comes the zone of extensive agriculture (wheat); then the zone of livestock raising; then the zone of trapping, hunting, and Indian trading; and beyond that "wilderness." The von Thünen model laid the foundations for the field of economic geography, establishing that, in market economies, land is allocated through the price mechanism; that the price of land is linked to transportation costs; that the combination of transportation and land price shapes the urban-rural edge; and that any changes to transportation networks will alter urban land markets and their linkages to the countryside.

Some of the most influential models in urban economics borrow from von Thünen's concentric rings. These include Homer Hoyt's famous study of one hundred years of land prices in Chicago, from 1830 to 1933, which showed how transportation technologies—the canals, railways, and highways—reordered land prices, land uses and city form;[28] and William Alonso's influential bid-rent theory, which continues to be used today to predict the shape and price of urban housing markets.[29] More recently, Paul Krugman's Nobel Prize–winning work on the "new economic geography" integrates these location theories with new trade theory to predict how and where cities are formed and the links between food-producing hinterlands and manufacturing-based cities.[30]

Economists often view urbanization as a "set of exchange relations," an attitude for which they have received numerous criticisms.[31] What I want to focus on in this book is the property-rights assumptions of these models. Alonso's bid-rent theory assumes that "consumers" (i.e., those who have the market power) bid for land and sort themselves out in urban space. Krugman's model assumes that farmers grow food and that manufacturers produce goods, and that farmers and manufacturers smoothly arrange themselves in space. Conflict between farmers and manufacturers over the same plots of land, not for agriculture or industry but for real-estate development, as in the case of contemporary India, finds no place in Krugman's model. Writing at the time of the 1848 revolutions, von Thünen himself was deeply aware of the property assumption underpinning his model, and he stressed that his theory represented "the owning classes."[32] He wrote that any class conflict could be resolved by bringing into the market the "free land" at the "frontier of the cultivated plain."[33] In Europe, with its landed gentry, the assumption of the "isolated state" (the title of his book) became necessary to allow for a smooth frontier expansion. North America served as the ideal site for von Thünen's model, because a frontier or wilderness "of unmeasured vastness" existed where land could be appropriated, often through the exercise of force, for little or no market price.[34] Now, of course, revisionist histories show us that what von Thünen saw as "wilderness" in North America was actually Native American property, and that the expansion of the market into the American frontier, via transportation networks like the transcontinental railways, was possible only through a violent erasure of existing property regimes.[35]

In the parlance of economic geography, India's agricultural land represents the new frontier: until recently, these lands had no market price; they were "outside" the market (a claim that I contest in the Polanyian view below). In this view, the expansion of the economic corridors is bringing these residual lands into the market. But, unlike the colonial conquests of the past, the introduction of market relations for land in contemporary India is taking place in a context where the peasantry, including the marginalized Adivasis, have the power of the vote; the information explosion has substantially increased the awareness of the peasantry on the market price of their land; and social movements are demanding that the state protect the rights of the peasantry and enact strong constitutional barriers against expropriation carried out with the flimsy justifications of the "public purpose." In this context, the market expansion into the frontier cannot be reduced to a neutral "distance coefficient" in an economic model; on the contrary, it is shaped by vigorous contestations on the ground, as enfranchised groups bring their own aspirations of what it means to be global and urban to the changing meanings of land.

Marxist Views: Waste Land as Rent Gap

What the economists called the frontier, Marxist geographers reframed as the rent gap. In his influential rent-gap theory, the Marxist geographer Neil Smith developed the concept by picking up on an "oddity" in Homer Hoyt's otherwise smooth rent-gradient map for Chicago: the "valley in the land-value curve between the Loop and outer residential areas . . . that indicates the location of those sections where the buildings were mostly over forty years old and where the residents rank lowest in rent-paying ability."[36] Paying attention to the "valleys" that economists had previously smoothed out in their models, Smith built his theory of the rent gap, which he defined as the difference between capitalized ground rent and potential ground rent, the former being the price of land given its present use, the latter being the predicted price of the land when it is developed to its "highest and best use." Such rent gaps exist because certain regions are devalued vis-à-vis others, an essential process for capitalism, as it allows for the "seesaw theory" of capital: whenever capitalism confronts a crisis of falling profits, it resolves this crisis through a movement from a developed to an underdeveloped region, itself often produced by the planned lack of capital investment in that region in a prior phase of development.

Smith's rent-gap theory became influential in explaining the process of gentrification in western cities from the 1980s onward, when capital started moving back into inner cities that had been abandoned in the postwar years. The redevelopment of inner-city lands led to rising rents and displacement, and the rent-gap theory became a rallying cry for Marxists to challenge the housing crisis. Whether they are the open frontier of the American West or the low-income neighborhoods between the Loop and the outer residential areas in Chicago, Smith's work was seminal in pointing out that these rent-gap regions do not exist on a frontier outside the capitalist economy but are instead actively devalued regions within the system, an intrinsic part of the locational seesawing logic of capitalism.[37]

Theorizing from a different place, the large-scale land-use changes in the global south are commonly referred to as the "new enclosures" or the "global land grab."[38] National governments, international donor agencies, and investors deploy the narrative of the "yield gap" to justify the conversion of "so-called 'marginal, empty, and available' lands across the globe" into large-scale, mechanized agricultural production.[39] As with the rent gap, the land grab narrative is mobilized by environmental and agrarian justice activists to challenge transnational and often speculative land transactions.

If we apply the rent-gap theory to India's corridor regions, the waste lands owned and occupied by the Adivasis are the regions with the highest potential for the rent gap: colonial and postcolonial land policies actively devalued these lands, and they now hold out the market promise of windfall profits. But, unlike the clear-cut class conflict in Smith's antigentrification struggles or in the land grab struggles, in which the owners and occupiers of formerly devalued land resisted en masse the incursions of financial capitalists seeking to realize the rent gap by dispossessing the existing land users, the outcomes in contemporary India have been mixed.[40] Under certain conditions, Adivasi owners of waste land support the re-valuation of their land in order to assert their autonomy from the oppressive caste hierarchies of Maratha landowners.

Since agrarian classes are at the forefront of protests in India's corridor regions, and since it is agrarian land-use categories that are being mobilized for urban change, we need to bring in the South Asian agrarian studies scholarship to understand the distinct variety of agrarian capitalism in India, produced by the inextricable intersections of caste and class.[41] In the early decades post-Independence, the Nehruvian state implemented its first phase of land reforms, which aimed at abolishing the Brahmin *zamindars*, the non-cultivating propertied classes that mediated revenue relations between the colonial state and the peasants. The main beneficiaries of these land reforms were the Sudras, who occupy the lowest rung in India's caste hierarchy (the "upper castes" being Brahmins, Kshatriyas, and Vaishyas). The later Green Revolution further consolidated these beneficiaries into a surplus-producing agrarian propertied class. The rise of the Sudras, or the "backward classes," as they are categorized in the Indian Census,[42] into a formidable electoral constituency by the late 1970s has been heralded as the "second democratic upsurge."[43] If the first democratic upsurge was universal adult franchise in 1947, when upper-caste elites still retained power in national politics, the 1977 elections were a decisive watershed for the second democratic upsurge: the backward-class legislators won more than 10 percent of the Parliamentary seats, and their share in Parliament has increased since then. The Sudra *varna* (or caste) itself is made up of a large number of subcastes called *jatis*, and certain jatis have now emerged as "dominant castes," meaning castes that have a higher ritual status in the sacralized hierarchy than either the Dalits or the Adivasis, and that "wield preponderant economic and political power" in the countryside.[44]

The Marathas are the dominant caste in Maharashtra. In the first half of the twentieth century, alongside the anticolonial struggles, they were part of a vigorous anticaste movement that challenged the ritual superiority of the "upper" castes. The Marathas share kinship networks with another Sudra jati, the Kunbis. The Maratha-Kunbi caste bloc became consolidated into a numerically strong electoral constituency by the 1960s. This constituency is economically stratified, ranging from wealthy Maratha elites to poor Kunbi landless laborers. It sends the largest number of elected representatives to the state legislature and is concentrated in the western region of the state.[45]

The Green Revolution is a key development program that facilitated the transformation of certain backward classes, such as the Marathas, into dominant castes. Unlike the Nehruvian state, which sought to balance economic growth across the national space, the Green Revolution program—piloted in 1961 and implemented in two phases, from 1965 to the early 1980s—was driven by the rationale of "picking out the best and most favorable spots" for intensive agricultural development.[46] Irrigation water became a crucial precondition for the selection of the "intensive agricultural areas."[47] The Green Revolution subsidies of high-yielding seeds, fertilizers, and water were concentrated in areas "where supplies of assured water created 'fair prospects of achieving rapid increases in production.'"[48] In Maharashtra, the Marathas who controlled the state legislature had the political power to draw irrigation waters to their constituencies; the Maratha-Kunbis further benefited by capturing the seed, fertilizer, and water subsidies under the Green Revolution program.

In the wake of the Green Revolution, in an intense "mode of production" debate, scholars tried to categorize surplus producers like the Maratha-Kunbis in relation to peasant categories derived from the west.[49] An elite sliver of Marathas are wealthy; they are capitalist farmers and fit the descriptors of an agrarian bourgeoisie. The vast majority of the Maratha-Kunbis, however, do not fit this category. In western Maharashtra, most sugarcane growers had control over their means of production—that is, they had secure access to land in the form of private-property rights. But these cash-crop growers were not large landowners, and their landholding size on average was less than 2.5 acres, which in the Indian Census classifies them as marginal farmers. Nevertheless, their marginal plots of land were irrigated: though they did not control the routing and flow of the irrigation canals, their shared caste affinity to the Maratha agrarian elites, who controlled the state-level irrigation department, ensured that they had access to the flow of water and other state subsidies. These marginal farmers also depart from typical "bourgeois" descriptors by not hiring wage labor and thus not controlling labor power. Lloyd and Susanne Rudolph have called these dominant-caste marginal farmers the "bullock capitalists," "cultivators who rely more on family labor and their own human capital than on wage labor and machines."[50] K. Balagopal calls them the "provincial propertied class," sections of the peasantry that align with the rural rich, "aided by the fact that caste usually functions as a common link between the two classes, though there are plenty of conflicts between them."[51] Further complicating the issue are the landless within this constituency, with localized concentrations in the eastern regions of Marathwada and Vidarbha in Maharashtra, where almost 20 percent of the populations are landless Kunbis.

The dominant castes, then, include agrarian elites, the middle peasantry, and the landless. Especially influential in the corridor regions are the "middle peasants," who have "secure access to land and cultivate it with family labor"[52] but who are also able to gain access to state subsidies by capitalizing on their caste privileges. Even though they are marginal landowners, they remain a formidable political voice in the corridor regions by virtue of their caste- and land-based sources of agrarian power. These caste identities make for unexpected alliances that often go against class interests. The Maratha agrarian elites should be in class alliances with the urban industrialists who control Mumbai; the poor Kunbis should align with poor Adivasis. Instead, caste identities divide otherwise aligned class interests and bond otherwise antagonistic class interests. Region here completes the caste/class/space triumvirate, because the dominant-caste bloc was shaped by colonial agrarian land-revenue systems and industrial histories. In northern India, the Sudras experienced harsher caste discrimination, making their rise to national politics momentous for plebeian politics, but in southern India the Sudras had already started consolidating into provincial propertied classes long before the 1970s.

Much of the critical South Asian scholarship is situated within the field of agrarian studies and was written during the peak Green Revolution years. Even more recent work, like Sharad Chari's, analyzes agrarian-industrial linkages in the 1990s, meaning before the liberalization reforms had taken effect in land markets. In his monograph *Fraternal Capital,* Chari describes how the Gounders (of peasant origins in Tamil Nadu) became industrial capitalists in a globally competitive knitwear cluster by the 1980s. Chari refers to the transformation as an instance of "subalterns accumulating capital."[53] But this class positioning of the Gounders is debatable. As a regionally specific Sudra jati, the Gounders were formerly subordinate cultivators who gained economic and social power through the land reforms and the Green Revolution. They enjoyed a ritual status higher than that of the Dalits or Adivasis, and, as Chari himself persuasively shows, they were able to draw on their caste identity both to access state subsidies and to perpetuate exclusionary labor arrangements that exploited Dalits. Though Chari's analysis draws attention to agrarian-industrial linkages, it is still from a period preceding the liberalization of agricultural land markets.

My analysis of the corridor regions asks what is happening to these agrarian propertied castes/classes in the current era of postliberalization land commodification. What are the changes in the land-based sources of agrarian power of the dominant castes, in a context where the price of land increases at a faster rate than either agricultural or industrial profits? The corridor regions are the sites of a new agrarian-urban electoral geography, as the carefully constructed caste/class constituency of a state-controlled agrarian society now unravels in the midst of market and urban shifts.

The new flow of private capital into formerly protected agricultural land is producing new collisions and collusions among agrarian and industrial elites, who are now contesting for the same plots of land. The land-based power of the middle peasantry is being disrupted both by the entry of urban firms into agricultural land markets and by the empowerment of disadvantaged castes, whose formerly unproductive waste lands are now being re-valued in a liberalizing and urbanizing economy. I specifically draw attention to the unexpected finding of the revaluation of waste lands near economic corridors, asking how this incidental phenomenon might crack open possibilities for a new emancipatory politics for Adivasis. As the South Asian scholarship makes clear, class is an inadequate category for analyzing social relations in India; class relations cannot be understood without refracting them through the lens of caste. And these caste/class relations are unevenly produced through space.[54] By focusing on the same economic corridor as it passes through three varied agrarian propertied regimes within the state of Maharashtra, I demonstrate that the analytic of caste/class/space is central to examining the corridor region.

Polanyian Views: Waste Land and the Double Movement

The creation of new economic corridors and corridor cities in former Green Revolution regions raises a question about the sequencing of development. Land commodification is an old debate, but the Indian case is a unique experiment because the market reforms in land are being introduced in the context of a functioning electoral democracy. Scholars have addressed this democratic-market question in a number of ways. Ashutosh Varshney, for instance, distinguishes between elite and mass reforms and argues that the Central Government selectively initiated liberalization reforms, opening up "elite" sectors to the market but leaving untouched "mass" sectors that are bound to affect the plebeian electorate.[55] In a similar vein, Rob Jenkins argues that the economic reforms have been strategically and selectively implemented. He points to the Special Economic Zone (SEZ) policy as a practical response to the public outcry against the wave of liberalization in a democratic society. In this context, policy-makers capitulated to public opposition to liberalization not by reducing the scope of the economic reforms but by shrinking the extent of the territory to which the new reforms will apply. When the full range of market- and urban-oriented reforms are applied to a "patchwork of tiny hyper-liberalized jurisdictions dotting the country," political resistance to these policies will be fragmented and less effective.[56] Partha Chatterjee points to the paradox that, precisely when the state introduced liberalization reforms that allowed "hegemonic corporate capital" entry into land and labor markets, there was also an explosion of social welfare programs aiming to provide the poor with basic safety nets. The conditions of an electoral democracy, he argues, make it unacceptable to leave marginalized groups to fend for themselves, partly because of the threat of political instability if the displaced groups turn into "dangerous classes." The social welfare programs are thus attempts by the state to reverse the effects of primitive accumulation.[57]

Zooming in on the liberalization of land markets, recent books such as *Liberalization, Hindu Nationalism and the State* by Nikita Sud and *The Price of Land* by Sanjoy Chakravorty trace a shift in land policy from earlier state-oriented regimes of land governance that balanced growth and welfare to deregulated regimes that prioritize growth over welfare.[58] Chakravorty's work is particularly relevant because he identifies pricing as the critical issue in the ongoing land conflicts. He distinguishes between conflicts over "the right price of land" and those over "priceless" land; for the latter, he cites as examples the temples of Khajuraho and other historical buildings that have no substitute and are irreplaceable.[59] But Chakravorty does not get into the thorny question of who decides which lands have a market price and which are priceless. The difficulty in answering this question has plagued many fields. The relatively new design field of critical conservation seeks to go beyond a mere acceptance of certain buildings as representing of an architectural heritage and instead to ask whose history is being preserved and, in turn, whose future is being made. The scholarship on legal pluralism is deeply attentive to both economic and noneconomic claims on land, and how the contesting claims on land drawn from history, religion, de facto use, notions of fairness, and other rationales can be resolved, by whom, and through what procedures.[60] Similar questions confront the efforts to urbanize and liberalize India: which categories and geographies of land—irrigated land that produces food, grazing and common land, waste land—should be opened to market relations and which should be protected, keeping in mind that these land categories are not immutable and have themselves been socially produced by earlier development policies? As importantly, who decides?

To answer this question, it is instructive to turn to the political economist Karl Polanyi's insights from *The Great Transformation*, first published in 1944.[61] Land, Polanyi argues, is a fictitious commodity, in that it is not an object that was originally produced for sale on the market. Polanyi challenges the economic fallacy of a self-regulating land market—the assumptions that a land market can spontaneously regulate itself through adjusting to the demand-and-supply logic of the price mechanism and that land markets can be disembedded from politics, religion, and social norms; he describes this fallacy as a "stark utopia."[62] Land can never be reduced to a mere commodity because, as the negative consequences of an unrestrained, commoditized land market become apparent, people resist: "they refuse to act like lemmings marching over a cliff to their own destruction."[63] This is what Polanyi famously calls the "double movement": efforts to commodify land being met by countermovements to slow down the rate of change and/or protect certain lands from the incursions of the market.

If the Polanyian concept of the double movement is transposed to India, the liberalization reforms represent the market movement. But, unlike the enclosure movements of the sixteenth to nineteenth centuries that Polanyi was writing about, India's contemporary land-use change is not a first-time transformation of a resource into a commodity. It is well documented that India's land markets were commodified under colonization.[64] In postcolonial India, the imperatives of the Green Revolution—to increase food production—required that the fungibility of agricultural land be restricted. The state introduced various land laws (such as the land-ceiling acts) to disincentivize the conversion of agriculturally productive land into real estate. It was the crops grown on these lands, rather than the land itself, that were traded by a state-mediated process of price setting. The status of this land as outside the market, then, was produced by postcolonial development policies. The protected land under agrarian capitalism was as fictitious as the postliberalization attempt to create a transnational real-estate market. The making of a new fictitious commodity in land is now being contested in myriad ways, not least by agrarian propertied classes who consolidated power under the earlier phase of agrarian capitalism with their protected lands. Even the most marginalized Adivasi groups, far from being lemmings, have the power to vote and some agency in resisting unrestrained market change. The contestation over the making of a new fictitious commodity in land is being fought both on the streets and in Parliament, over the enactment of India's new land-acquisition law, the Right to Fair Compensation and Transparency in Land Acquisition, Rehabilitation and Resettlement Act (LARRA).[65]

In Polanyian terms, the market movement is being resisted by countermovements, but, departing from deterministic class-based analyses, the reactions to postliberalization land commodification vary among members of the same class. Take the instance of the Maratha-Kunbi landowners in western Maharashtra. In one region, the Maratha-Kunbi middle peasantry applied pressure on bureaucrats to protect their fertile agricultural land from acquisition; these protective countermovements have now found their way into the LARRA, which mandates that, as far as possible, the state should use only waste land for urban expansion. But in an adjacent agrarian region, the same category of the Maratha-Kunbi middle peasantry voluntarily converted their fertile agricultural lands into an urban township, choosing both to transform their protected agricultural land into real estate and to transform their stakes in land from those of agricultural landowners to those of real-estate shareholders.

The Adivasi responses to the postliberalization land commodification are most unexpected. Adivasi property regimes vary across India. In many parts of the country, Adivasis or tribals have collective ownership of their land. In regions like western Maharashtra, Adivasis have private-property rights, but only over marginal one- to two-acre plots of waste land that were economically worthless in an agrarian society. As advantageously located waste lands are re-valued into desirable market assets, Adivasi landowners are leveraging this moment of change to gain new recognition for themselves. Using their control over a high-demand market asset as a negotiating chip, Adivasis in certain regions in western Maharashtra are now demanding entitlements like water, which they should have had access to as a basic public service but which was denied to them out of caste discrimination. They are also refusing to work on the lands of the dominant castes unless they receive higher wages. These advantageously located Adivasi landowners are willing, even eager, to enter the emergent real-estate market.

It is not only the re-valuation of waste land and their new market power as landowners that increase the Adivasis' negotiating power. Further amplifying their voice are other democratic fixes, including the "reserved seats" policy for Schedule Tribes in local governments and the Mahatma Gandhi National Rural Employment Guarantee Scheme (MGNREGS), which guarantees all rural residents one hundred days of employment annually at minimum wage for the building of rural public works. The younger-generation male Adivasis in one of the book's case-study regions, Khed, are using these new changes to break away from their dependency on dominant-caste landowners and to assert a new caste/class identity of autonomy and dignity. Yet these celebratory experiences of postliberalization land commodification are also uneven: in the property regime adjacent to Khed, changes to land markets have led to widespread Adivasi displacement.

Contrary, then, to the sanguine predictions of neoclassical economic models and to the Marxist logic of dispossession, the reaction to postliberalization land commodification in India has been uneven and unpredictable, often with members of the same social class responding differently to land-use change. Polanyi anticipated that we cannot predict the class basis of the double movement. We cannot assume that the countermovement will be led only by the working class or the non-propertied constituents; periods of economic downturns have shown how the capitalist fractions insist on state protection to shield them from the uncertainties of the market.[66] Unaddressed by Polanyi is the real-estate desire by groups that depend on their land for subsistence needs and that stand to lose the most from these market deals. To unpack the regional variations of specifically located caste/class constituents of postliberalization land commodification, we need to view India's ongoing land conflicts not as conflicts over either market or nonmarket relations in land. Instead, the core of the conflict lies in the complex negotiations about which lands to expose to new market relations and which to protect, and in the balance of class powers at the negotiating table when these decisions are made. The corridor regions resemble what Timothy Mitchell calls the frontier, which he defines not as a "thin line" that separates market from nonmarket relations, but as "a scene of political battles" in capitalist societies, where various groups struggle and clash over the inclusion and exclusion of land in market relations.[67]

Democratic-Market Encounters

The political contestation in India over the making of a new fictitious commodity in land is situated within the context of the 1991–93 institutional reforms. In 1991–93, the Central Government introduced two simultaneous sets of reforms: economic liberalization and decentralization. These reforms produced a wave of new market relations in an otherwise tightly regulated, state-led economy. Market advocates argued that the slow pace at which public decisions are made in India resembled a system with the engine of a bullock cart and the brakes of a Rolls Royce.[68] In the 1990s, the Central and state governments repealed agrarian-era land laws, such as the land-ceiling acts, which prevented private landowners from consolidating large tracts of land. New laws in 2002 further eased the entry of private capital into agricultural land markets by allowing foreign investment in real estate. In her work on the creation of transnational real-estate markets in Gurgaon, Llerena Searle highlights the fact that global capital does not simply enter a new land market.[69] Instead, she shows the work involved in the making of new transnational real-estate markets in India: the "booster" stories that persuade investors to buy land in anticipation of future returns; the painstaking standardization of valuing, building, accounting, and marketing that helps to integrate local land markets into a globally legible financial asset; and the emergence of new intermediaries (in this case, real-estate developers) that connect interlinked markets and liaise between foreign investors and local builders.

These market reforms have driven the enactment of new urban laws—such as the Integrated Township Policy, the Hill Station Regulation, and the SEZ Act—which ease the entry of firms not only into agricultural land markets but also into the governance of the new corridor cities. The laws authorize the formation of new governance structures, in which corporate firms take over traditional local-government functions, including zoning and basic-service provision. In effect, they create local private authorities for the governance of the new corridor cities.

If the 1991 liberalization reforms represent the market movement, certain sections of the 1992–93 democratic decentralization reforms represent the Polanyian countermovement. Before these reforms, the federal nature of the Indian democratic system designated land in India as a state subject, meaning that land laws were under the jurisdictional control of state governments, not the Central Government. Because the state governments controlled the implementation of land reforms and land-use policies, different agrarian regions produced specific configurations of agrarian propertied classes. Local governments, meanwhile, remained largely neglected institutions. It was only with the decentralization reforms that new life was injected into local government politics. The 73rd Constitutional Amendment, enacted in 1993, envisioned the Gram Panchayats (rural local governments) as key sites of democratic decision making. The reforms constitutionally mandated regular local-government elections. They introduced a quota system mandating that 33 percent of local-government representatives should be women and members of underrepresented castes and religions. In the words of Patrick Heller, these reforms introduced "232,278 voter-accountable institutions where none existed before [and created] a whole new political class of 3,000,000 elected representatives [that] in principle included 1/3 of seats set aside for women and proportional representation of SC/STs [scheduled caste/scheduled tribes]."[70] Most important for this book, the reforms created a new democratic institution in the form of the Gram Sabha—a public assembly open to every citizen in a particular Panchayat.

The decentralization reforms envisioned the Gram Sabhas as necessary institutions that conferred power directly to the citizens. They deemed the Gram Panchayat, with its elected representatives, as the executive branch of the local government, and the Gram Sabhas as the village "legislature."[71] The reforms mandated that Gram Sabhas be held at least twice a year and that all eligible voters of the village be allowed to participate in these public assemblies. The Gram Sabhas have the power to "discuss and review all development problems and programs of the village, select beneficiaries for the beneficiary-oriented programs, and plan for the development of the village economy."[72] If, for instance, the Central Government allocates grants for a specific social-welfare program to the Gram Panchayat, the Gram Sabha assemblies can ensure transparency in the selection of beneficiaries and the allocation of funds. As an aspirational ideal, the Gram Sabhas ensure an economic democracy in which all citizens can make their voices heard on the types of development and jobs they want for their villages.

The twin institutional reforms of liberalization and decentralization are fundamentally changing the nature of land and property relations in two interrelated ways: they are changing the role of land within different forms of capitalism (then agrarian, now urban), and they are changing the relationship of the state to land. Formerly, the economic value of agricultural land in a state-controlled agrarian society derived not from the price of the land but from the price of the crops grown on the land. Before liberalization, there was no real-estate market in the way it is understood in the west. Now, as the liberalization reforms remake agricultural land into a more fungible commodity, both agrarian and urban fractions of capital compete to stake their claims on the profits from the emergent real-estate markets. At the same time, the dirigiste state formerly expropriated land for developmental projects and paid landowners a compensation price set by government diktat, with nothing at all for land occupiers; the Central and state governments retained a monopoly over locational and land-use decisions. Now, the decentralization reforms have reterritorialized the state. When the Central or state government wants to create a new urban jurisdiction (e.g., a corridor city), they must contend with empowered Gram Panchayats and the newly instituted Gram Sabhas. What we see here is a restructuring of the local state, earlier absent from any locational or land-use decisions but now a key site of conflict over postliberalization land commodification. The local state itself is getting transformed, mirroring the wider institutional democratic-market tensions, with development companies and Gram Sabhas jostling with one another to make the new rules for governing the corridor cities.

The normative concern of this book is how to keep these processes of postliberalization land-use change and land commodification contestable and open to the public.[73] The Gram Sabhas are an important new local institution that can ensure the inclusion of previously excluded groups in these processes. But, despite the decentralization mandate that Gram Sabhas be empowered as sites of local democracy in action, the agrarian propertied classes—which were themselves shaped by the uneven flows of resources and subsidies under earlier agricultural modernization programs—exert substantial influence on how the Gram Sabhas are mobilized.

The geographical focus of this book is the Mumbai-Pune corridor region. In Chapter 1, I examine the successive eras of infrastructural development, situated within the dominant development paradigms of their times—the colonial-era railways, the irrigation canals of the postcolonial developmental state, and the postliberalization economic corridors—all of which produced distinct geographies of uneven development. One original contribution of this chapter is its mapping of the land prices of 242 villages from 1996 to 2016—from the year when the expressway was announced to almost fifteen years after its completion. Some of these 242 villages are located very near the Mumbai-Pune Expressway; others are more distant from the expressway but received the largest number of irrigation canals in the 1960s and 1970s. Mapping the changing land prices in this corridor region illustrates how the economic value of agricultural land, which earlier derived from its proximity to irrigation canals, is now being recalibrated based on the land's proximity to the new economic corridors. This chapter sets the stage for the following three chapters, which track how specific agrarian pasts shape the urbanizing present.

The Mumbai-Pune corridor region contains spectacularly diverse property regimes. The most agriculturally developed region in Maharashtra is the sugarcane region. At the turn of the twentieth century, this region was an agro-ecological scarcity zone. A dense concentration of irrigation canals has since transformed it into one of the most agriculturally productive regions of the country. India is the second largest exporter of cane sugar after Brazil, and more than 40 percent of India's sugar comes from cooperatives in this region. Magarpatta City is built on former sugarcane fields, and it represents a case of agrarian privileges reproduced in an urbanizing context. Along the western coastline of the state of Maharashtra lies an ecologically sensitive mountain range, the Western Ghats. A densely forested area and one of the four major watersheds of the country, the Western Ghats are second only to the Himalayas as a "hotspot of biodiversity."[74] Ironically, these forests, which are home to major rivers and the largest density of dams in the country, also contain vast tracts of agriculturally unproductive waste lands. The Western Ghats represent the excluded zones of an uneven agrarian past: these dammed hinterlands were devalued in the process of developing the sugarcane region. Now, Lavasa Lake City is being built on these forest lands.

In between these developed and underdeveloped regions are mixed landscapes with undulating terrain and patchy areas of irrigation canals. At the intersection of the lower slopes of the Western Ghats and the plains is the Khed taluka. The routing of the canals in Khed follows topographical features: the canals traverse the plains but bypass the hillocks that intersperse the plains. Khed City is an SEZ development in this mixed region. In each of these three interlinked but differentiated agrarian regions, the precise configuration of agrarian land-based social relations influences how the twin laws of liberalization and decentralization are enacted on the ground. Map 1 shows the western Maharashtra region and the corridor cities located within each of the three property regimes.

Chapter 2, "From Sugar to Real Estate," analyzes the case of a 600-acre township—Magarpatta City—within the former agriculturally developed region of well-irrigated sugarcane fields. At this location, a group of sugarcane landowners voluntarily pooled their agricultural land and formed a real-estate company wholly owned by erstwhile landowners, who hold shares in proportion to the acreage of land they gave up for the new township. I argue that Magarpatta City represents a wider movement among the sugar elites from an agrarian to an urban economy. In the former, state-controlled agrarian society, the Maratha elites consolidated power over the countryside through their control of irrigation canals and sugar-rich land. Now, with the restructuring of land markets, the agrarian promoters of the new corridor city are mobilizing the same political linkages to generate urban profits; just as the sugar elites shared the profits of the sugar cooperatives with the Maratha-Kunbi sugarcane growers who were members of the cooperatives, they are now sharing the profits of land redevelopment by including the former sugarcane growers as shareholders of the new company. Left out of both the cooperatives and the new companies are the landless laborers who used to work on the sugarcane fields. In other words, the propertied bias of the agrarian era is being reproduced in the urbanizing and liberalizing era. Moreover, since existing agrarian networks were mobilized for the new land commodification, a Gram Sabha was never formed in this region. Had one been formed, the nonpropertied agrarian groups could have exercised their voice, but the agrarian elites were too entrenched, and they succeeded in excluding the laborers' voices and in reproducing agrarian privileges and exclusions in the new corridor city.

Chapter 3, "From Forests to IPO," focuses on Lavasa Lake City, located in the formerly underdeveloped regions of the Western Ghats. The lake city is the

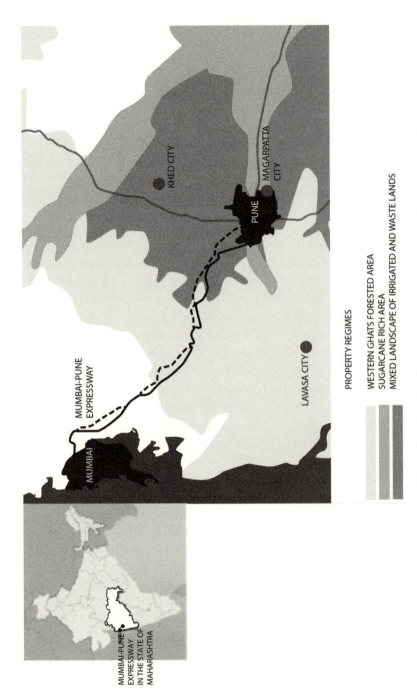

Map 1. The Mumbai-Pune corridor region, showing diverse property regimes and the three case-study locations.

PROPERTY REGIMES

WESTERN GHATS FORESTED AREA
SUGARCANE RICH AREA
MIXED LANDSCAPE OF IRRIGATED AND WASTE LANDS

MUMBAI-PUNE EXPRESSWAY

MUMBAI

KHED CITY

PUNE

MAGARPATTA CITY

LAVASA CITY

MUMBAI-PUNE EXPRESSWAY IN THE STATE OF MAHARASHTRA

first real-estate development in India financed via an initial public offering (IPO). It sprawls across 25,000 acres and is nearly one-fifth the land area of the Municipal Corporation of Greater Mumbai. The Mumbai-Pune Expressway opened up these forest lands, which previously were remote and disconnected because of a lack of access roads, to new rushes of private capital. The current redevelopment of the forest land is geared toward foreign investors and distant shareholders. Significantly, the urban promoter of the corridor city is facing numerous legal charges of fraudulent land transactions and environmental violations. The region contains a mix of some of the poorest Maratha-Kunbi middle peasantry and other Adivasi constituents, many of whom are landless. From the 1920s onward, successive rounds of building big dams to irrigate the sugarcane fields have submerged these forest lands and forcibly relocated their residents to adjacent districts. Gram Sabhas have not been formed in any of the villages because their populations are too splintered. In other words, by denying the residents the right to stay put,[75] the displacements undermined their capability to come together for collective action.

Chapter 4, "From Waste Land to SEZ," focuses on the 4,213-acre Khed City, located on mixed lands of irrigated fields interspersed with waste land. This region is representative of a vast majority of former Green Revolution regions. Its irrigated lands in the plains are owned predominantly by Maratha-Kunbi middle peasantry, who grow vegetables for export to Mumbai, Pune, and the surrounding cities. Their lands are interspersed with waste lands relegated largely to Adivasis. When the state government tried to acquire land in four Khed villages on behalf of an industrial-firm-turned-SEZ-promoter, the middle peasantry protested. They lacked the forms of capital that the sugar elites possessed to make an urban transition themselves, but they were organized enough as an electoral constituency to make their voice heard. This chapter tracks the initial conflicts between the urban promoter and the middle peasantry and the mediating role of regional bureaucrats in negotiating a solution of a joint land company with agrarian landowners and industrial firms as shareholders. Khed City merits attention both because the SEZ company includes as shareholders historically antagonistic groups—industrial capitalists and agrarian landowners, the Maratha middle peasantry and Adivasi agricultural laborers—and because the Gram Sabha became the site for negotiating new land commodification. A key insight in the Khed case concerns the re-valuation of former waste land, thanks to its conversion into an SEZ development. As stated above, younger-generation male Adivasis are capitalizing on the rising market value of their lands in order to break away from their patron-client relationships with the middle peasantry and assert a new politics of recognition for themselves.

As these three cases make clear, it is only under certain conditions that the Gram Sabhas can be activated and open up a space for previously excluded groups to challenge inherited agrarian power relations and to exercise their voice in the ongoing negotiations. One of these conditions is the relative power of middle peasantry vis-à-vis the agrarian elites and the incoming urban firms. In cases where the agrarian propertied power is either too entrenched (Magarpatta) or too dissipated (Lavasa), past agrarian privileges and exclusions are reproduced in an urbanizing context. Agrarian regimes like Khed, however, hold promise for a new politics of disruption and inclusion, in which agrarian-urban encounters create opportunities for previously excluded agrarian groups to enter the fray and stake new claims for themselves.

For this to happen, the Gram Sabhas must be not only activated in the first place but also conducted in a democratic way. All three corridor cities entail the making of new jurisdictions; urban promoters are carving territories out of existing local governments and governing these new territories with the formation of new authorities: the Magarpatta Township Development and Construction Company Limited, the Lavasa Corporation Limited, and Khed Economic Infrastructure Private Limited. These new authorities are taking over the traditional functions of urban local governments, including zoning and service provision. Yet these market movements are being interrupted by democratic politics: the companies have to jostle for power with the Gram Sabhas. Particularly in regions like Khed, which has the enabling conditions for the activation of the Gram Sabha, what does it mean to engage in the public sphere as a shareholder?

When the promoters of the new corridor cities transform landowners into shareholders, they are creating a new form of local government, which I call the "shareholder city." I use the term "city" to emphasize the governance aspects of these jurisdictions. The corridor region resembles what Henri Lefebvre in the mid-twentieth century called an "urban society" and what Neil Brenner and Christian Schmid more recently called "planetary urbanization" that renders inadequate city-village distinctions.[76] In the context of this book, the term "city" remains relevant, as the "city" in "shareholder cities" signifies the legal status of the jurisdiction that links territory-authority-polity in a social contract: the boundary of the city defines a territory; laws, such as the decentralization law, grant a public authority the power to make and enforce rules for governing this territory; and the boundary also delineates the polity that has the power to hold the authority accountable for its actions.

I am critical of the new shareholder cities because they attempt to restructure the local state in such a way as to redraw the public/private boundaries of these new jurisdictions. In his brilliant defense of the public sphere, Paul Starr reminds us that privatization is not merely aimed at shifting assets and services to the private sphere; instead, it constitutes a "reordering of claims in a society": "The terms public and private sum up a whole structure of rules and expectations about the proper conduct and limits of the state. To say some activity is public is to invoke claims of public purpose, public accountability, and public disclosure. To say something is private is to claim protection from state officials and other citizens. The theory of property rights sees privatization as a reassignment of claims to the control and use of assets, but it misses the special claims of the public sphere in a democratic society—claims for greater disclosure of information . . . [and] for rights of participation and discussion."[77]

In the shareholder cities, the "rights of participation and discussion" are premised on landownership. These propertied norms threaten to undermine the democratic ideal of one-person/one-vote. The shareholder cities are changing not only the public/private boundaries of the city but also who has claims on the city. At stake here is the notion of the democratic city, where, irrespective of their position in society, all individuals have equal claim-making power on the public authority that governs the city. The shareholder model of compensating landowners with shares in the new real-estate development is, instead, a variant of land readjustment or land pooling, which is gaining popularity as a mode of resolving land conflicts in other parts of India. In land readjustment, instead of shares, smaller but serviced and higher-priced plots of land are returned to the landowners. Though focusing on the price of land may be the most expedient way of gaining consent from the middle peasantry, what gets eclipsed in these negotiations are the bigger distributional questions about the reallocation of land and land-based social power among new users. Worst of all, the voices of nonpropertied citizens in these negotiations are silenced altogether.

A View from the Gram Sabha

This book draws on eighteen months of qualitative fieldwork, from 2011 to 2012, in the western Maharashtra region, followed by annual visits (of three to five months in duration) to the new corridor cities from 2013 to 2015.[78] The normative focus of the book—on keeping land-use change contestable by entrenching these decisions in the local democratic institution of the Gram Sabha—emerged from my own fieldwork experience of negotiating access to the corridor cities. I started my fieldwork by mapping out the institutional actors involved in the process of land-use change in each of the corridor cities. The agrarian elites, the middle peasantry, and the users and owners of the forests and agricultural lands emerged as central protagonists whose lives and livelihoods are being fundamentally remade by the building of the new corridor cities. My ability to gain access to these protagonists varied in the three cases. "Access" in qualitative research implies not just entry into the research site and into the lives of the participants but the creation of a more enduring relationship, building trust and a rapport with the research participants.[79] In the course of my fieldwork, the means I had to use for negotiating access to the three corridor cities revealed the degree of publicness of those cities.

The easiest corridor city to gain access to was Khed City. My first set of interviews in Khed City was with the elected representatives of the Khed Gram Panchayats. Norms of access applied here: from earlier fieldwork in peri-urban Bengaluru, I had learned that the dominant-caste agrarian landowners are often the gatekeepers in caste-segregated villages. Accordingly, I started the Khed City fieldwork by making contact with the Maratha-Kunbi elected representatives and then spent time in the Adivasi settlements within these villages. Khed City was the easiest corridor city to gain access to because I did not need permission to enter the local democratic offices (including the Gram Panchayat office) or to attend the Gram Sabhas. The public spheres, which were the sites of the land-use negotiations for Khed City, were open and thus truly public.

During one of the Khed Gram Sabhas, I met Meena *tai*, a feisty sixty-year-old Mali (a backward-class but not dominant-caste group) who lived in the village. In 2005, the Central Government had introduced the Mahatma Gandhi National Rural Employment Guarantee Scheme (MGNREGS), guaranteeing all rural residents one hundred days of employment annually for the building of public works. Meena tai had recently filed a Right to Information petition to get information from the Gram Panchayat on the beneficiaries selected for the MGNREGS, because some of the non-Maratha backward-class residents suspected nepotism: with elected representatives selecting family members and close friends and excluding other citizens.

During the Gram Sabha, in front of elected representatives and bureaucrats from the local to the district levels, Meena tai demanded that the Gram Panchayat display the list of beneficiaries outside its office, in the spirit of transparency and democratic accountability. It was her duty as a citizen, she said, to *takleef dena*—literally, "give trouble," though a more accurate interpretation would be "ask uncomfortable questions and challenge the status quo." Citizens like Meena tai apply pressure on their elected representatives not just while casting their votes but also through regular interactions in the Gram Sabha. Through the Gram Sabhas, I met many other active citizens influenced by and influencing the building of Khed City.

The corridor city that was most difficult to gain access to was Magarpatta City. During my first few weeks in Pune, I went to Magarpatta City with the naïve view that security guards or domestic workers would point me to the houses of the agrarian landowners-turned-shareholders. They did not. I then tried to get an interview with Satish Magar, an urban developer of sugar origins. After five months, a family friend who knew a business associate of Satish Magar finally got me a half-hour with him. It was an informative interview, yielding deep insights on real-estate development in India. At the end of the discussion, he agreed to introduce me to one of the agrarian landowners-turned-shareholders, who would drive me around on a tour of the township and introduce me to other shareholders of sugar origins. I had two months of interviews with these shareholders. When I returned to Pune the following year and called the agrarian landowner-turned-shareholder who had given me the tour, hoping to meet with him again, he kindly but firmly refused to talk to me until I had received permission from Satish Magar for a second round of interviews. I did not follow up with Satish Magar this time, as I was eager to move my fieldwork out of Magarpatta City into the adjacent areas. At the edges, where the corridor city meets other urban and rural local governments, I experienced the stark distinctions between the private city and the public city.

Equally difficult in terms of access was the Lavasa Lake City. At Lavasa, I gained access to the owners and occupiers of the forest lands through a social movement, the National Alliance for People's Movements (NAPM). My earlier attempts to meet residents in the region had met with limited success: the charged conflict over land had made residents distrustful of outsiders and unwilling to talk. Not a single Gram Sabha assembly had been held in the region; the institution existed only on paper. The NAPM, however, has been closely involved in the region's land struggles, and it was through their Pune activist that I was first introduced to landowners who opposed the development. My interviews with these landowners revealed the fragmented nature of the region's households: earlier dam-induced displacement had scattered families across distant relocation sites; the poor availability of irrigation waters (which had been diverted to the Maratha-controlled sugar-rich regions of western Maharashtra) had forced family members to migrate to Pune and Mumbai in search of work. These families continue to be splintered: I conducted around half of my interviews in the Western Ghats region but the other half with family members who live and work in Pune but make occasional visits back to their villages. Unlike the Khed region, where the Gram Sabha provides a common public place for all citizens to gather, the Western Ghats region lacks these local democratic institutions.

My varied experiences in gaining access to the corridor cities became a proxy for the varied publicness of the land-use decision-making process. Though corporations have triumphed over the Gram Sabha in the Magarpatta case, the Gram Sabha remains a force to be reckoned with in Khed City. The Khed Gram Sabha granted me, a researcher from an elite Western university, with caste/class privileges in her home country, a glimpse into the workings of local democracy as a social practice. It has granted backward-class women like Meena tai the democratic power to demand information, a fair allocation of resources, and respect from her elected representatives. Such public negotiations have opened land-use decisions to public scrutiny. Of course, the Gram Sabha meetings remain far from ideal: they can sometimes become "talking shops";[80] their politics can be performative; and, even with democratic fixes, access to them can continue to be mediated by the intersections of class, caste, and gender. Nevertheless, at their best, these public assemblies are forums where all the citizens can gather as a collective to exercise their voice. Even the powerful Marathas have to articulate their interests in ways that are acceptable to the wider public. Consent by the Gram Sabha grants legitimacy to the rules made to govern the polity. These democratic processes may be painfully time-consuming and slow; they may even be inefficient. But they provide much-needed brakes for slowing down and sometimes reversing the direction of change for a country that is careening at a dizzying pace toward an uncertain, market- and urban-oriented future.

CHAPTER 1

From Railways and Big Dams to Economic Corridors

Billboards are the new skyline for the region around the Mumbai-Pune Expressway. The newly constructed economic corridor is punctuated by signs that draw attention to its potential as one of the "best investment options . . . for bungalows, farm plots and estates." In anticipation of the proposed Pune International Airport, the precise location of which has been the subject of intense speculation, a billboard in front of an unfinished five-story apartment complex advertises its proximity to the airport—and to a new lifestyle of international travel—by proclaiming "Book your flat and fly to Singapore." The billboards echo an aspirational ideal of world-class living, with slogans inviting buyers to "an amazing lifestyle," "the home with a view attached," and "the right to be a world citizen." They are part of a branding strategy that also includes new brochures from the Maharashtra Industrial Development Corporation (MIDC), which has an acquired land bank of over 50,000 hectares of land in the western Maharashtra region for new industrial development.

In February 2016, the MIDC announced its plan to host Foxconn, the Taiwanese electronics giant, on one of its land banks in Talegaon, 30 kilometers from Pune. Media and policy sources tout the Foxconn investment, at $5 billion, as the largest foreign direct investment (FDI) in India, and Foxconn chose this location because of its proximity to the Mumbai-Pune Expressway and the proposed Pune International Airport.[1] It also has plans to coordinate with the domestic firm Bharat Forge to build an airstrip adjacent to the proposed Pune International Airport that will carry exclusively Foxconn cargo. Similarly, the agricultural lands in Supa Village, located around 70 kilometers from Pune, are the hub of a "dedicated industrial zone for Japanese

Figure 1a. Billboards in the Mumbai-Pune corridor region. Here a new apartment complex along the Pune-Nashik Highway advertises its proximity to the proposed Pune International Airport. The billboard on the left says: "Book your flat & fly to Singapore . . . . ."

Figure 1b. Billboards in the Mumbai-Pune corridor region. Billboards along the Mumbai-Pune Expressway (MPE) and the MPE region promise world-class living.

companies."[2] Also mediated by the MIDC, the Supa Japanese Industrial Zone enumerates its locational advantages in a brochure of its own: "well connected to major cities of Maharashtra such as Mumbai, Pune, Aurangabad and Nashik by national highways, also well connected to international airports in Pune, Mumbai and the upcoming Navi Mumbai International Airport, and to Maharashtra's major ports such as Mumbai Port Trust, Jawaharlal Nehru Port Trust and Dighi Port."

These billboards and brochures project enticing urban visions for the agricultural lands along the new economic corridor. But the corridor is also the site where these visions are routinely and vigorously contested. In stark contrast to the serene futures promised by the billboards, the Mumbai-Pune Expressway and the nearby highways are frequently occupied by turbulent protests. One of the most successful of these highway protests was staged by agrarian landowners resisting the forced acquisition of their land by the MIDC for Khed City, a 3,500-acre Special Economic Zone (SEZ) (the focus of Chapter 4). Nor was this the only protest to be spearheaded by the politically organized and powerful Maratha-Kunbi agrarian propertied class.

Map 6, of Maharashtra's new infrastructures, shows them to be concentrated in the western region of the state, which is also home to one of the country's strongest agrarian lobbies, the sugar elites. These agrarian elites control some of the most fertile sugarcane fields in the country, which contribute to more than 40 percent of India's cane-sugar exports. The overlay of the new economic corridors onto fertile agricultural lands makes western Maharashtra an instructive arena for analyzing land conflicts through a locational lens. The case is particularly instructive when we cast a historical gaze on its geography of agrarian capitalism. The western Maharashtra region has not always been fertile. In fact, at the turn of the twentieth century, it was so arid that commercially viable agriculture was not possible. During that time, the region that is now eastern Maharashtra had assured rainfall and black cotton soil, making it a thriving agricultural center of cotton production. By the 1970s, however, the map of Maharashtra's agriculturally productive and unproductive lands had been flipped, with the western region becoming one of India's richest agricultural zones and the eastern region declining into one of the poorest and most economically backward regions of the country.

This chapter has two aims. The first is to historicize and politicize the geography of uneven agrarian land markets in Maharashtra. When we say that the Mumbai-Pune Expressway, as part of a wider raft of postliberaliza-

REGIONS OF MAHARASHTRA:

KONKAN: THANE, MUMBAI, RAIGAD, RATNAGIRI AND SINDHUDURG DISTRICTS

WESTERN MAHARASHTRA: NASHIK, AHMEDNAGAR, PUNE, SATARA, SANGHLI AND KOLHAPUR DISTRICTS

MARATHWADA: AURANGABAD, JALNA, BEED, PARBHANI, LATUR, NANDED AND OSMANABAD DISTRICTS

VIDARBHA: BULDHANA, AMRAVATI, AKOLA, YAVATMAL, WARDHA, NAGPUR, CHANDRAPUR, BHANDARA AND GADCHIROLI DISTRICTS

Map 2. The state of Maharashtra divided into districts.
Each district is subdivided into talukas.

tion infrastructures, was routed through the fertile lands of an organized agrarian propertied class, it begs the question of how these fertile and waste lands were produced in the first place. I use three eras of infrastructural development—the colonial-era railways, the irrigation canals of the Green Revolution period, and the economic corridors of the postliberalization era—to illustrate the uneven development of agrarian and then urban capitalism in Maharashtra. Perhaps because spatial inequality is more visible than other forms of inequality (such as income inequality), it often provokes a public backlash, which then forces the state to adjust its uneven development politics to prevent further social unrest. Here, I draw attention to the politically influenced routing of railways, irrigation canals, and economic corridors, showing how each of these networked infrastructures was situated within a historically specific political-economic context, and how each era of land markets accretes on the former to produce a distinct geography of uneven development.

The second aim of the chapter has direct policy relevance. By excavating the production of uneven development, I seek to politicize the categories of land that are the basis of India's new land-acquisition act, the Right to Fair Compensation and Transparency in Land Acquisition, Rehabilitation and Re-settlement Act (LARRA). This Act has "special provisions to safeguard food security"[3] and contains a number of clauses that regulate the geography of urban expansion: "no irrigated multi-crop land shall be acquired under this Act; such land may be acquired subject to the condition that it is being done under exceptional circumstances, as a demonstrable last resort . . . ; wherever multi-crop irrigated land is acquired, an equivalent area of culturable waste-land shall be developed for agricultural purposes."[4] LARRA has an under-lying premise of technocratic rationality: it assumes that any irrigated land expropriated for urban expansion can be compensated for by the redevelop-ment of some other waste land for agriculture. Yet these categories of irri-gated land and waste land are in fact the basis of regional social power. Through sociospatial segregation, the more powerful agrarian propertied classes have either influenced the flow of irrigation canals through their land or appropriated the irrigated lands; the bypassed lands have been relegated to subordinate caste/class groups. This chapter shows how the categories of "multicrop" land and "waste" land are themselves the result of the uneven routing of previous irrigation infrastructure, which selectively watered cer-tain lands and bypassed others. In the postliberalization era, the new eco-nomic corridors are accreting on these unevenly irrigated agrarian land markets, and in the process they are producing conflictual, land-based so-cial transformation.

Uneven Development: Railways, Irrigation Canals, and Economic Corridors

I have periodized Maharashtra's infrastructural history into the eras of rail-ways, irrigation canals, and economic corridors because these infrastructures were the national development priorities during their times. In the colonial period, railways and irrigation made up the bulk of infrastructural invest-ments in British India. Historians have written about the military, economic, and social considerations that drove the colonial empire's massive railway in-vestment from 1860 to 1930. The railway networks were selectively routed through regions of military importance—in order to concentrate troops rapidly in those regions that were prone to uprisings—and of economic value, in order to connect the cotton-growing hinterlands of the colonial periphery to the provincial capitals, the port cities of Calcutta, Bombay, Madras, and Lahore. Following the 1878–79 famines, infrastructural priorities shifted and the railway lines were extended to famine-prone areas as "protective" rather than "profitable" lines. At the same time, investment in irrigation went up from less than 20 percent before 1880 to over 60 percent after 1880.[5]

On the heels of Independence in the early 1950s, following a Soviet style of planning, the Central Government's Planning Commission began prepar-ing Five-Year Plans for allocating public expenditures across economic sec-tors and geographic regions. These Five-Year Plans are an instructive source for tracking the country's shifting infrastructural and development priori-ties. Figure 2 maps out the key shifts from the 1950s to the present. Aside from defense, the irrigation and transportation sectors account for the heavi-est public-sector investment. But the share of public expenditure on irriga-tion infrastructure registers a steady decline from the 1950s to now, while the combined investment of both public and private sectors in certain types of transportation infrastructure, including economic corridors, has shot up in the postliberalization period, from the 1990s to now.

A closer reading of the Five-Year Plans alerts us to some qualitative shifts within the water and transportation sectors. The share of public-sector ex-penditure in irrigation was at its highest, at 19.1 percent, in the first Five-Year Plan (1951–56): this was the time of big dam-building. It then spiked again to 17 percent during the agricultural-modernization program of the Green Revolution (1969–74). Since then, it has steadily declined and was less than 4 percent in 2007–12. It increased slightly to 7.2 percent in the twelfth Five-Year Plan, but canal waters are now being diverted to meet the water needs of the new corridor cities. By contrast, the share of public expenditure on transportation has remained more or less steady, beginning at 19.1 percent in the first Five-Year Plan, dipping down in subsequent plans, but now rising back up to 19 percent in the current plan.

What has changed is the type of transportation infrastructure, from roads and railways to economic corridors and international ports and airports. In

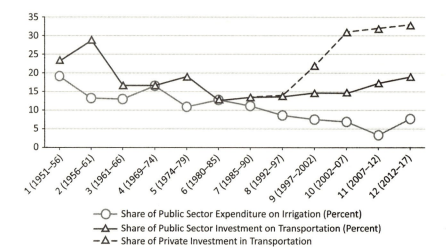

-O- Share of Public Sector Expenditure on Irrigation (Percent)
-▲- Share of Public Sector Investment on Transportation (Percent)
-△- Share of Private Investment in Transportation

Figure 2. Investment in infrastructure from the Five-Year Plans. Sources: Based on data from Five-Year Plans prepared by the Planning Commission, Government of India, available at planningcommission.nic.in/plans/planrel/fiveyr/welcome.html; Transport/Infrastructure sections in the annual economic surveys, Government of India, available at Indiabudget.nic.in/previouses.asp; reports by expert working groups, Government of India, on infrastructure policies in the 1990s, available at www.rakeshmohan.com/reports.html; and National Transport Development Policy Committee, *Trends in Growth and Development of Transport* (New Delhi: Government of India, 2013).

the early decades after Independence, the first democratically elected government knew that they had inherited a colonial-era, unevenly routed railway network that had been designed to serve an imperial world economy. Moreover, the country had just come out of a debilitating partition from Pakistan, and national leaders saw an urgent need to connect the areas along the border to the national transportation network. Road- and railway-building thus became deeply tied to nation-building. Guided by the rationale of political integration, policy elites made these road and railway networks crisscross evenly across national space. Today, in the era of postliberalization infrastructure, mobility rather than connectivity is driving infrastructural decisions. Broader, faster expressways are being built parallel to existing ones. Older airports are being decommissioned for larger, world-class ones. Cities are vying with one another to build metros, which have become de rigueur ingredients of world-class cities. Though actual public-sector expenditure on transportation is 19 percent under the current plan, since the mid-1990s the public sector has been offering in-kind subsidies to attract private capital into the infrastructural sector. The Five-Year Plans do not reflect these in-kind subsidies—which include the leasing or sale of additional land for property redevelopment adjacent to economic corridors and airports.

The three infrastructural development eras—railways, irrigation canals, and economic corridors—produced different policies of allocation across the urban-rural divide, and each caused a spatially uneven distribution of power and inequality among various caste/class groups. I focus here on the state of Maharashtra, but I also show how Maharashtra diverged from and converged with wider patterns of urban change.

Railways, Cotton, and Empire

The state of Maharashtra was formed in 1960, when the erstwhile Bombay State was reorganized into the states of Maharashtra and Gujarat. Bombay State had been part of the colonial-era Bombay Presidency, which was territorially divided during the 1947 India-Pakistan Partition, with the region remaining within the boundaries of India getting reorganized into Bombay State. The state of Maharashtra, as we know it today (see Map 2), has distinct regions shaped by past colonial histories of public works and land tenure.

The present-day region of Vidarbha (earlier called Berar or Varhad) is an exceptionally fertile agrarian zone, particularly the districts of Amravati, Akola, Buldhana, and Yavatmal. Its black loamy soil earned it a reputation among locals as being a region where "not a pebble can be found for several miles."[6] These districts also receive assured rainfall, and together these agro-climatic conditions made the region the epicenter of imperial cotton production at the turn of the nineteenth century. One of India's largest and oldest business conglomerates, the House of Tatas, set up the Empress Mills there in 1878. When the British began their extensive railway-building enterprise in the late nineteenth century, they routed the lines in such a way as to connect India's raw-material-producing hinterland to the factories in London. Within the Bombay Presidency, railway mileage increased by 70 percent between 1881 and 1891.[7] The routing of the railway lines served the interests of the imperial economy by connecting the cotton-growing areas of present-day eastern Maharashtra, Gujarat, and northern Karnataka to the port city of Bombay; ships then carried the cotton from Bombay to the textile mills in

Lancashire.[8] The new railroads dramatically changed the economics and experience of distance in India: they shortened the two-month journey from the cotton-growing regions to Bombay to a twenty-four-hour passage.[9] One of the earliest of these railway lines, a 190-kilometer stretch from Yavatmal to Bombay, was recently in the news; for some strange reason, it was never taken over by the Indian Railways post-Independence, and it is now the only private railway line owned by a British company in a country with a nationalized railway system.[10]

For the British Raj, cotton was "white gold," and the Varhad region was the epicenter of the empire's cotton trade. From the Amravati district of Varhad, the world's rates for cotton were declared. When the American Civil War in the 1860s briefly interrupted the U.S. supply of cotton to England, the Varhad region became the primary supplier to Lancashire's mills. As the historian Sven Beckert has argued, the U.S. Civil War thus became not only a crucial turning point in the history of the American nation but also the spark for an explosive transformation of the worldwide web of cotton production and, with it, of global capitalism.[11] The short-lived spike in Indian cotton prices (which ended with the end of the American Civil War in 1865) led to investments in expensive land reclamation projects in Bombay,[12] giving us the now-familiar urban form of the island city.

By contrast, the Bombay Deccan region of Bombay Presidency (comprising the present-day districts of Pune, Nashik, Ahmednagar, Satara, and Solapur) remained arid, with poor, unreliable rainfall, and was classified as an agro-climatic "scarcity zone" (see Map 3).[13] The "life of the people [in this region was] a gamble on rain,"[14] and until the late nineteenth century, this western region could support only dry-crop subsistence cultivation.

Yet, in the twentieth century, over the span of a few decades, Maharashtra's geography of agriculturally productive and unproductive land became almost a mirror image of what it had been in the late nineteenth century. By the 1970s, the western arid region had become the sugar bowl of the country. What makes the transformation all the more dramatic is the fact that sugarcane is a water guzzler and is hardly the expected choice of crop for a "scarcity zone." Moreover, while western Maharashtra has become a thriving sugarcane producer, the Varhad region, now called Vidarbha, in eastern Maharashtra, has been in the news for its growing spate of farmer suicides: in the past decade, nearly 300,000 Vidarbha farmers have committed suicide. The current disparity between the eastern and western regions is especially jarring when one realizes that the financial capital of the country, Mumbai (formerly

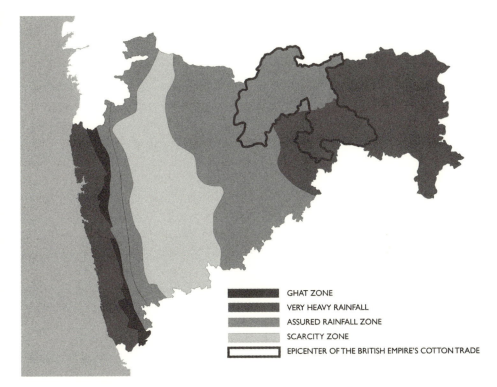

GHAT ZONE
VERY HEAVY RAINFALL
ASSURED RAINFALL ZONE
SCARCITY ZONE
EPICENTER OF THE BRITISH EMPIRE'S COTTON TRADE

Map 3. Fertility of the regions based on the degree of rainfall (the boundary indicated is of the present-day state of Maharashtra). Source: Data from Maharashtra's Water Resources Department.

Bombay), located on the western edge of the state, is only 600 kilometers away from the "suicide capital," Vidarbha.

Infrastructural politics is about the prioritization of certain types of infrastructure over others. But it is also about the uneven routing of these networked infrastructures. Depending on the routing plans, infrastructural benefits are capitalized in the values of certain plots of land and not in others. Western Maharashtra, previously arid, benefited from the routing of a dense network of irrigation and other infrastructural networks. Map 4 shows the territorial synchrony between the locations of major irrigation canals and the country's richest sugar cooperatives. For instance, the first sugar cooperative in India, the V. Vikhe Patil Cooperative Sugar Factory, was set up in 1950 in the drought-prone Ahmednagar district, which receives scanty, irregular rainfall of less than 600 millimeters per year. The cooperative was

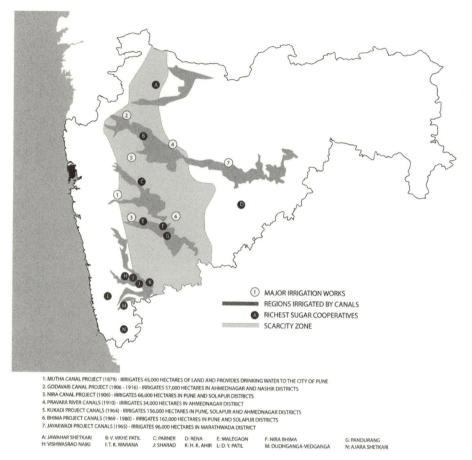

MAJOR IRRIGATION WORKS

REGIONS IRRIGATED BY CANALS

RICHEST SUGAR COOPERATIVES

SCARCITY ZONE

1. MUTHA CANAL PROJECT (1879) - IRRIGATES 45,000 HECTARES OF LAND AND PROVIDES DRINKING WATER TO THE CITY OF PUNE
2. GODAVARI CANAL PROJECT (1906 - 1916) - IRRIGATES 57,000 HECTARES IN AHMEDNAGAR AND NASHIK DISTRICTS
3. NIRA CANAL PROJECT (1906) - IRRIGATES 66,000 HECTARES IN PUNE AND SOLAPUR DISTRICTS
4. PRAVARA RIVER CANALS (1910) - IRRIGATES 34,000 HECTARES IN AHMEDNAGAR DISTRICT
5. KUKADI PROJECT CANALS (1964) - IRRIGATES 156,000 HECTARES IN PUNE, SOLAPUR AND AHMEDNAGAR DISTRICTS
6. BHIMA PROJECT CANALS (1969 - 1980) - IRRIGATES 162,000 HECTARES IN PUNE AND SOLAPUR DISTRICTS
7. JAYAKWADI PROJECT CANALS (1965) - IRRIGATES 96,000 HECTARES IN MARATHWADA DISTRICT

| A: JAWAHAR SHETKARI | B: V. VIKHE PATIL | C: PARNER | D: RENA | E: MALEGAON | F: NIRA BHIMA | G: PANDURANG |
| H: VISHWASRAO NAIKI | I: T. K. WARANA | J: SHARAD | K: H. K. AHIR | L: D. Y. PATIL | M: DUDHGANGA-VEDGANGA | N: AJARA SHETKARI |

Map 4. Territorial synchrony between the scarcity zone and the richest sugar cooperatives in the state. Sources: Data on large dams and irrigation canals are from the Government of Maharashtra, "Maharashtra Water and Irrigation Commission Report" (1999); Maharashtra Water Resources Regulatory Authority, Government of Maharashtra, "Major and Medium Irrigation Projects in Maharashtra" (includes a GIS map on existing and proposed sub-basins for planning); and Central Water Commission, Government of India, National Registry of Large Dams (2009). Data on sugar cooperatives are from the Maharashtra State Cooperative Sugar Factories Federation Limited, available at www.mahasugarfed.org/aboutus.htm.

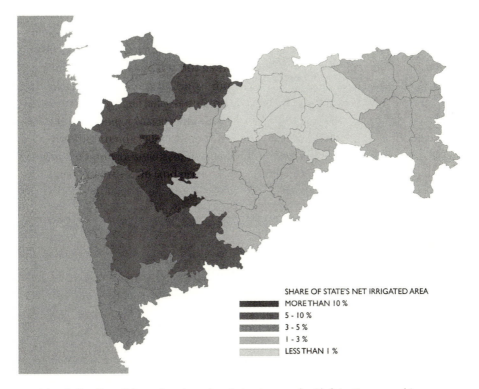

SHARE OF STATE'S NET IRRIGATED AREA
MORE THAN 10 %
5 - 10 %
3 - 5 %
1 - 3 %
LESS THAN 1 %

Map 5. Fertility of the regions based on irrigation surplus/deficit. Compare this map with Map 3, and notice how the Vidarbha districts (particularly the Amravati, Akola, Buldhana, and Yavatmal districts), which were the epicenter of the imperial cotton trade, are now a region with the highest irrigation backlog, and how the scarcity zone of western Maharashtra now attracts the highest share of the state's irrigation. Source: Based on data from the Government of Maharashtra, "Report of Fact Finding Committee on Regional Imbalance in Maharashtra" (2014).

made possible by the building of the Pravara River Canals, which irrigate some 34,000 hectares of land in the Ahmednagar district.

Just as the nineteenth-century, colonial-era railways unevenly connected distant places and splintered proximate ones, twentieth-century irrigation canals produced a new geography of prosperity and poverty. With irrigation, the categories of agriculturally productive and unproductive land no longer derived from attributes such as soil conditions and rainfall, but became socially produced by the geography of infrastructure. Wherever the canals went, they transformed arid lands into agriculturally prosperous zones; wherever they did not go, the bypassed regions slipped into economic decline. To make sense of the political economy of this biased routing of irrigation canals and the new uneven geographies they created, we must turn our attention to the making of a new agrarian propertied class in western Maharashtra.

Irrigation, Sugar, and the Making of the Agrarian Propertied Classes

Large-scale irrigation canals were first introduced in the Bombay Presidency as a form of famine protection. In the mid- to late nineteenth century, India witnessed grave famine outbreaks in the midst of an agricultural boom.[15] Indian nationalists attributed the famines to the expensive railways, which they argued had crowded out other investments, including much-needed spending on irrigation canals. The Indian nationalist Dadabhai Naoroji derided railway policy as a "pitiless drain to Europe"; he described "the magic wheels of the train [resulting in] empty stomachs" in the colony.[16] The famines triggered large-scale peasant protests, among the largest of which were the Deccan Riots of the 1870s in the Bombay Deccan region. The Indian nationalist movement had started making inroads into the countryside, and in a bid to restore political stability among the agitated peasantry, the colonial state started investing in major irrigation works in these famine-ridden regions. In the Bombay Deccan, the first of these canals was the Mutha Canal Project of 1879, constructed in the drought-prone Pune district. Located on the river Krishna, this dam became part of a dense network of dams in the Sahyadri mountain range, including the more recent Varasgaon dam, completed only in 1987 (the focus of Chapter 3).

Before the irrigation canals, the arid, famine-exposed region of the Bombay Deccan could support only dry crops like millet and sorghum for household consumption. The construction of big dams and the irrigation canals that flowed from these dams started as famine-protection works under colonial rule. But they became a key developmental policy under the later, postcolonial agricultural-modernization program, producing an uneven agrarian development that continues to exert an influence on contemporary land politics. In the early decades of the twentieth century, during colonial rule, vast irrigation networks were expanded to the present-day districts of Pune, Nashik, Ahmednagar, Solapur, and Satara. The newly irrigated lands opened up what Donald Attwood calls the "irrigation frontier"[17] and what Neil Smith popularized as the "rent gap."[18] Studies during that period show that in 1917, an acre of dry millet or sorghum would fetch a gross income of about 12 rupees. With canal irrigation, however, the same plot of land could support a perennial crop like sugarcane that would fetch an income of nearly 618 rupees.[19] Though the massive investment in irrigation canals was primarily driven by the political need to quell uprisings, the colonial state did want some financial returns on these infrastructural investments, and using the expensive canals to grow dry subsistence crops made little sense. In the early 1900s, the executive engineer for irrigation in the Pune district, M. Visvesvaraya—who later became the dewan and noted technocrat in Mysore/Bengaluru—proposed the switch from dry crops to sugarcane, a cash crop that consumed a vast amount of water, required irrigation all year round, and had a ready and profitable market.[20] The "irrigation frontier" was small in terms of its total land area: by 1936, the six major canal systems in the Bombay Deccan had irrigated less than 2 percent of the net sown area. But in terms of the market price of agricultural land, the expensive irrigation canals, wholly subsidized by the colonial state, increased the profits of the sugarcane cultivators by nearly fifty times.

If the irrigation canals transformed an arid, famine-stricken region into a new "irrigation frontier," they simultaneously devalued the Western Ghats region, where the dams were located. It was not only the British who built dams during the colonial period; indigenous industrial capitalists did so as well. Around 40 kilometers from the Mutha canal project is the Mulshi dam, built by the industrial house of the Tatas in the 1920s. Before the construction of the dam, these mountainous regions contained lush mango groves, trellises of karvada (a type of fruit), and fields of high-quality rice.[21] The dams submerged vast tracts of this low-lying, fertile, rice-growing area, and by the 1930s the region (comprising the present-day talukas of Mulshi, Maval, and Velhe) had become an almost deserted stretch of barren land. Deprived of their livelihoods, forest dependents in the region started migrating to the cities of Mumbai and Pune for work, and those left behind were literally plunged into darkness: until as late as the 1980s, their villages did not even have the basic amenities of electricity and drinking water. The scholar Rajendra Vora recently captured the region's politics in the 1920s, recounting the remarkable history of the "world's first anti-dam movement," staged by peasants under the socialist leadership of Pandurang

Mahadev Bapat (popularly known as "Senapati") against the dam's builders, the Tatas.[22] Because the Tatas were backed by the leaders of the Indian nationalist movement, the anti-dam movement did not succeed.

In short, within the western Maharashtra region, the biased routing of irrigation canals produced an uneven geography—fertile sugarcane fields in drought-prone regions, which received irrigation waters from big dams located in the river-rich Western Ghats region, with the latter becoming agriculturally underdeveloped due to dam flooding. The biased routing of irrigation canals also produced stark inequalities between western and eastern Maharashtra. A number of reports were published in the 1970s and 1980s on these irrigation disparities. In 1983, the state government appointed a Fact-Finding Committee that showed how public expenditures were disproportionately skewed toward the western region at the expense of the Marathwada and Vidarbha regions. The committee concluded that eastern Maharashtra was lagging far behind its western counterpart due to an "infrastructural backlog."[23] In the sector of irrigation, it estimated that the backlog in Marathwada and Vidarbha accounted for nearly 63 percent of the total state backlog. More recent reports have similarly found that some of the "most agriculturally distressed and backward districts" in India are concentrated in the eastern regions of Maharashtra.[24]

We can see that today's geography of fertile and waste lands, the basis of the current land-acquisition and land-taxation systems, was socially produced by the uneven routing of irrigation canals. This biased routing started off as famine protection under the colonial state; but why did it continue into the postcolonial period? We cannot understand the postcolonial geography of irrigation canals without connecting it to Maharashtra's electoral politics. During the peak years of the anticolonial nationalist movement in the 1930s, nationalists from the Bombay Presidency included people like Y. B. Chavan, who later rose to prominence as one of the most influential Congress politicians in post-Independence India. These politicians established their political legitimacy by participating in the anticolonial struggle. But at the same time that the nationalist movement was locked in a struggle against external colonizers, states like Maharashtra experienced another struggle—against internal colonizers, the upper-caste Brahmins. As Suhas Palshikar argues, these regional anticaste movements constructed new political constituencies by fusing together "backward" caste groups that dominated local areas into a statewide identity. The new electoral constituencies became known as the "dominant castes," and their rise to power in the 1980s, in both state legislatures and the nation's Parliament, has been heralded as the "second democratic upsurge."[25]

In Maharashtra, the new dominant caste was the carefully constructed Maratha-Kunbi cluster.[26] The regional caste geography in what is now Maharashtra is variegated and complex. Maharashtra contains 252 Sudra jatis, and these subgroups are categorized in the Census as Other Backward Classes, eligible for affirmative-action programs.[27] The caste status of the Marathas is contested: some argue that they are Sudras, others that they are upper-caste Kshatriyas.[28] To become a viable electoral constituency, the Marathas formed a coalition with one of the numerically largest Sudra jatis, the Kunbis. Other Sudra jatis, such as the Malis and the Lingayats (who are now important caste groups in the three corridor cities), retained political power in certain "local pockets" of the state: for instance, the Solapur and Kolhapur districts have always elected Lingayats as Members of the Legislative Assembly (MLAs), and the Amravati district has always elected Malis.[29] But the fusing of the Maratha-Kunbis into an electoral constituency enabled this caste cluster to scale its political power beyond local politics and gain control over the state legislature. As noted in the Introduction, the dominant castes are a heterogeneous class, ranging from wealthy landowners to landless laborers. What they have in common is a shared historical opposition to high-caste Brahmins and a somewhat similar ritual status in the sacralized power structure of the caste hierarchy. The Maratha-Kunbis, constituting almost 36 percent of the population of Maharashtra, are dispersed across the state, but the epicenter of their power is western Maharashtra. Some of the most influential Marathas, who controlled the state-level Congress party in the 1960s and 1970s, came from western Maharashtra. Gaining control of the state legislature also gave these Marathas control of the key resource of water: since the formation of the Maharashtra state in 1960, the state cabinet portfolio for irrigation has always been controlled by a Maratha politician of sugar origins.

In the early decades after Independence, because of India's unique sequencing of development—the country achieved universal suffrage when it was still a predominantly agrarian society—agrarian voters mattered most to the politicians. The "votes were in the countryside"[30] and sugar cooperatives became a key institution through which the Maratha caste and the Congress political party gained legitimacy among the agrarian voters, embedding themselves deeply into the electoral geography of Maharashtra. In the first two decades post-Independence, western Maharashtra's sugar cooperatives became the bedrock of Congress-Maratha politics. These decades were a formative time, in which different factions attempted to take control of new institutions and entrench themselves within the political system. For the fledgling Maratha caste group, which started off with only modest economic power in the 1950s, the sugar cooperatives became a key organizational device for the consolidation of wealth, status, and power. They enabled the wealthy Maratha landowners to retain control over the Maratha-Kunbi caste bloc because, while they worked on the democratic principle of "one person, one vote," they were managed by a board of directors, who decided on the appointment of staff, the purchase of equipment, and the sale of sugar—decisions that directly and decisively affected the economic lives of small-scale cane growers. Only the wealthy Maratha growers had the resources to contest the cooperative elections, which at times had a larger voter turnout than even the regular political elections. The small cane-growers did not challenge the large growers, despite their blatant exertion of power, because the cooperatives at least guaranteed them an assured income.

The sugar cooperatives were also important instruments of political mobilization for the Congress party. They served as major contributors to political campaigns, with the large cane-growers often diverting the cooperative profits to finance election campaigns, meaning that prices paid by the cooperatives to their farmer members dropped by as much as 20 percent during electoral years.[31] The cooperative factories also hosted election meetings and other campaign events. The directors were in turn rewarded by the Congress, which supported them as political candidates for the state legislature. Thanks to these arrangements, in the span of three decades—from the 1950s through the 1970s—the large Maratha cane-growers gained considerable power both in the regional economy and in state-level politics, earning the epithet of "sugar barons" or "sugar kulaks" in popular discourse. The intertwined relationship between sugar cooperatives and politics has led some to comment that, in Maharashtra, "you cannot understand our sugar co-ops without understanding our politics, nor can you understand our politics without understanding our sugar co-ops."[32]

Before elaborating further on the sugar cooperatives, I will make a brief excursus here on the urban-rural development politics in India during this period, to situate the Maharashtra cooperatives within wider national trends. During the 1950s, India's development was organized around capital-intensive, industrial/steel towns and non-capital-intensive, agricultural cooperatives.[33] As part of the Third World political project, Nehru's economic policy objected to the modernization theorists' argument that the "darker nations" were poor because they were traditionally backward; rather, the root cause of backwardness was colonialism.[34] In order to cut India's ties of dependency to the West, the Nehruvian state sought both to invest in state-led industrialization as a means to economic self-sufficiency and to focus industrial development in economically backward regions that had been left out of the circuits of colonial capitalism. The big dams were expected to be "nuclei of regional growth," and 120 industrial townships were founded during this period, concentrated in the most economically backward states of Madhya Pradesh, Bihar, and Uttar Pradesh.[35]

The large allocation of capital toward heavy and basic industries meant that agricultural productivity (mainly for cheap food for the cities) had to be improved by other, non-capital-intensive means. The agricultural strategy took the form of institutional reforms, including land reforms and agricultural cooperatives.[36] These commodity cooperatives aligned with the "mixed economy" ideology of newly independent India: unlike collectives, they upheld the ideals of private property rights, but at the same time they provided small-scale owner-cultivators with state support to participate successfully in the market economy. These small peasants were the backbone of the Congress from the time of the anticolonial nationalist movement, when they organized to rally against the famine outbreaks caused by colonial economic development. As the peasant castes came to form regionally specific dominant castes, the cooperatives became influential institutions that were subsidized by the state and gave the electorally organized "middle peasantry" access to larger agricultural markets.

A confluence of unexpected events in the early 1960s—the Indo-China war in 1962, the death of Nehru in 1964, and famines in the mid-1960s— disrupted the urban-rural politics of the Nehruvian era. Institutional reforms had not led to an increase in food production, and some members of the political class, as well as some international-development experts, mounted a trenchant critique of the Nehruvian state's expenditures on urban industrial development when more than 75 percent of the population still lived and worked off their land.[37] The proposed new agricultural-modernization program of the Green Revolution, strongly backed and funded by U.S. international-development agencies, eschewed the ideal of balanced economic growth from the earlier era and instead concentrated its irrigation infrastructure in strategic nodes.

As an economically prosperous state, Maharashtra had not received any of the public-sector industrial townships of the Nehruvian era. Colonial-era

Bombay had developed an indigenous urban capitalist class, and the city still retained its strong industrial (and later financial) base. The sugar cooperatives, meanwhile, continued uninterrupted, first under the Nehruvian wave of cooperatives and then during the Green Revolution program. During the political tenure of Vasantrao Naik, who was the chief minister of Maharashtra from 1963 to 1975 and who is heralded as the father of the Green Revolution in Maharashtra, the sugar cooperatives benefited from an infusion of state subsidies for seeds, fertilizers, and water.

By the 1970s, the sugar cooperatives functioned more as political than market institutions, and the standard norms that govern market institutions rarely applied to them. Sugar was classified as an essential commodity under the 1955 Essential Commodities Act, a welfare policy for the subsidization and public distribution of certain commodities listed as essential to low-income groups. This Act mandated that all sugar factories, private and cooperative, sell 65 percent of their sugar as "levy sugar" to the Central Government, to be distributed at below-market rates to households below the poverty line. The sugar cooperatives were thus assured of guaranteed sales to the government, and more than 40 percent of the "levy sugar" was procured from western Maharashtra.[38]

Assessments of the performance of western Maharashtra's sugar cooperatives vary. Critics argue that the government's "regulatory intrusions" distorted the functioning of the market and offered misplaced incentives by encouraging a water-intensive crop to flourish in a water-scarce state.[39] Pointing to the heavy subsidy from the state government—90 percent of sugar-cooperative finances came from debts to the cooperative banks with state guarantees, and over three-quarters of the 10-percent equity was a direct handout from the state budget—they also argue that the cooperatives were "a medium for siphoning off funds from the treasury into the coffers of the kulaks."[40] B. S. Baviskar and Donald Attwood, two of the foremost scholars on western Maharashtra's sugar cooperatives, disagree.[41] They concede the heavy reliance of the cooperatives on state subsidies, but they argue that these subsidies were helpful: though sugar production is usually dominated by immense plantations, Maharashtra's sugar cooperatives were unique in forging alliances among marginal, small, and large cane-growers. Attwood and Baviskar also argue that the sugar cooperatives were institutionally checked not by market competition but by political competition, and that the intensely fought cooperative elections staved off "despotism."

Both the critics and the supporters of the cooperatives agree that they needed strong state support. The state's coffers during that period were largely filled by surpluses from Mumbai's thriving industrial economy. The city's industrial capitalists tolerated these diversions for the sake of agrarian political stability that was guaranteed to them as a result. Just as the agrarian surplus from the eastern region was diverted during the colonial era to build Bombay, the agrarian sugar economy of the post-Independence period was linked to the city's urban economy, but in an inverse relationship: this time, the industrial surpluses from the city were diverted to the agrarian countryside.

Economic Corridors, Real Estate, and the Emergence of New Constituencies

Since liberalization, the infrastructural priorities in Maharashtra have shifted from big dams to economic corridors. The new megaprojects, which the state government calls its "marquee infrastructural projects," include the Navi Mumbai Airport, the Pune Metro Rail Project, the Nagpur Metro Rail Project, the Mumbai Trans Harbour Link and Multimodal International Passenger and Cargo Hub Airport, and the development of the Navi Mumbai Airport Influence Notified Area (NAINA) Smart City around the new Mumbai international airport. The shift in infrastructural priorities stems from the growing pressures of territorial competitiveness faced by India's various state governments. With the liberalization of the economy, the state governments are now in fierce competition with one another to attract private investment to their territories. The newly instituted "India State Competitiveness Report," jointly published annually by the Indian business daily *Mint Asia* and the India-based Institute of Competitiveness, has consistently ranked Maharashtra as the most competitive state in India. In the "Mumbai Meets Manhattan: Magnetic Maharashtra" report, the MIDC, an industrial parastatal, attributes the state's competitive edge to, among other factors, its infrastructural priorities, which "focus on creating opportunities for global businesses to invest in the state while at the same time ensuring that the state continues to strive for higher standards of business-friendly policies and approval processes." The MIDC brochures contain seductive images of the new infrastructures, including the Mumbai-Pune Expressway. Map 6 shows their location.

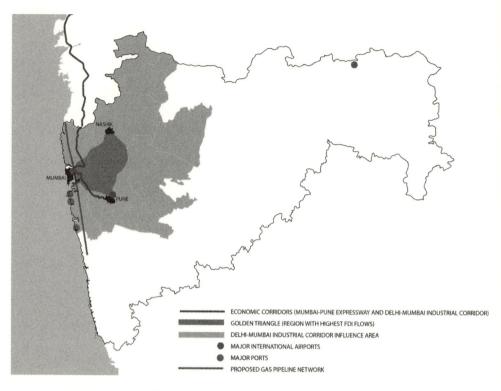

Map 6. Location of Maharashtra's postliberalization "marquee infrastructure projects." Source: Based on Maharashtra Industrial Development Corporation brochures.

Notice that these "marquee infrastructure projects" have a locational bias. Except for Nagpur (the dot in the Vidarbha region in eastern Maharashtra),[42] all the new infrastructures are located in western Maharashtra. In one of the few works written so far about the locational politics of postliberalization development, Sanjoy Chakravorty uses data from the Centre for Monitoring Indian Economy (CMIE) to map the geography of post-1991 private capital.[43] Chakravorty finds that two important determinants of post-reform private investment are "the existence of any investment in the pre-reform era and the existence of new private investment in the neighboring districts in the post-reform era."[44] Unlike the Nehruvian era, when public-sector industries were set up in economically lagging regions, partly under consideration of correcting uneven development, postliberalization private capital flows to already economically prosperous regions. These flows of capital produce what

I call "corridor regions"—comprising the new economic corridors and the corridor cities—clustered in the former developed regions of an agrarian capitalist economy. One type of new corridor city is the SEZ, and the locations of the SEZ areas reveal a clear geographical bias. Of the 154 SEZ areas established in 2009 by the SEZ Act, most are concentrated in a few districts that had strong economic growth prior to liberalization.[45]

The decision to concentrate the "marquee infrastructure projects" in regions with prior market linkages often results in duplicated infrastructure projects. It is not uncommon for the new economic corridors, for instance, to run almost parallel to existing highways. A case in point is the Mumbai-Pune economic corridor. In the 1990s, the Mumbai-Pune Expressway was a high-priority project for the newly liberalized Maharashtra state government. Early feasibility studies showed that the regions of Mumbai and Pune accounted for nearly 72 percent of the factories, 77 percent of employment, 88 percent of working capital, and 86 percent of the industrial output of the entire state.[46] Though Mumbai and Pune were already connected by an existing highway, the studies found that it took nearly five hours to cover the 180-kilometer distance. Between Mumbai and Pune lie the mountainous Western Ghats, and during the monsoon season the five-hour trip could be lengthened to almost fifteen hours, due to frequent landslides. A faster corridor, argued the studies, could reduce the distance between the two cities to under two hours of traveling time, leading to significant savings in logistical costs and transforming the region into a globally competitive information-technology corridor. Though at that time the cities of Mumbai and Pune were also connected by a functioning railway line, the feasibility studies, reflecting wider transportation shifts in national development politics, argued that the financial model of the Indian Railways—which heavily subsidized passenger travel with high-cost freight charges—was not useful for a new economy in which competitiveness relied on low freight costs.[47] The Mumbai-Pune Expressway was thus a pioneer not just because it was the country's first economic corridor but because it represented a new mode of financing and governing public infrastructure. As the country's first public-private highway project, it was built under the build-operate-transfer model, and the expressway concessionaires have been permitted to levy tolls to recover their capital costs.

During interviews with some of Mumbai's most left-leaning journalists and academics, I was surprised to learn that, though strongly critical of the new, exclusionary urban developments in the western Maharashtra region, they had nothing but praise for the Mumbai-Pune Expressway. The policy justifications for it—reduced travel time, savings in fuel consumption by vehicles, economic development, reduced accidents—had so pervaded popular discourse that it seemed simply common sense for the two cities to be reconnected by a high-speed corridor. The journalists' and academics' support for the project did not lessen even when I shared with them data from the state government on the traffic count for the expressway: cars and jeeps accounted for nearly 70 percent of the expressway traffic; light commercial vehicles made up 11 percent; trucks, 6 percent; buses, 7 percent; and the 3- and M-axles, another 7 percent.[48] Though one of the main rationales for the economic corridor was to reduce logistical costs and improve the economic productivity of the region, the tolls are so high that the main beneficiaries of the new corridor are privately owned cars and not public-transport vehicles or freight carriers.

The earlier era of irrigation canals flipped the geography of agriculturally productive and unproductive lands and enabled the making of a new constituency: the Maratha-Kunbi agrarian propertied class. Now, the new economic corridors are building on these uneven agrarian pasts; the prior market linkages in developed agrarian regions are now desirable locational attributes in the decision-making calculus of the new urban firms. But the economic corridors not only settle on formerly agrarian land markets, they also unsettle them in unexpected ways. In the next section, I will delve into the re-valuation of waste lands. As the Congress-Maratha-sugar politics are unraveled, this re-valuation re-maps the geography of unevenness and produces new constituencies within the western Maharashtra region.

Re-valuing Waste Lands

For a systematic analysis of the recalibration of land markets from the era of irrigation canals to that of economic corridors, I collected the ready reckoner rates for 242 villages in the western Maharashtra region. The ready reckoner rate—also known as the annual schedule of rates, circle rates, or guidance values—is a government-defined rate for land. Every year, the state government's Department of Registration and Stamps revises the ready reckoner rates based on market studies. The rates serve several purposes: they set the benchmark for land transactions so that buyers are not cheated by sellers charging exorbitant rates for property; more importantly, they are used for revenue purposes—stamp duty is levied on every property transaction based on these rates, and urban governments charge property tax based on these rates. The revenue rationales for the rates, as well as the institutions, like the Department of Registration and Stamps that governs property transactions, have their provenance in colonial-era land-revenue systems, when agricultural land was one of the main sources of public revenue. The colonial state implemented an elaborate system of land classification that underpinned the taxation system. Though the agricultural land tax was abolished in postcolonial India, these land categories are still used, and they have now become the basis for determining compensation prices for land acquisition as well as for setting the ready reckoner rates.[49]

The ready reckoner rates vary for different categories of agricultural land. Among the categories that Maharashtra uses, I focus on two to make my argument on the changing role of landed property under different forms of agrarian and urban capitalism.[50] I contend that agricultural land in an agrarian society derives its economic value primarily from its fertility, which is socially produced by the uneven routing of irrigation waters. In a liberalizing and urbanizing economy, the determinant of the economic value of land changes, with location trumping fertility as the main calibrator of land price. Thus, proximity to economic corridors now matters as much as, if not more than, proximity to irrigation canals. The two land categories that are central to this argument are (1) *dongarpad*, or "uncultivable waste lands," and (2) *bagayat*, or "multicrop land." The most agriculturally unproductive lands are the dongarpad lands. This land category, which traces its origins back to the colonial land-revenue system, is "situated on the tops or spurs of hill ranges,"[51] is unfit for profitable cultivation, and therefore has the lowest agricultural value. The most agriculturally productive land, and therefore the most valuable land in terms of revenue, are the bagayat lands, where more than 50 percent of the land is irrigated by either canals or wells.

To analyze how the price of dongarpad and bagayat lands have changed during the transition from an agrarian to an urban economy, I collected the ready reckoner rates in the Mumbai-Pune corridor region from 1996 to 2016. I chose 1996 because the Mumbai-Pune economic corridor was proposed in this year. In anticipation of the new corridor cities, land prices in the corridor region had already started increasing sporadically by 1996, but in general it was not until after the new economic corridor was completed that clear trends began to emerge in the fertility-location switch. The 1996 prices, then, still reflect agrarian determinants of land price, but the effects of market- and urban-oriented change on the corridor region are evident in the 2016 land prices.

Within the corridor region, I collected ready reckoner rates for 242 villages and census towns located in seven talukas: Panvel, Khalapur, Mawal, Mulshi, Haweli, Baramati, and Khed. I selected these talukas because six of them (with the exception of Baramati) fall within the Golden Triangle region, and the Mumbai-Pune economic corridor directly passes through them or indirectly exerts an influence on their land markets (for instance, though it does not directly pass through Mulshi taluka, the new corridor city Lavasa Lake City was built there because of the taluka's proximity to the new economic corridor). All of these six talukas, which differentially benefited from the earlier irrigation canals, are now proximate to the new economic corridor.

The seven talukas exemplify different property regimes. The Mulshi and Mawal talukas are the most underdeveloped regions from an agrarian past, but they are now being re-valued due to their proximity to the economic corridor. The Haweli taluka is a formerly developed agrarian region that now also benefits from its proximity to the new economic corridor. By contrast, the Baramati taluka was also a developed agrarian region—indeed, it was the most developed region in the previous era, and it is now the home constituency of Sharad Pawar and the epicenter of sugar politics—but it falls outside the Golden Triangle and is relatively distant from the economic corridor. The Khed region contains a mixed geography of multi-crop and waste lands, but its waste lands are now being re-valued due to their advantageous location close to the economic corridor. The Panvel and Khalapur talukas, due to their proximity to Mumbai, started industrializing in the 1940s, and they are now benefiting further from their proximity to the economic corridor.

How do these talukas relate to the earlier geography of agrarian capitalism at the turn of the nineteenth century? The Mulshi and Mawal talukas are the ghat regions, rich in rivers but devalued by dam flooding. The Haweli, Baramati, and Khed talukas are located in the "scarcity zone"—the former two were the epicenter of the later irrigation canals and sugar cooperatives; Khed received a patchwork of irrigation waters, with the lands on the plains getting water but those on the hills getting bypassed. Map 7a shows the location of the talukas vis-à-vis irrigation canals and economic corridors. Map 7b illustrates the changing prices of waste land (dongarpad) and multi-crop land (bagayat) for the years 1996 and 2016.[52]

Several trends are evident in these land-price maps. The 1996 land prices are from a time when agricultural productivity was still the main metric for valuing land markets and when the land markets had not started to adjust to the new development priorities of the economic corridors and related logistics infrastructures. Agricultural land was still tightly regulated, and a real-estate market had yet to be formed. The economic value of agricultural land derived not from the price of land but from the price of crops grown on the land. In 1996, therefore, land prices for bagayat land were higher than those for dongarpad land, but not by much. The main calibrator of the economic value of land was fertility, and the 1996 maps reveal the spatial mismatch between the sources of water for the irrigation canals and the beneficiaries of these canals. The talukas of Mawal and Mulshi occupy the ecologically rich mountain ranges of the Western Ghats, which is the source for some of the major rivers on the Indian subcontinent. These talukas have one of the highest densities of dams in the country, but they do not have any multicrop irrigated land; they are bereft of irrigation waters. See, for instance, the villages

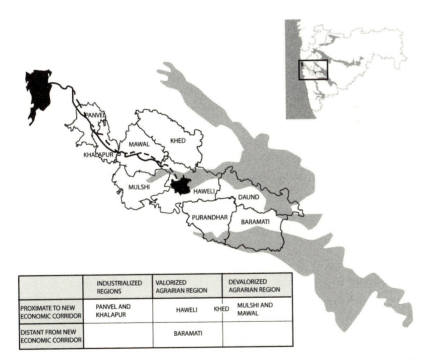

	INDUSTRIALIZED REGIONS	VALORIZED AGRARIAN REGION		DEVALORIZED AGRARIAN REGION
PROXIMATE TO NEW ECONOMIC CORRIDOR	PANVEL AND KHALAPUR	HAWELI	KHED	MULSHI AND MAWAL
DISTANT FROM NEW ECONOMIC CORRIDOR		BARAMATI		

Map 7a. Key map of the talukas for which land prices were collected and mapped.

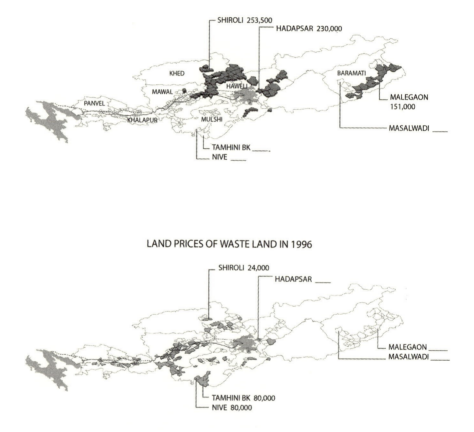

LAND PRICES OF IRRIGATED MULTI-CROP LAND IN 1996

SHIROLI 253,500
HADAPSAR 230,000
KHED
MAWAL
HAWELI
BARAMATI
PANVEL
MALEGAON
151,000
KHALAPUR
MULSHI
MASALWADI
TAMHINI BK
NIVE

LAND PRICES OF WASTE LAND IN 1996

SHIROLI 24,000
HADAPSAR
MALEGAON
MASALWADI
TAMHINI BK 80,000
NIVE 80,000

Map 7b. Changing land prices along the Mumbai-Pune economic corridor.

LAND PRICES OF IRRIGATED MULTI-CROP LAND IN 2016

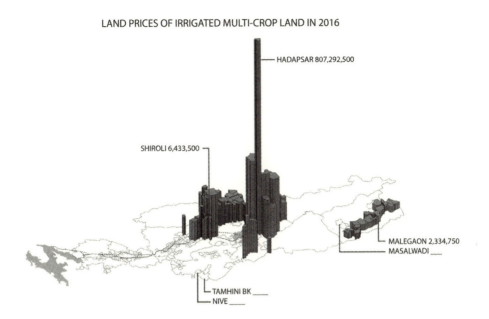

HADAPSAR 807,292,500

SHIROLI 6,433,500

MALEGAON 2,334,750
MASALWADI ____

TAMHINI BK ____
NIVE ____

LAND PRICES OF WASTE LAND IN 2016

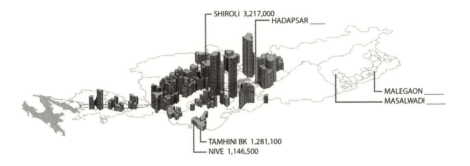

SHIROLI 3,217,000
HADAPSAR ____

MALEGAON ____
MASALWADI ____

TAMHINI BK 1,281,100
NIVE 1,146,500

of Nive and Tamhini Bk, both of which were flooded when the Mulshi dam was built in the early 1900s. These settlements have no multicrop land, only waste land priced at a low 80,000 rupees per hectare in 1996. On the other hand, notice that the talukas of Khed, Hadapsar, and Baramati have an abundance of well-watered multicrop land. Sharad Pawar has retained a stronghold over the state irrigation department and has ensured that irrigation waters flow in the direction of his home constituency, Baramati.

In Baramati, a dense and thriving cooperative complex dominates the cluster of villages in the southeast part of the taluka: three sugar cooperatives; a grape cooperative geared toward the wine export market; dairy cooperatives that supply milk to conglomerates like Britannia Industries and Schreiber Foods; thirty-one district cooperative banks that channel funds into these commodity cooperatives; and an education trust that controls a 150-acre education complex, which has now expanded into an information technology, biotechnology, and engineering college. It is worth noting that Malegaon, the epicenter of Pawar's cooperative complex, has rich agriculturally productive land that, in 1996, was priced at 151,000 rupees per hectare; in other words, the agrarian profit came not from the land itself but from the sugar grown on that land. Irrigation waters, however, do not flow evenly within Baramati. The richly irrigated sugarcane fields and the cooperative complex are concentrated in the southeastern part of the taluka; as one travels toward the northern and western boundaries, where Baramati meets Purandar and Daund, the irrigated countryside gives way to dry fields. The cluster of villages to the northwest, for example, including Masalwadi, does not have any multicrop land.[53] Also notice that the talukas of Panvel and Khalapur do not have any multicrop land. These talukas were identified in the 1973 Bombay Regional Plan as areas fit to absorb the urban-industrial expansion of Bombay, and because they were earmarked for urbanization, no irrigation canals were extended to them.[54] The left-leaning academics and journalists I spoke to have pointed to the lack of farming in these talukas and their vast swathes of agriculturally unproductive land in their support of the Mumbai-Pune economic corridor, but they do not realize that the new LARRA clause builds on earlier, socially produced uneven categories of land.

The 2016 land prices reveal key patterns in the agrarian-to-urban land transformation in western Maharashtra. The most advantageously located taluka in the region is Haweli. The city of Pune, located within Haweli, exerts its agglomeration shadow on its neighboring villages, and it is also one of the book-ends of the Mumbai-Pune Expressway. Notice that all the land catego-

Table 1. Land Prices of Representative Villages and Census Towns in the
Mumbai-Pune Corridor Region (Land prices in Indian rupees)

TALUKA	VILLAGE/ CENSUS TOWN	1996		2016	
		IRRIGATED LAND	WASTE LAND	IRRIGATED LAND	WASTE LAND
Mulshi	Nive	—	80,000	—	1,146,500
	Tamhini Bk	—	80,000	—	1,281,100
Baramati	Malegaon	151,000	—	2,334,750	—
	Masalwadi	—	—	—	—
Haweli	Hadapsar	230,000	—	807,292,500	—
	Fursungi	536,625	74,250	22,403,250	9,336,000
Khed	Shiroli	253,500	24,000	6,433,500	3,217,000

Note: These land prices are not adjusted for inflation. If one wants to calculate the land-price increase, the following method of compounded rate can be used: The compounded rate of increase for Hadapsar, for instance, works out to 62 percent. Corresponding inflation during this period was about 6 percent per annum. So, the percentage increase in land price from 1996 to 2016, adjusted for inflation, is 62 − 6 = 56 percent.

ries in Haweli registered a skyrocketing increase in price from 1996 to 2016—in particular, Hadapsar, the site of one of the most fêted recent real-estate projects, Magarpatta City, and recently incorporated within Pune Municipal Corporation. Hadapsar's land prices shot up in price from 230,000 rupees per hectare in 1996 to 807,292,500 rupees in 2016. Though LARRA prohibits the state from acquiring irrigated land in the interests of food security, Magarpatta City represents a wider trend of agrarian elites becoming key players in urban real-estate markets by voluntarily converting their irrigated lands into urban townships. To get a sense of land prices just outside the city boundary, see the prices for Fursungi, which is adjacent to Hadapsar but continues to be governed by Gram Panchayats. Because Fursungi has not been incorporated within the Pune Municipal Corporation, its land prices are lower than Hadapsar's, but its irrigated land has still gone up in price, thanks to its proximity to Pune, from 536,625 rupees in 1996 to 22,403,250 rupees in 2016. The Hadapsar region is the focus of Chapter 2, which examines the making of Magarpatta City.

Another trend evident from this data is that the economic corridor has opened up previously disconnected land to new influxes of private capital. In Table 1, see the 2016 land price for waste land in Mulshi. These waste lands were relatively worthless as economic assets in 1996, having a market price averaging only 80,000 rupees per hectare; now, they fetch around 1,200,000 rupees per hectare, going up to more than 7,500,000 rupees in certain villages located adjacent to the Mumbai-Pune economic corridor. The location of these re-valued waste lands merits attention: they are clustered around the dams that both submerged the low-lying fertile areas and transformed the higher-elevation areas into isolated waste lands. The making of these waste lands displaced forest dependents to relocation sites in drought-prone talukas like Daund. But the profits from the re-valuation of these waste lands are now being entirely captured by firms from Mumbai, whose shareholders are not local residents but distant (often foreign) investors.

It is worth noting that though the price of waste land in Mulshi has increased, it has not done so to the same extent as Hadapsar's irrigated lands. Because the Mulshi and Mawal talukas were bypassed by the Green Revolution, they did not develop the forms of market linkages needed for market-oriented urbanization. The precise nature of these market linkages is the topic for another book, but, for now, I want to emphasize that talukas bypassed during the Green Revolution and now connected to the new economic corridors are witnessing speculative rather than industrial development. The remaking of these forest lands into a new corridor city, Lavasa Lake City, is the focus of Chapter 3.

One of the most unexpected findings from these land-price analyses is the 2016 price of advantageously located waste land vis-à-vis disadvantageously located multicrop land. Now that location trumps fertility as the main determinant of land price, the previously undesirable waste land of an agrarian economy is a desirable market asset. Compare, for instance, the map of waste land in 2016 with that of multicrop land during the same year. Notice that waste lands in Khed are now valued at almost the same price as the multicrop land in Baramati. This trend becomes more striking when we compare the land prices of villages in Khed and Baramati. Shiroli, a village in Khed, is advantageously located at the intersection of two new postliberalization transportation infrastructures: the Mumbai-Pune Expressway and the proposed new Pune international airport. Multicrop land in Shiroli has increased at a faster rate than the waste land, the former now being priced at 6,433,500 rupees and the latter at 3,217,000 rupees. However, the waste land in Shiroli now fetches a higher market price than even the most irrigated land in Malegaon. Malegaon, in Baramati, is the heartland of Pawar's sugar politics, but its irrigated land fetches 2,334,750 rupees, which is lower than Shiroli's waste land priced at 3,217,000 rupees.

These waste-land re-valuations are unsettling existing caste hierarchies. Long histories of sociospatial segregation produced a land-based form of social hierarchy, with the Maratha-Kunbis appropriating the irrigated multi-crop land and the Adivasis being relegated to the undesirable waste land. Now, the rising value of advantageously located waste land is disrupting these agrarian sources of land-based power. In the Khed region, younger-generation Adivasis, belonging to the Thakkar collective, are seeing themselves in a new light within their changing caste- and land-based society. Both the rising price of their former waste land and the availability of informal industrial work in the urbanizing Golden Triangle region hold the promise of a transition from a caste-ridden agrarian past to a hopefully caste-equal urban future. These economic shifts, together with the reserved seats for Scheduled Tribes in local governments, are leading to demands not only for material redistribution but for a new politics of recognition. In the Khed region, many younger-generation Thakkars are now refusing to work in the fields of Maratha-Kunbi landowners, leading to an acute agricultural labor shortage in the region. A common refrain among Maratha-Kunbi landowners is *"Maz-door nahi milte"* (Workers cannot be found). Just a decade earlier, the agricultural wage rate was 16 rupees a day; now the landowners complain that "no one comes for less than 100." The Thakkars and other agricultural laborers have started negotiating their wage rates based on the standard set both by the informal industrial economy and by the Central Government's guaranteed-employment social welfare program, the Mahatma Gandhi National Rural Employment Guarantee Scheme. The re-valuation of advantageously located waste land is the focus of Chapter 4.

The next three chapters focus on the restructuring of land markets in the Mumbai-Pune corridor region and the emergence of new agrarian-urban constituencies in place of older, agrarian, land-based social relations. Before moving to the case studies, I will end this chapter by looking at the changing geography of agrarian to urban uneven development and the political implications of these uneven spatial transformation.

The Politics of Uneven Development

In its 2009 *World Development Report* (*WDR*), the World Bank acknowledged for the first time that geography is central to economic development.[55] With a focus on uneven development, the report argues that policy efforts at spatial redistribution have proven futile and that uneven development is an inevitable correlate of economic development. The central message of the report is that "economic growth will be unbalanced; to try to spread out economic activity is to discourage it." It claims that when policy-makers seek to balance economic development and to redirect growth from prosperous to impoverished areas, they are unnecessarily interfering with the market logic of agglomeration. At its simplest, "agglomeration" here means the economic advantages of proximity, namely the ability of firms in an industrial cluster to share inputs that exploit economies of scale, to match the skills of labor to those needed by the firms, and to learn from spillovers of knowledge and ideas.[56] The challenge for governments, then, is to "allow, even encourage, unbalanced economic growth, and yet ensure inclusive development."

The *WDR*'s policy of deliberate uneven development has attracted much criticism.[57] Of particular significance is the complete neglect of history, despite the fact that economists are now becoming more and more aware of the path dependencies created by earlier institutional formations in later economic performance.[58] Despite the *WDR*'s intent to bring spatial dimensions into economic development, this blindness to history leaves out questions that are central to this book, namely why and how current, uneven urban development is building on past, uneven agrarian capitalism. However, the report's recommendation of unbalanced economic growth finds strong resonances in the spatial policies of both the Green Revolution and the new postliberalization infrastructure-development programs.

The uneven spatial effects of the Green Revolution have been well researched, most notably by Francine Frankel, who analyzes the "economic gains and political costs" of the program.[59] The program provided heavy subsidies of water, seeds, and fertilizers to certain strategic agrarian regions, thus producing a clear geography of economic prosperity that arced from the northwest to the southeast of India. These food-surplus regions represented the economic gains of the program; it was successful in ensuring an increase in food production and keeping the threat of famines in check. But the gains came at a high cost. Alongside the arc of new agricultural prosperity, a parallel arc developed of economic impoverishment. The region from the northeast to the southeast, covering vast swathes of central India, became a sorely neglected zone. Now, these regions are the site of a raging civil war with the Maoists, also called the Naxalites. Indigenous groups and the rural poor are caught in a crossfire between the state and extra-legal left-wing groups, and former prime minister Manmohan Singh has referred to the area as

"India's greatest internal security challenge." The irony of the Green Revolution is that, though it was pushed forward by the United States in the 1960s at the height of the Cold War, to avert the threat of communism or the "red revolution," the deliberate policy of uneven spatial development led to the transformation of the neglected regions into the Maoist-controlled "Red Corridor." The state of Maharashtra exemplifies this phenomenon: the easternmost district of Maharashtra, Gadchiroli, has been neglected since the early twentieth century, and it is now part of the wider swath of the Red Corridor.

The policy response to the Red Corridor has been a massive surge in road-building. The economic corridors are not the only transportation programs in postliberalization India. A parallel road-building program—equally ambitious, at least in terms of the scale of its coverage—is the Pradhan Mantri Gram Sadak Yojana (PMGSY). Launched in 2000, the PMGSY is a road-development program that focuses on improving connectivity in "rural" areas of the country. "Rural" here has a specific connotation: the program largely concentrates on sixty districts in nine states where the Naxalites are active, identified by the Central Government's Ministry of Home Affairs as "Left Wing Extremism affected areas."

While the entire PMGSY had an aggregate investment of 14 billion rupees as of January 2016, the estimated cost of a single economic corridor, the Delhi-Mumbai Industrial Corridor (DMIC), is almost ten times more, at 100 billion rupees. The parastatal in charge of the DMIC belongs to a new generation of nimbler and more market-savvy quasi-public agencies that meet the needs of foreign investors: the DMIC Authority, for example, is headquartered in a posh hotel suite, and its CEO is well known for his branding strategies, which have been used to promote tourism in the country.[60] The PMGSY, by contrast, is implemented by the Border Road Organization, a public agency with a clear political mandate of national security. The Border Road Organization's mission is to "construct and maintain operational road infrastructure for the armed forces in inhospitable, far flung border areas."[61] In other words, the new economic corridors are geared to global economic integration, while the new rural roads are driven by concerns about political integration.

This parallel strategy of building economic corridors for richer regions and basic roads for poorer regions is an attempt to bridge the spatial divide, but it fails to take into account the agrarian history that produced these spatial divides in the first place. The DMIC website argues that the "*raison d'être* of the DMIC is that agriculture has failed to create adequate livelihood opportunities; therefore, setting up industrial nodes would help employment generation; the DMIC believes it can create more than 25 million jobs in the next seven years."[62] But these claims overlook the more complex, urban-rural market linkages put in place by the earlier agricultural-modernization programs, which created the background conditions for the new urban-oriented economic corridors. When market analysts from Credit Suisse see the new rural roads of the PMGSY as sufficient triggers for economic productivity— "once there is connectivity, hitherto isolated hamlets become part of larger clusters of 200–300 villages with 50,000–100,000 consumers, against 1,000–2,000 previously; this allows for economies of scale, specialization and flourishing of microenterprises"[63]—they similarly ignore the raft of other public policies that are needed for the development of regional economic clusters. The PMGSY road-building program works on the untested assumption that a lack of roads means a lack of market integration.[64] But the density of roads tells us little or nothing about the existence or shape of urban-rural market linkages, and we cannot assume that there is a simple causality between the building of new rural roads and better economic activity.[65]

My critique of the PMGSY program is not to assert that the Red Corridor conflict is only about economic neglect. As recent scholarly work on these regions shows, the Naxal conflict in some regions is about being "unseen by the state"; in other regions, it is about exploitative core-dependency relations between the mineral-rich forests occupied by Adivasis and the resource wants of a liberalizing and urbanizing society; in many cases, it is also underpinned by strong assertions of tribal sovereignty and identity.[66] In short, the Naxal conflict in the non–Green Revolution regions is as variegated and complex as the market-driven urbanization in former Green Revolution regions. My broader claim is that the deliberate policy of uneven development espoused by the World Bank has untenable political costs. The need for legitimacy should compel India's Central and state governments to temper their policy of uneven development. Even the colonial state had to reverse its development policies when famine broke out in the Bombay Presidency, shifting public spending from railways to irrigation canals. The postliberalization Indian state is pursuing a dual developmental policy to bridge the spatial divide, but it is doing so without meaningfully intervening to correct the earlier and present geographies of uneven development.

CHAPTER 2

From Sugar to Real Estate

Pune is surrounded by a verdant countryside of fertile sugarcane fields; this is one of the most agriculturally prosperous regions of the country. It is hard to believe that just a few hundred kilometers east is the drought-prone and suicide-ridden region of Vidarbha. The Pune region owes its prosperity to a rich network of sugar cooperatives, generously subsidized by the state government, and backed by powerful Maratha politicians, the most recent being Sharad Pawar. The sugar-rich regions of western Maharashtra send the largest number of elected representatives to the state legislature.

The past few decades have seen new aspirations forming among the sugar elites. As Pune started an explosive outward urban growth from the 1980s onward, the sugar elites saw a new opportunity in city-building. Satish Magar, one of the sugar elites in the Magarpatta area, took the lead in convincing sugarcane farmers to pool their fragmented agricultural land into an integrated township, a primarily residential development catering to the burgeoning urban middle class. The 600-acre Magarpatta City is the first integrated township in the Pune region, advertising itself as near to Pune but far from its crime and congestion. Magarpatta City, completed in 2006, became the precedent for a new form of urbanization, in which agrarian landowners become shareholders in new real-estate companies and thus continue to retain control over their landed assets. Following the commercial success of Magarpatta City, other agrarian landowners from the Pune region started consulting with the Magarpatta company to replicate the Magarpatta model in their areas. The company is now developing the Nanded township—700 acres in size, about 15 kilometers from Magarpatta—and there are three more similar projects in the pipeline.

Magarpatta City is held up in media and policy circles as an exemplar of the form of urbanization that should be replicated in other parts of the countryside. The township is celebrated as an example of "inclusive capitalism"[1] and "a shining example of how urban areas can expand to accommodate the needs of urbanisation without hurting the interests of rural landowners through forced or unfair acquisition."[2] In her analysis of this phenomenon, Neha Sami refrains from celebrating the Magarpatta experiment but instead situates it within theories of urban politics.[3] Sami characterizes the integrated township as an ad hoc set of coalitions that will arise whenever mayors and city governments lack the authority to control urban development; individuals who can successfully build coalitions in these fragmented institutional landscapes step in and become power brokers. I agree with Sami on the relative powerlessness of city governments in such cases and about the fragmented nature of the political power involved. But I depart from her characterization of ad hoc politics and argue instead that experiments like Magarpatta City represent a wider trend of agrarian elites adjusting their politics and economics to the rewards and risks of a newly liberalizing economy. These agrarian elites, who started gaining legitimacy as part of the anticolonial and anti-Brahmin movements of the early twentieth century, seized power in the state legislatures soon after Independence. Though regional agrarian histories vary, the national-development programs of land reforms and the Green Revolution benefited these constituents and helped to transform them into an affluent agro-capitalist class. In Maharashtra, the Maratha elites articulated and advanced their interests through the sugar cooperatives. Now, in an urbanizing and liberalizing economy, the sugar elites are adapting old agrarian institutions into new organizational forms; the urban promoters of sugar origins are mobilizing the same political and economic networks that made the sugar cooperatives possible on arid land in the 1960s and 1970s for the new urban townships.

In narrating the shift from sugar cooperatives to real-estate companies, this chapter makes two claims. First, it examines whether certain agrarian property regimes are better prepared than others to reap the benefits of urban- and market-oriented change. More specifically, it investigates the question of whether all regions with agrarian cooperatives have the forms of capital needed to make a smooth transition from an agrarian to urban economy. Here, a comparison with Gujarat is instructive. Central Gujarat is home to another wildly successful agrarian cooperative experiment, milk cooperatives, and the region is dominated by the organized agrarian constituency of the Patidars (or Patels). But, unlike the sugarcane-rich regions of western Maharashtra, the Patidars did not adapt their dairy cooperatives into urban real-estate companies. I elaborate below on this comparison to emphasize that it is not just the presence of agrarian cooperatives but the property relations within those cooperatives that matter. The sugar cooperatives are premised on private property rights: even the most marginal sugarcane grower is part of the cooperative, but membership is restricted to landowners, excluding nonpropertied cultivators. The dairy farmers, on the other hand, graze their livestock on common grazing land, and landownership is not a prerequisite for cooperative membership. The comparison challenges the conventionally held view that the cooperative form of organizing property is an "alternative to capitalism."[4] Instead, these property forms need to be investigated within their political and economic contexts and linked to the local power structures in which they are embedded. In western Maharashtra, the presence of the sugar cooperatives did not protect agrarian users from postliberalization land commodification but instead facilitated new market relations in land.

Second, I compare the Magarpatta experiment with another, earlier "farmers' company," Bhama Construction Limited. The idea for Bhama was floated by Sharad Joshi, the charismatic UN bureaucrat–turned–leader of an agrarian movement, the Shetkari Sanghatana, which swept into power in the western Maharashtra countryside in the 1970s. Joshi was a successful organizer, capable of fostering collective action among large numbers of agrarian constituents. Despite his organizational prowess, however, Joshi was unable to implement his idea of the "farmers' company." Comparing Satish Magar with Sharad Joshi underscores the fact that not all voluntarily consolidated agricultural lands can be smoothly transformed into urban real estate. Magarpatta City was made possible when certain agrarian constituents applied pressure on the state government to reregulate agricultural land for real-estate developments. The making of these urban real-estate markets was politically mediated: sugar elites like Satish Magar, who had political networks with state-level politicians, were successful in gaining legal exceptions to convert their otherwise protected sugarcane land to an urban township; due to his oppositional stance to state-level politicians, Sharad Joshi was denied these legal privileges. The Magar and Joshi comparison, therefore, illuminates the nuances of how agrarian networks are shaping new urban real-estate laws.

Cooperative, Inc.

> Recitals of a legendary past: What started as a project
> to help farmers gain the full benefit of their land use
> has today spun into a dream for thousands who set out
> in search of a better life. Urban cities of Maharashtra
> faced the problem of unauthorized constructions and
> haphazard development. Pune city was also a patch of
> unplanned layouts that was destined to be a marionette
> in the hands of wealthy industrialists. Until 120 farmers
> of Magarpatta came together with a dream to create a
> new way of life. They pooled in their ancestral lands
> held by them for over 300 years and proposed the idea
> of "Magarpatta City"—an innovative township, to the
> Pune Municipal Corporation and the Government of
> Maharashtra.

This is how Magarpatta is marketed in its brochure "The Story of Magarpatta— The Pride of Pune City," with the aspirational subtitle "Life as It Should Be." The completed and functional Magarpatta City is a higher-income enclave of apartments, row houses, bungalows, food courts, information technology (IT) complexes, schools, and 120 acres of gardens and lawns. A block away from this dense urban environment, vestiges of the 1990s landscape remain in the few sugarcane fields surrounding Magarpatta City. These sugarcane growers, like the Magarpatta ones, have ambitions to be developers, but they are holding on to their plots, waiting for land prices to soar higher before starting their own residential and commercial developments.

Before the 1990s, the Hadapsar Gram Panchayat was the site of fertile sugarcane fields. The largest landowning family in Hadapsar were the Magars, a politically influential network whose most prominent member, Annasaheb Magar, had been a Member of Parliament for the Congress Party in the 1970s. During his political tenure, Magar channeled many development projects to his home constituency of Hadapsar, including the creation of a cooperative sugar factory to benefit the local sugarcane growers. The 1980s saw a wave of

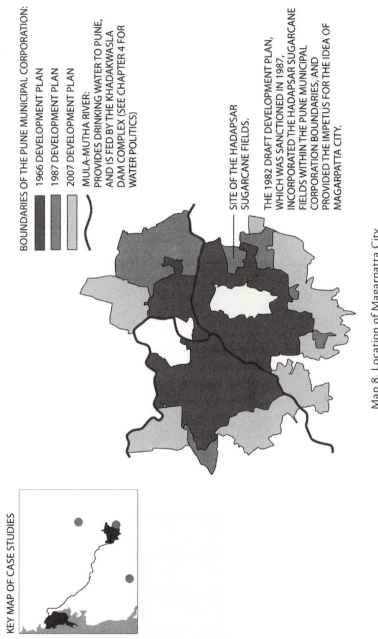

KEY MAP OF CASE STUDIES

BOUNDARIES OF THE PUNE MUNICIPAL CORPORATION:

1966 DEVELOPMENT PLAN

1987 DEVELOPMENT PLAN

2007 DEVELOPMENT PLAN

MULA-MUTHA RIVER:
PROVIDES DRINKING WATER TO PUNE,
AND IS FED BY THE KHADAKWASLA
DAM COMPLEX (SEE CHAPTER 4 FOR
WATER POLITICS)

SITE OF THE HADAPSAR
SUGARCANE FIELDS.

THE 1982 DRAFT DEVELOPMENT PLAN,
WHICH WAS SANCTIONED IN 1987,
INCORPORATED THE HADAPSAR SUGARCANE
FIELDS WITHIN THE PUNE MUNICIPAL
CORPORATION BOUNDARIES, AND
PROVIDED THE IMPETUS FOR THE IDEA OF
MAGARPATTA CITY.

Map 8. Location of Magarpatta City.

Figure 3. Magarpatta City interspersed amid sugarcane fields waiting to be developed.

urbanizing changes sweep over the Hadapsar area. In 1982, the Pune Municipal Corporation's Draft Development Plan marked Hadapsar as a future urban zone, which meant that the Magars' lands could be forcibly acquired in the future by the government under the Urban Land Ceiling and Regulation Act (ULCRA). The purpose of this Act was to redistribute urban lands: land beyond a certain acreage would be acquired by the government and used for public purposes, like housing for the urban poor. Hadapsar was also facing acute agricultural labor shortages, because the laborers who had lived and worked on the sugarcane fields were now finding alternative employment in Pune's informal industrial economy. With the impending threats of land acquisition and agricultural labor shortages, Annasaheb's nephew, Satish Magar, saw an opportunity in land development. He experimented with an innovative real-estate idea and eventually convinced the small and marginal sugarcane growers in Hadapsar to pool their agricultural land, convert the aggregated territory into an urban township, and set up a real-estate company, the Magarpatta Township Development and Construction Company Limited (MTDCCL), owned entirely by these sugarcane farmers.

Magarpatta City is an instance of land readjustment, an idea based on the principle of a "property rights exchange."[5] The land-readjustment agency, which could be a public or private agency, assembles fragmented agricultural lands in a particular area, deducts a percentage of the land for public infrastructure or for sale to cover the cost of local infrastructure, and re-allocates the remaining lands to the original landowners in proportion to the size of the landholdings given up. Land readjustment has several advantages over the pure state mode of land assembly (eminent domain) and the pure market mode (individual market transactions). First, existing landowners are not displaced from their lands. Second, land readjustment overcomes the common challenge of determining the just compensation price for acquired land or the fair-market value for market transactions. In regions around India's new economic corridors, land prices are skyrocketing to unprecedented levels, sometimes as high as 150 times the original land value after land-use conversion. In such cases, it is difficult for policy-makers and buyers of agricultural land to predict how much the land will increase in price; the first round of land exchange may take place without conflict, but in later rounds adjacent landowners who have seen the rapid increases in land price may realize that the earlier condemnees or sellers got an unfair deal.

The embittered nature of later acquisitions is evident in the case of Hinjewadi, the IT cluster set up on formerly agricultural land at the edge of Pune.

The earlier land acquisition for phases I and II proceeded calmly, but in the later phases the agrarian landowners put up a stiff resistance against land acquisition, having realized that, though the industrial parastatal had compensated the earlier landowners at 200,000 rupees per acre in 2003, when the prevalent market price was only 100,000 rupees, in less than three years the land values in Hinjewadi had more than quadrupled. Including landowners as shareholders, by contrast, allows them to remain beneficiaries of future increases in the land price.

Third, land readjustment allows existing landowners to capture the profits from land redevelopment, unlike in eminent domain or individual market transactions, where the state agency or private developer captures these windfall profits. Fourth, the compensation price for expropriated land or the price of land in market transactions is determined by the location of the plot of land: land that is closer to the infrastructure fetches a higher price than plots at a greater distance. In land readjustment, all landowners within the project boundary benefit regardless of the location of their plot of land; the main criterion in allocating profits is not location but the size of the plot within the project boundary.

The Magarpatta case is a variant of land readjustment: rather than readjusted plots of land, shares in the real-estate company are returned to the landowners. The company was organized to ensure that each landholding family receives shares equivalent to the acreage of land that they gave up for the new development. Satish Magar deliberately formed a company rather than a cooperative so that a professional staff with real-estate expertise could manage the company but ownership would be retained by agrarian landowners. The company has rules to ensure that ownership is not transferred at any point from the agrarian landowners to outsiders: the company shares cannot be publicly traded; they can only be traded among the landholding families. Within a household, shares are allocated equally among all adult members, including women. The company is unique in including women as property beneficiaries, and their inclusion is particularly innovative in the patrilocal context of India, where women are expected to move to their husbands' homes and villages after marriage and have often been denied a share in land on the specious argument that giving them rights over an immobile asset will increase the rate of absentee landownership. Magarpatta circumvents this regressive practice by granting women a financial interest in the land via equity shares. In a context of coercive land acquisitions and displacements, the Magarpatta case seems laudable both for its noncoercive mode of land assembly and for sharing the profits from land redevelopment with existing landowners, including women.

To get a ground-up view of this experiment in land readjustment, I needed to speak to the landowners-turned-shareholders. I reached Pune in December 2010 and for the next few months tried, unsuccessfully, to gain access to the sugarcane shareholders. Researchers studying gated communities have noted the difficulty in entering these developments,[6] which, unlike public cities, are regulated as private property. In gated communities, the public's right to enter urban spaces can be treated as what is referred to in property law as a nuisance (i.e., an undue interference with the enjoyment of private property). Physical entry into Magarpatta City is possible, at least for urban middle-class Indians like me, who dress in a certain way and can display elite markers, such as a clipped English accent, if needed. But it was not physical access that I wanted; rather I hoped to gain access to the sugarcane shareholders themselves. With some naïveté, I had assumed that talking to the security guards and hanging out in the residential parks of the new apartment complexes would enable me to find out where the sugarcane shareholders lived. This plan failed: the security guards grew suspicious after the first day. The residents in two of the parks I visited were mainly IT professionals, most of them not from Pune, and they had no idea which of their neighbors were former farmers.

I then visited the MTDCCL office and left my business card to request an appointment with Satish Magar—in vain. After five months of trying to secure an interview, however, a family friend who knew Satish Magar arranged for me to have a thirty-minute meeting with him. After the interview, Satish Magar introduced me to a sugarcane shareholder, Kishore Magar,[7] who now works in the marketing division of the MTDCCL. Over the course of the next six weeks, Kishore Magar drove me around the township, introducing me to five sugarcane shareholders and their families. I had open-ended interviews with these shareholders that ranged from an hour to sometimes an entire day, complete with a hospitable home-cooked lunch.

Satish Magar is a savvy businessman. He has developed a strong brand image for the new integrated township that advertises a new form of urbanization, with farmers as developers. He calls Magarpatta a "city within a city,"[8] and he places the farmer at the center of urbanization: "At a time when urbanization is fueled by foreign direct investment [FDI], the investors in our [Magarpatta] township are farmers; this is farmers' direct investment."[9] In the late 1980s, when the sugarcane landowners in Hadapsar Gram

Panchayat were facing acute labor shortages, many marginal growers, owning less than 2.5 acres of land, started selling their land in individual transactions to developers. Satish Magar's family owned around 40 percent of the
sugarcane fields in Hadapsar Village, and he convinced his neighbors to not
sell their land individually but instead to pool their lands to develop an urban township.

The importance of the size of the agrarian landholdings becomes evident
when one examines the ongoing contestation over Khed City (see Chapter 4).
Even though Khed City is only 40 kilometers away from Magarpatta City and
the state has passed the Integrated Township Policy to facilitate agrarian-to-
urban transitions, the Khed landowners had to rely on Revenue Department
bureaucrats to mediate their land assembly. Their difficulty in fostering voluntary collective action is not surprising, however, when one looks at the land
records for their villages: a 2-acre plot of land in Kanersar Gram Panchayat
in the Khed region, for instance, is co-owned by seventy-eight landowners,
many of whom do not even reside within the Khed region and have migrated
to Mumbai and other neighboring cities.[10] The Khed region is thus representative of much of agricultural land in India, which is highly fragmented
in size and fractionated in ownership.[11] The more consolidated pattern of
landownership in the Hadapsar region made it easier for Satish Magar to
take the lead in collectively assembling land from other sugarcane growers.
His extensive landholding is connected to the region's history of sugar cooperatives, when the sugar elites owned large tracts of land interspersed among
the lands of more marginal sugarcane growers.

In addition to the consolidated pattern of landownership, what enabled
the formation of Magarpatta City were the relations of trust cultivated
through years of belonging to the same sugar cooperative. Ramesh-kaka, a
seventy-year-old landowner-turned-shareholder who gave up 4 acres of his
land for the Magarpatta township, gave his account of the negotiations leading up to the township, which spells out the role of sugar cooperatives in forging trust between Satish Magar and the small sugarcane-growing families:

> I have been farming here since 1965. Hadapsar, Mundhwa, all of these
> areas were rich sugar-growing areas. The best fields were here. The ca-
> nal from Khadakwasla Dam comes here for agriculture, we do not
> have any water problems. . . . In 1993, our Magar family had a meet-
> ing, and all of us were convinced of the [Magarpatta] project. We gave
> a signature, we did not ask anything, we just gave our signature, we

trusted Satish Magar. Annasaheb Magar became an MP [Member of
Parliament] from here. He made a market here; it is the biggest market in Pune. He started a sugar factory here for the farmers, 20 kilometers from here, started in 1969. All our sugarcane from here went
to this factory. As Annasaheb Magar helped us, Satish Magar is also
helping the farmers with the township.[12]

Ramesh-kaka's narrative highlights the huge risks taken by small and
marginal owner-cultivators in joining Satish Magar's unique land experiment. Being a member of a sugar cooperative is one thing; being a shareholder of a real-estate company is something else. It is relatively easy to
convince sugarcane cultivators to join a cooperative because sugarcane is a
highly perishable commodity—sugar cannot be extracted from sugarcane
unless it is processed within twenty-four hours of harvesting.[13] This creates
a strong incentive for sugarcane cultivators to send their crops to a sugar cooperative. Landowners, on the other hand, have the option of holding on to
their land indefinitely, in anticipation of higher market prices, and it takes
more effort to convince them to give it up for equity membership in a company. Moreover, in joining a sugar cooperative, cane-growers are, at most,
risking one harvest by turning over their crops to the cooperative. Members
of a land-shareholding company, on the other hand, face higher sunk costs
and higher opportunity costs. Even if it took Satish Magar more than a single meeting to convince Ramesh-kaka and the other cane-growers to sign up
for his experiment, it would not have been possible if not for the bonds of
trust between the Magar political elites and their plebeian neighbors.

Satish Magar has now gained a reputation as a farmer-developer. When
the 1997 Development Plan for Pune again expanded the municipal boundaries to incorporate twenty-three new villages, Satish Magar used his reputational capital as a farmer-developer to convince agrarian landowners
outside the western edge of Pune to form a new integrated township, Nanded
City. The MTDCCL is the developer of the now-completed Nanded City;
the company's shareholders own 51 percent of the Nanded City shares,
with the remaining 49 percent owned by the Nanded landowners. As the
Magarpatta model expands to other sugar-cooperative regions, the earlier
rounds of sugarcane shareholders will benefit from these successive township developments.

The cooperatives, then, are a key organizational vehicle in enabling past
agrarian relationships to be carried into an urbanizing present. Agricultural

Figure 4. Villas of the Magarpatta sugarcane-landowners-turned-shareholders.

cooperatives were a crucial part of the Green Revolution program: they were the conduits through which seeds, fertilizers, and credit were channeled to agrarian constituents in return for their electoral support. Extrapolating from the Magarpatta case, can we say that all regions with successful agricultural-commodity cooperatives will make an easier transition into urban real estate? An instructive comparison for our purposes is that of sugar versus milk cooperatives, which illustrates that it is not just the cooperative form of organizing commodity production but the property relations of cooperatives that matters in times of economic change.

Unlike the sugar cooperatives, which became political institutions for both the Maratha elite and the Congress Party, Gujarat's milk cooperatives were controlled by technocratic elites, with the U.S.-educated Dr. Verghese Kurien leading the organization. Starting in the 1960s, Dr. Kurien scaled up the central Gujarat dairy-cooperative model into a national development program called Operation Flood, which received substantial funding from UNICEF, OXFAM, the European Economic Community, and the World Bank. In his influential work on cooperatives in India, B. S. Baviskar offers a number of reasons for the differences between the political and the technocratic management of milk and sugar.[14] One explanation is caste politics. The Patidars who initiated the dairy cooperatives at a regional scale in 1946 were worried that the expansion of the cooperatives into distant villages would result in the rival and numerically preponderant "backward-class" group of the Barias taking control of the cooperatives. The Patidars thus deliberately opted for a depoliticization of the milk cooperatives in order to keep milk out of caste and party politics.[15] Another explanation is that sugarcane is a cash crop, usually making it the major source of a household's income. Sugar-cooperative members are therefore highly motivated to get involved in cooperative politics, to ensure that the board of directors' decisions do not negatively affect their livelihood. Income from milk, on the other hand, is usually a supplementary source of income, making it less imperative for the milk-cooperative members to get involved in the cooperative's day-to-day affairs. As a result, the milk cooperatives did not get politicized and it was possible for Dr. Kurien to retain technocratic control over them.

I contend that the main difference between sugar and milk cooperatives lies in their property relations in land, which explains why the former has become a conduit for reproducing agrarian land-based privileges in an urban economy and the latter has not. The sugar economy relies on private property rights: sugarcane landowners, no matter how marginal, may be members of the cooperative, but agricultural laborers may not. Members of the milk cooperative, on the other hand, need only access to land, not ownership of it. The World Bank, in its evaluation of Operation Flood,[16] pointed to the fact that dairy farming has a low barrier to entry—just ownership of one or two cows—and this low bar makes dairy cooperatives a more viable alternative to targeted poverty-alleviation programs. Most dairy farmers rely on common grazing lands for their livestock; what they own, the cows themselves, cannot be easily converted into anything else.

The reorganization of sugar cooperatives into real-estate companies highlights the fact that the cooperative form does not always act as a bulwark against land commodification. If nonpropertied constituents have a voice in the current land debate over land-use change, it is highly likely that they will prioritize dairy, rather than sugar, cooperatives as the institutional conduits during a transition. A renewed dairy-cooperative policy would result in a different land-use pattern of protected land in the commons.

Agrarian Elites in "Land, Liquor, and Learning"

In recounting his experience of owning and living in an urban township, Ramesh-kaka extolled the "world-class" virtues of Magarpatta City. In the mid-1990s, as part of a tour organized by the Maratha Chamber of Commerce and Industry, Satish Magar traveled with a group of other sugarcane farmers to San Jose in California and to other cities in the United States. Ramesh-kaka took part in this tour, and Magarpatta, to him, has all the attributes of living in a "foreign country." This is particularly true of its infrastructural services, including electricity, roads, plumbing, and internet services, which are provided by the Magarpatta City Property Management Services (PMS)—a private company owned by Satish Magar's brother. Magarpatta residents pay property taxes to the Pune Municipal Corporation (i.e., the municipal government), but they also pay maintenance charges to PMS for the private services within the township. In comparing Magarpatta City to other new townships coming up in the Pune region, Ramesh-kaka proudly proclaimed the benefits of the former:

> Amanora, Blueridge [nearby townships], they are not like Magarpatta. Here, the standards are very high, *ek dam safety* [absolute safety], it's like a foreign country. If we have any problem—drainage, lights, roads,

we call our services company, PMS. Someone will be here within five minutes. You will not find this anywhere in the world. Anywhere else, they give you a house, and then they will tell you to go to the corporation after that. We pay property taxes to Pune Municipal Corporation, though most of our services are maintained by PMS. We paid a one-time 3.5 lakhs [3,500,000 rupees] for maintenance, and all the services are maintained from that interest. No corporation person comes here. Everything is done by PMS. This is the number one city in India, a world-class city.[17]

When Ramesh-kaka proudly stated that Magarpatta works perfectly without the state ("no corporation person comes here"), he overlooked the crucial role of the state government in granting legal privileges to Satish Magar regarding land and water—first in the form of exemptions, and then in the form of new laws. Highly visible to Magarpatta residents are the private service providers, like PMS, who distribute water and other utilities within the township boundaries. What is invisible to them is the strong role of the state in ensuring that water, power, and other networks are channelled up to the boundary walls of the township.

Though Magarpatta residents may be oblivious to the hand of the state in their lifestyle, other people, who are deprived of basic services so that Magarpatta and Nanded can get their constant utility supplies, are not. A public-interest litigation filed by a Right-to-Information (RTI) activist charges the Water Resources Department of "illegally" installing a permanent valve in the Khadakwasla Dam to divert water to Nanded City.[18] In an earlier, agrarian economy, the Maratha elites controlled land and water resources through the sugar cooperatives; now sugar elites like Satish Magar are leveraging the same political and social networks to mobilize these key resources for urban real-estate development. Magar is frank and open about the support he received from the Nationalist Congress Party (NCP) during the planning stages of Magarpatta. The NCP was in power in the early 1990s, when Magar first started approaching public officials for approval to convert agricultural land to urban uses. India has a highly prohibitive land-conversion regime, which is partly a vestige of the colonial era, when agricultural land taxes were a significant source of government revenue, but also a product of the socialist years, when policies were put in place to curb "speculation and profiteering from land."[19] The ULCRA prevents landowners from consolidating urban land beyond a certain acreage, and the Maharashtra Land Revenue Act prohibits nonagriculturalists from purchasing agricultural land. These regulations initially prevented the sugar elites from becoming real-estate developers, but Magar's close political connections with top state-level politicians enabled him to get exemptions from both of them.

Sharad Pawar, the founder and leading political figure of the NCP, was the chief minister of Maharashtra at the time when the Magars began the land-conversion process. As a former Congress politician and a sugar elite, Pawar had close professional relationships with Annasaheb Magar's family. More recently, Satish Magar's political connections with Pawar have been strengthened by a personal relationship: on one occasion, when the sugarcane shareholder drove me around the township, the backseat of his car was piled high with wedding invitations that he said had to be distributed for the upcoming wedding of Satish Magar's daughter to Sharad Pawar's nephew. The exemptions that Magar has received are not limited to Magarpatta City; they have now been formalized in the state government's Integrated Township Policy, for which the chief architect is none other than Magar himself. Thanks to this policy, any urban development larger than 100 acres can apply to be an integrated township, gaining exemptions from the restrictive land-conversion regulations. And it is this enabling piece of legislation that has allowed Magar to replicate the Magarpatta success in other sugar-cooperative regions, including Nanded City.

The creation of the Integrated Township Policy was not motivated solely by short-term financial gains for well-connected sugar elites like Satish Magar, but also by the long-term political calculations of savvy politicians like Sharad Pawar, as they prepare the Maratha-Kunbi sugarcane constituency for a market-oriented urban economy. As can be seen in the land-price maps in Chapter 1, Hadapsar land prices shot up due to the advantageous location of these lands near Pune, the Mumbai-Pune Expressway, and the Delhi-Mumbai Industrial Corridor. The sugarcane lands in Baramati, Pawar's home constituency, did not register similar price hikes because the taluka is farther away from Pune and the economic corridors. In these more distant regions, Sharad Pawar has been introducing new agro-industrial policies. Starting in the mid-1980s, he exhorted his agrarian constituents not just to enter but to embrace economic liberalization. His speeches at sugar-cooperative factories and the Maratha Chamber of Commerce and Industry targeted agrarian youth, urging them to quit agriculture and move into the urban economy. His pro-liberalization stance was so unequivocal that the former prime minister, Manmohan Singh, in his foreword to *Fast Forward*—a compilation of Pawar's speeches—highlighted "Sharadji's commitment to the economic reforms and liberalization we initiated in 1991" and noted that in the 1980s, "when Rajiv Gandhi had taken many bold steps towards modernizing our economy, Sharadji supported these initiatives."[20]

There were a number of reasons for Pawar's prescient pro-market, pro-urban policy stance. For one, he recognized the ascendance of and growing opposition from the urban-oriented Bharatiya Janata Party (BJP) and Shiv Sena. When the BJP–Shiv Sena coalition seized control of the state legislature in 1995, breaking the Congress Party's uninterrupted rule since the creation of the Maharashtra state in 1960, one of the coalition's first policies was a frontal attack on the Congress's organizational base, the sugar cooperatives. State subsidies for the cooperatives came under harsh scrutiny, and the BJP–Shiv Sena coalition rallied for a halt to the "zoning of sugarcane," which prevented sugarcane farmers from selling cane to factories outside their zone. Removing this restriction undermined the control of the sugar elites over their formerly territorially bounded members. More importantly, Pawar recognized that it was no longer enough to control only the agrarian economy for electoral success; with the liberalization reforms, it was imperative to forge new alliances across the urban-rural divide.

When Pawar became the state's chief minister in 1988, he initiated new development plans that incentivized export-oriented agriculture, horticulture, and agro-based industries. These plans enjoined farmers to adopt new communication and other IT technologies in their export-oriented agricultural ventures.[21] When he took over the central government's agriculture portfolio in 2004, these state-level changes were translated into national policy through changes in FDI policy, allowing almost total foreign investment in floriculture, horticulture, the development of seeds, animal husbandry, pisciculture, aquaculture, and the cultivation of vegetables and mushrooms (agriculture is otherwise protected from FDI). In Pawar's home constituency of Baramati, agrarian landowners are now diversifying from sugar to another commodity that has bright economic prospects due to the growing urban middle class—grapes for wine production. As his constituency of sugarcane growers shifts to grape cultivation, Pawar has been taking active steps to change liquor regulations to protect and promote Maharashtra's nascent wine industry.[22] The sugar elites are also investing their agrarian surpluses in educational empires. These state-level politicians have the regulatory power to gain access to large tracts of land needed for college and university campuses, and so, in the words of Rob Jenkins, "the sugar barons" have now earned for themselves the "derisive title of educational barons."[23]

The Magarpatta experiment is thus part of a larger movement of former sugar elites who are shifting out of agriculture into the new money-spinning sectors of "land, liquor, and learning."[24] New policies for agro-industries and integrated townships have enabled these agrarian elites to create and then to capture the benefits from new markets in real estate, wine, and private education. Crucially, the policies also ensure that the Maratha-Kunbi middle peasants in these regions share in the profits of a liberalizing economy, thus giving electoral stability to the sugar elites amid a market-oriented transition.

"Bharat v. India" in a New Liberalizing Context

While Satish Magar was pacing the state government's corridors of power, trying to persuade politicians to grant him key exemptions for the implementation of his integrated township, another agrarian activist was trying to get a similar proposal off the ground. In 1997, Sharad Joshi, the charismatic leader of an agrarian movement called the Shetkari Sanghatana,[25] floated a "farmers' company" called Bhama Constructions Limited, which he touted as the "second Green Revolution."[26] The company would issue farmers shares in any new real-estate development, allocating the shares proportionally to the contributing landowners and equally within a household. Despite their similarities, however, the idea of Bhama remained grounded while the idea of Magarpatta took off. Joshi admits that it was the favorable exemptions granted to Magarpatta that made it possible, exemptions he did not receive. But why did Magar and not Joshi receive them? A brief excursus here on the Shetkari Sanghatana will be helpful in establishing Magarpatta's political moorings.

Joshi shot to fame in the late 1970s, during the Green Revolution, as the leader of a popular agrarian movement. He, along with other fiery agrarian leaders such as Charan Singh and Mahendra Tikait in Uttar Pradesh, were part of the "new farmers' movement." Scholars use the adjective "new" to distinguish the 1970s agrarian movement from earlier peasant movements, such as the 1870s Deccan Riots, that comprised the nonpropertied cultivating class. In contrast, the new farmers' movement drew its membership from owner-cultivators who were operating within a commoditized agrarian economy. The demands of the new movement reflected its membership demographic: the Shetkari Sanghatana, for instance, made many demands about agricultural prices (lower taxes, debt relief, deeper subsidies on seeds and fertilizers, and better procurement prices) but were silent on agricultural minimum wages.

During this time, Joshi coined the popular slogan "Bharat v. India," pitting India's urban interests against rural ones: "Bharat" stood for the rural and oppressed majority of the country, and "India" was the anglicized and urban few. But the slogan, as well as the timing of the agrarian movement, is puzzling. The rise of the movement in the 1980s coincided with what is called India's "second democratic upsurge," when backward-class politicians of agrarian origins gained considerable power in the Central Government and for the first time took on portfolios other than the obligatory Ministry of Agriculture responsibilities that had earlier been reserved for them. Joshi's "Bharat v. India" slogan echoes Michael Lipton's charge of "urban bias"—the idea that development policies in poor countries enrich the cities and impoverish the countryside—but the Liptonian argument makes little sense in western Maharashtra, where the diversion of capital was the other way around, from the city to the countryside.[27] As outlined in the previous chapter, the agrarian sugar cooperatives were market failures, but they were propped up by generous subsidies from the public coffers and by rural-biased irrigation infrastructure—and the main sources of revenue for the public coffers were the industrial surpluses from Mumbai. Moreover, the Shetkari Sanghatana took root in the Nashik, Pune, and Ahmednagar districts, the very regions that had received abundant irrigation waters and contained thriving sugar cooperatives.

The "Bharat v. India" slogan makes more sense, however, if we interpret it to mean not an inability to generate surpluses in an agrarian economy but an inability to invest these surpluses in an urban one.[28] If we map out the geography of the new farmers' movement, we see that it emerged in agriculturally thriving regions, many of which were beneficiaries of the Green Revolution program. Agrarian landowners in these regions were generating large surpluses and yet were blocked from investing them in the urban economy. As historians like Rajnarayan Chandavarkar have shown, Bombay's industrial capitalism traces its origins to the nineteenth-century colonial era, when indigenous capital belonging to specific ethnic communities, such as the Parsis and Ismailis (Bohras and Khojas), was invested in cotton-textile factories.[29]

One of the largest industrial houses in India today, the Tatas, traces its lineage back to these times. Because Bombay's economy was controlled by an industrial class that was ethnically distinct from the agrarian landowning classes, they prevented the latter's agrarian surpluses from entering Bombay. However, well aware that state-legislature politicians relied on the numerically strong agrarian countryside for their votes, Bombay's industrial class tolerated the diversion of capital from city to countryside for the sake of political stability. The Shetkari Sanghatana, therefore, were reacting against the industrial monopoly that was denying them access to Bombay's economy.

Joshi was also a vocal critic of the sugar elites who controlled the cooperatives, and it is this older rivalry that explains why Satish Magar's township proposal received exemptions but Joshi's did not. The sugar cooperatives worked on the democratic principle of one person, one vote, but the large sugarcane landowners who had the resources for the vigorously fought and expensive elections always populated each cooperative's board of directors. The directors made all the major decisions, including the prices at which the cooperative would purchase sugarcane from its members, and it was common practice for the directors to lower cane prices and invest the remaining profits in activities that disproportionately benefited themselves. Among the common recipients of such investments were private educational institutes, and western Maharashtra's sugarcane-rich regions are dotted with large educational empires set up by sugar elites like Sharad Pawar and D. Y. Patil. Because of these diverted profits, the Shetkari Sanghatana's agitation around agricultural prices drew strong support from the small sugarcane growers, whose economic prospects were frequently thwarted by the decisions of the directors. While industrial capitalists prevented the agrarian class from investing its surplus in the urban economy, the sugar elites depressed the surplus-generating potential of the smaller owner-cultivators. Joshi was emphatic that his agrarian movement benefited all farmers—marginal and large[30]— but his opposition to the cooperative leadership points to his assumption that the "India" in his slogan comprised both agrarian and urban elites who were preventing the smaller propertied classes from reaping the benefits of agrarian capitalism.

Joshi's "Bharat v. India" narrative is now being reshaped in the context of a liberalizing economy. Raju Shetti, a Lingayat mechanical engineer from an agrarian family in the sugar-rich district of Kolhapur, was a member of Shetkari Sanghatana. In 2002, he split from the new farmers' movement and formed his own nonparty agrarian movement, called the Swabhimani Shetkari Sanghatana (SSS; "Swabhimani" here means dignity). In 2004, he entered electoral politics with the formation of the Swabhimani Paksha political party. Like Joshi before him, Shetti focused his earliest agitation, in 2002, on the price of sugar. Since then, he has had repeated success in forcing higher sugarcane prices for owner-cultivators, and the website of his farmers' movement lists the "battle of sugarcane price" as one of its main issues: "The battle of sugarcane tops the agenda of the Swabhimani Shetkari Sanghatana. Sanghatana has mobilized mass movement of farmers against organized loot of sugar cane producing farmers by the cooperative sugar lobby. It is because of the series of agitations and protests by the SSS that sugarcane prices have been raised up to 1300 rupees. However the battle still continues."[31]

The politics over price broadened beyond sugarcane when Shetti entered democratic politics. As a Member of Parliament, he has been a vocal participant in the land-acquisition debates. His land politics reflects his astute reading of the changing role of land in the new economic-corridor regions. Sugarcane landowners, even the small and marginal ones, now see urban land development, rather than agricultural profit, as the more lucrative mode of generating surplus. In regions where the price of advantageously located agricultural land is registering astronomical hikes, small agrarian landowners aspire to become builders. These small-scale agrarian landowners, however, lack the political connections of the sugar elites to gain the legal exemptions needed to pool their fragmented lands and form real-estate developments. Even the new Integrated Township Policy is biased toward the sugar elites: only a development larger than 100 acres is eligible for land-conversion exemptions. The main beneficiaries of the policy are thus traditional elites like Satish Magar, who already have consolidated plots of land as well as mobilized resources for convincing other landowners to pool their lands. And not only do small-scale agrarian landowners lack the enabling legislation, they also face the threat of having their lands forcibly acquired by the Maharashtra Industrial Development Corporation (MIDC) for urban expansion.

Both in Parliament and on the streets, Shetti has agitated against the forced acquisition of agricultural land for Special Economic Zones (SEZs)—including Khed City. Shetti is not against owner-cultivators entering a liberalizing real-estate market, but he is against excluding them from the benefits of the new urban economy. Reflecting the real-estate aspirations of his constituents, he has made not just the price of crops grown on the land but the price of land itself a key political issue. His arguments against the land-acquisition bill reflect his preference for models like Bhama Construction

Limited, in which the state would have refrained from coercively acquiring agricultural land and instead facilitated the entry of owner-cultivators into the lucrative urban sectors of "land, liquor, and learning." Just as Joshi saw Bombay's industrial capitalists as blocking the entry of owner-cultivators into an urban economy, Shetti sees the new SEZs as urban aggressors against rural interests. Like the "battle of sugarcane price," the battle of land price revolves around the conflict of how surpluses will be allocated between agrarian elites on the one hand and small owner-cultivators on the other.

Bypassed Gram Sabhas

Two kilometers from Magarpatta City is a basti (an informal settlement). The basti is home to 810 residents,[32] belonging to a mix of Mali and Dhangar caste groups. These residents worked as laborers on the lands of the small sugarcane growers of Hadapsar in the 1970s and 1980s. Most of them migrated to Pune before that from drought-prone villages in the neighboring Sholapur district in the late 1960s.

After talking to the sugarcane shareholders, I was eager to explore the edges of Magarpatta City, to see the land uses at the boundaries where the integrated township meets Pune city. Walking around the township, I chanced upon Shankar-ji, a resident of the basti, and struck up an acquaintance with him. I visited the basti periodically from June to September 2012, and Shankar-ji introduced me during this time both to other residents of the basti and to local politicians for the Hadapsar neighborhood. A Mali tailor in his fifties, Shankar-ji is one of the oldest residents of the basti. In the 1980s and 1990s, he used to work on the sugarcane fields. He recalls the change in this area over the past two decades:

> Satish Magar was the biggest farmer then; he had a large poultry farm, he studied in Dubai. All the other Magars were small farmers. I used to work for them when they did not even own a cycle. If someone wanted a *bidi* [a local, hand-rolled Indian cigarette], they had to borrow money to buy it. They were that poor. Some lands were 2 acres, others 5 acres, some even had less than half an acre. But now they have become rich. We used to eat together when I worked on their farms; now I cannot go to their houses. They have large flats; now they are on another level.[33]

Figure 5. Informal settlement of agricultural laborers who worked on the lands of the Maratha-Kunbi sugarcane growers.

Significantly, Shankar-ji and his younger nephew held opposing views on Magarpatta City. The nephew, in his early twenties, had recently started working as a security guard in the urban township. His uncle explained that he had used his past contacts with the sugarcane growers to secure the job for his nephew. Enamored of the curtain-walled office building, the neatly arranged and maintained villas, and the manicured green spaces, the new guard wished all of India could look like Magarpatta City. The township, he said, was paradise: "As India's *nandanvad* [paradise] is Kashmir, Pune's nandanvad is Magarpatta."[34] The uncle dismissed his nephew's bright-eyed optimism as the naïveté of a "young boy who does not know anything about *bazaar ka rate* [the cost of living] and family responsibilities." Ruing their severance from the Hadapsar land, even if they had only worked as laborers there, the uncle explained: "When we worked on the field, we used to get the vegetables for free. We used to eat fresh food. How could they [the landowners] not allow us to take the vegetables—we were growing it, we worked there, they were eating because of us. Now, we go to the market for everything, it has become very expensive."[35]

In Magarpatta City, even the most marginal agrarian landowner is a shareholding beneficiary of the new real-estate developments. The smallest sugarcane shareholder in Magarpatta, who gave up 0.12 acres of land, now owns two apartments in the township, worth 2,400,000 rupees; he receives dividends from his township shares and rental income from the leased office buildings (all of the office buildings in Magarpatta are owned by the company and rented out to firms); moreover, he is a shareholder in the new Nanded City. Shankar-ji is also a landowner, but his plot of land is in the drought-prone region of Solapur. His aged parents continue to subsist on their Solapur fields. As the previous chapter showed with the mapping of agrarian land markets, the routing of the irrigation canals produced uneven geographies of agriculturally productive and unproductive land. The poverty of the Solapur waste lands forced Shankar-ji to migrate to Hadapsar in the 1960s, but those lands would not have been unproductive in the first place if irrigation waters had been channeled to Solapur. It was political decisions about the uneven routing of water resources that rendered certain lands "waste" and, by extension, certain landowners vulnerable to migration.

Now, not only are the agrarian-landowners-turned-shareholders in Magarpatta City capturing the urban real-estate profits, but they are also investing their dividends in new agricultural land. Unlike the younger-generation Magars, who have diversified into construction and other urban economic activities, Ramesh-kaka has bought agricultural land in Baramati. Distressed laborers migrating from the poor regions of northern Karnataka work on his lands. He has built a basti for these laborers, and he goes to Baramati once a week to supervise his fields. The contrasting experiences of Ramesh-kaka and Shankar-ji show how the uneven geographies of an agrarian past are shaping inequalities in an urbanizing present, when the location of agricultural land makes all the difference between those who can move into formal land markets and those who slip into landless poverty.

The decentralization reforms intended the Gram Sabhas to be a democratic fix and disrupt precisely these forms of entrenched power hierarchies. So the question then arises: why did the agricultural laborers (belonging to Mali, Dhangar and other nondominant castes) not exercise their voice through the Hadapsar Gram Sabha? The reason for their silence is that land is a state subject in India; the state legislature has the final authority to make land laws. Knowing where the regulatory power lay, Satish Magar bypassed the local government and sent his demands directly to state-level politicians. To make matters worse, this bypassing of local governments is now institutionalized in the Integrated Township Policy, which allows urban developments larger than 100 acres to get direct approval from the state government, exempting the developers from needing local government approval (see Appendix 1 for more details on these land-use exemptions).

In the two cases examined in later chapters, Lavasa Lake City and Khed City, the urban promoters similarly convinced state-level politicians to grant them regulatory approval for the making of their corridor cities. But, in both of these cases, the promoters were urban firms. Unlike Satish Magar, they were outsiders to the agrarian context, and they needed the Gram Sabhas' approval to grant them legitimacy in the eyes of both proximate landowners and distant investors. In Magarpatta City, Satish Magar derives his legitimacy from his family's decades-long involvement in the region, as patrons responsible for the welfare of those dependent on them. Unlike the urban promoters, Satish Magar did not require the Gram Sabha to foster collection action; instead he relied on his family's networks of trust, cultivated over forty years with the small growers of the sugar cooperatives, to convince them to make the uncertain transition from sugar to real estate.

Real-estate developments like Magarpatta City exemplify the shifting urban aspirations of agrarian elites, who are exercising their voice to stake their claim on an urbanizing future. The entry of these electorally strong agrarian elites into urban land markets spells a new era of urban politics. In an earlier, agrarian economy, the sugar elites diverted cooperative profits not only to deepen their pockets but to fulfill their political ambitions. Today, land is the new sugar. The urban profits from formerly agricultural land perform many of the same functions that the sugar cooperatives did, including enabling the sugar elites to retain control of resources and power. They also enable former sugar elites to forge new political and economic alliances across the urban-rural divide. The pathways of agrarian elites into urban real estate and urban politics vary by region. The Magarpatta case represents one such pathway, where the organizational form of sugar cooperatives was reworked to ensure the continuity of agrarian privileges in an urbanizing context.

===

CHAPTER 3

From Forests to IPO

Around 90 kilometers from Mumbai along the Mumbai-Pune Expressway, nestled within the ecologically rich Sahyadri Mountain range, you will find India's first privately financed city, Lavasa Lake City. This city was built on an ambitious scale. Spanning 25,000 acres, it covers approximately one-fifth of the land area of the Municipal Corporation of Greater Mumbai. Its promoter, Ajit Gulabchand—the CEO of the prominent Mumbai-based firm Hindustan Construction Company (HCC)—sees Lavasa Lake City as a bold response to the demands of accelerated urbanization: "[Lavasa] is a grand project. . . . It actually looks at the needs of India's urbanization—an estimated 400 million people will move to urban centers in the next 30–40 years. So, we really need to consider our urbanization needs and this project couldn't have come at a better time to create a kind of replicable model of a new city. The speed with which we will have to build these urban centers or enhance existing ones would need some kind of public-private partnership. And Lavasa is a model, an experiment in making that happen."[1]

Lavasa Lake City is an experiment in both urban finance and urban governance. It is the first urban development to be financed by tapping into India's newly liberalized equity markets. Lavasa Corporation Limited (LCL), the promoter company and a subsidiary of HCC, has regulatory approval to raise capital for the required 33,000 million rupees ($492 million) from public equity, including foreign institutional investors (FIIs). The lake city is also unique in having a private-sector firm as its Special Planning Authority (SPA). In a controversial move, the state government delegated its land-use planning powers to LCL, in effect granting regulatory control over the Lavasa Lake City jurisdiction to a firm. Gulabchand claims that these governance changes are necessary to package the city as an initial public offering (IPO) with a brand that is seductive and sellable to investors.

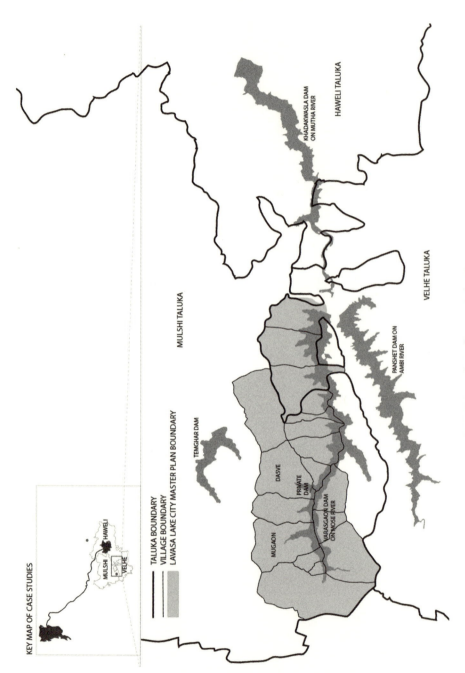

MULSHI HAWELI

VELHE

TALUKA BOUNDARY

VILLAGE BOUNDARY

LAVASA LAKE CITY MASTER PLAN BOUNDARY

MULSHI TALUKA

TEMGHAR DAM

MUGAON

DASVE

PRIVATE DAM

VARASGAON DAM ON MOSE RIVER

PANSHET DAM ON AMBI RIVER

KHADAKWASLA DAM ON MUTHA RIVER

HAWELI TALUKA

VELHE TALUKA

Map 9. Location of Lavasa Lake City.

Figure 6a. The completed Dasve township encircling the Varasgaon reservoir.

Figure 6b. The incomplete Mugaon township.

India's first private city is an audacious experiment in "frontier" expansion. The sprawling city is located in the Sahyadris, part of the ecologically fragile Western Ghats mountain range that stretches along the western coast of the Indian peninsula. Second in height only to the Himalayas, the Western Ghats range encompasses the most important "biodiversity hotspots" of the country. The range is home to some of India's biggest rivers and thickest evergreen forests. Before the arrival of the economic corridor, Mulshi taluka, in which Lavasa Lake City is located, was cut off from its surroundings. The Gram Panchayat of Dasve—which LCL has now transformed into a township, one of the five townships in Lavasa Lake City—was secluded. Tucked away amid the wild jackfruit and mango trees of the lush Sahyadri forests, the Gram Panchayat even lacked roads. Children had to trek almost an hour each way to reach the nearest primary school. In the 1990s, when employees of the promoter company were scouring the region for the right site, the lack of road access meant they had to rely on helicopters to survey the region.[2] But the Mumbai-Pune economic corridor has created a new market demand for these previously disconnected forest lands. LCL's IPO brochure boasts of the unique locational advantages of Lavasa Lake City:

> Lavasa lies at the intersection of the upcoming Delhi-Mumbai Industrial Corridor and the proposed Bengaluru-Mumbai Economic Corridor. Lavasa also lies in close proximity to the Mumbai-Pune corridor, one of India's largest economic corridors, which has an estimated population of 35.6 million as per the 2011 census of India and contributed 4,032 billion to India's GDP in 2011–2012. In light of the relative scarcity of land in Mumbai and Pune cities, we believe the pressure of economic activities and residential developments are spreading along the transportation links, namely expressway, highway and railway lines between the two cities, leading to the emergence of a new corridor of economic development. We expect that Lavasa, because of its location and size, will benefit from this economic activity.[3]

Gulabchand plans to tunnel new roads through the Sahyadri forest lands that will directly connect the new city to the Mumbai-Pune Expressway and reduce the travel time to Mumbai.[4] The economic corridor is opening up the vast swathes of forest lands between the cities of Mumbai and Pune as new areas for capital expansion.

The growing market demand for these lands derives from their advantageous location adjacent to the economic corridor, which makes them ripe sites for investment. Look, for instance, at the land prices in Mulshi, which contains only waste land, from 1996 to 2016. The closest village or census town to the Lavasa villages for which ready reckoner prices were available is Tamhini Bk, which was submerged in the 1920s by the building of the Mulshi Dam. In 1996, waste land in Tamhini Bk fetched 80,000 rupees; in 2016, the price of that same land had shot up to 1,281,000 rupees. To put these prices in perspective, the price of irrigated land in Malegaon (Baramati) is 2,334,750 rupees; the price of waste land in Shiroli (Khed) is 3,217,000 rupees. The price of waste land in Tamhini Bk has not increased at the same rate as the waste land in Shiroli (note that the waste land in Shiroli has a higher market price than even the most irrigated land in Malegaon). The lower price of the Mulshi waste land may be partly due to the protests and litigation engulfing Lavasa Lake City. It may also be because the new corridor city lacks what economic geographers call "agglomeration effects."[5] The economic benefits of spatial proximity derive from a complex mix of social interactions, labor markets, and resource concentration, and these cannot be reduced to a simple factor like the presence or absence of roads. A new economic corridor is not enough to create an agglomeration economy. It can, however, open up new areas of investment for speculative capital. Lavasa Lake City today is both a weekend getaway for wealthy Mumbai residents and a financial asset for distant shareholders. The corridor city does not have any schools, markets, or other basic amenities for daily living, but it does offer branded golf courses and university campuses (such as a proposed campus for Oxford University, which was scrapped after Oxford pulled out of the deal following protests). Bereft of prior market linkages, the Mulshi region is now the site of speculative rather than productive capital. Only real-estate firms, not industrial firms, are investing in the taluka. Even Special Economic Zones (SEZs), which have been justifiably criticized as real-estate projects masquerading as industrial developments, are not being sited in Mulshi.

The Lavasa corridor city is either the new frontier or the rent gap, depending on your ideology. The process of converting forest lands into an IPO includes the redevelopment of these formerly devalued lands into market assets; the conversion of various forms of property rights (e.g., common land and state-controlled forest lands) into exclusive private property rights controlled by a firm; and the suppression of alternative (indigenous) forms of production and consumption to make way for privatized streams of profits. All in all, it closely resembles what David Harvey has called "accumulation by dispossession": "Since privatization and liberalization of the market was the mantra of the neo-liberal movement, the effect was to make a new round of enclosure of the commons [where] assets held by the state or in common are released into the market where overaccumulating capital could invest in them, upgrade them, and speculate in them."[6] Scholars writing with a view from the south resist the concept of neoliberalization, which, they argue, privileges the global over the local. In recent books, Gautam Bhan and Asher Ghertner write about the conjuring of world-class futures in millennial Delhi but also draw attention to the local actors—regional courts, low-level bureaucrats, and the slum residents themselves—implicated in these projects of "worlding cities."[7] In her dissertation, which focuses on Lavasa Lake City, Anokhi Parikh borrows from Susan Parnell and Jennifer Robinson's "post-neoliberal analytic optic" to show how the local Sarpanches (the elected heads of the Gram Panchayats) and *talathis* (village-level bureaucrats) are active land aggregators for LCL.[8] She also focuses on the National Alliance for People's Movements (NAPM) as the local actors resisting the new development. These works turn our gaze to local actors who are peripheral or neglected in global theories, reframing them as central protagonists in the production of new millennial developments. In the context of the debate on neoliberalization and city-making, I am particularly interested in a local institution that is overlooked in most, if not all, the recent urban analyses: the Gram Sabhas.

The Lavasa development has been mired in stiff opposition from environmental and social groups, brought together by the NAPM and its internationally known social-activist leader, Medha Patkar. The corridor city has also been interrupted and indicted by state agencies, including the central government's Ministry of Environment and Forests (MoEF) and the Comptroller and Auditor General (CAG), the central regulatory agency that audits public institutions. The city's promoter, Gulabchand, has countered these charges by arguing that LCL has "the support of the 18 Gram Panchayats." But the Gram Panchayats often do not represent the will of the people: they may be controlled entirely by elites. For this reason, the decentralization reforms introduced both quotas in local government elections (one-third of local representatives must be from formerly excluded groups) and a new local legislature in the form of the Gram Sabhas. The residents of Dasve and the adjacent Gram Panchayats are challenging Lavasa Lake City on the streets and in the courts; why are they not also mobilizing the Gram Sabhas to oppose the private city? In ten years of ongoing conflict, the Gram Sabhas have not been convened even once in the Mulshi villages. The focal question in this chapter is, therefore, why are the Mulshi Gram Sabhas unactivated?

I point to two interrelated reasons for the unactivated Gram Sabhas: the lack of a critical mass of dominant agrarian-propertied classes and the previous rounds of dam-induced displacement. The caste composition of the Mulshi propertied classes has disadvantaged them in two ways. First, these petty proprietary classes and forest dependents were not active in nationalist politics. Their marginalization before Independence continued into the post-Independence era. Mulshi has the highest density of dams in the state of Maharashtra, but sugar elites diverted water from those dams to their water-guzzling sugarcane fields in western Maharashtra during the earlier agricultural-modernization period. It was the relative electoral weakness of the Mulshi constituents that explains the uneven flows of water from the Mulshi region to the sugar-rich talukas of Haweli and Baramati. Second, the exclusions from an uneven agrarian past are now affecting the residents' democratic practices. The building of the Mumbai-Pune economic corridor has made accessible the elevated mountainous lands of the marginalized Mulshi residents that were previously out of reach for urban investors. But these residents have been prevented from staking their claims on these newly desirable lands by the previous rounds of dam displacement and distress migration that scattered them to distant sites, thus vitiating their ability to organize collectively and activate the Gram Sabhas as the sites for these negotiations.

If Magarpatta City exemplifies the reproduction of agrarian privileges in a new market- and urban-oriented context, Lavasa Lake City exemplifies the perpetuation of agrarian exclusions, as the very constituents that had to bear the costs of an earlier era of dam-building now face a second round of displacement with the new economic corridors. These new exclusions, however, are also opening up a violent new form of identity politics. Nativist political parties like the Shiv Sena and the Maharashtra Navnirman Sena (MNS) are inciting the poor, excluded Marathas to a retaliatory politics of vandalism and to bans against groups that are seen as oppressing the "sons of the soil"

Marathas. "Bharat v. India" politics is now manifesting itself as a brittle form of identity politics in these underdeveloped regions.

City as IPO: Movements and Countermovements

If built according to its master plan, Lavasa Lake City will eventually encompass five townships spread over eighteen Gram Panchayats in Mulshi. The first and only completed township is Dasve, which is modeled after the Italian seaside town of Portofino. The colorful red, orange, and yellow Mediterranean-themed buildings line a broad boulevard with cobblestones and cafés. Named Portofino Street, this boulevard evocatively recalls its Italian precedent. Dasve is a busy weekend and vacation retreat for Mumbai and Pune residents, dotted with huge billboards that promote a modern lifestyle in synchrony with nature: "Come home to nature," "Don't just exist, live unbound," "Live the lifestyle you truly deserve," "Live luxuriously by an enchanting lake." Yet, despite the serene and tranquil lifestyle sold by the Lavasa promoters, the hills and the city "are alive with the sound of controversy."[9]

Lavasa Lake City was made possible by the 1996 "Special Regulations for the Development of Tourist Resorts/Holiday Homes/Townships in Hill Station Type Areas," also referred to as the Hill Station Regulation, enacted by the state government of Maharashtra. This urban policy grants private developers exemptions from existing planning regulations for the development of tourist-oriented hill stations. It is inspired by the colonial precedent of nineteenth-century hill stations—Shimla, Mussoorie, Darjeeling—that promised the British respite from the summer heat in the plains. Lavasa Lake City is also inspired by a popular tourist destination in England, the Lake District. The Hill Station Regulation exempts hill-station cities of between 400 and 20,000 hectares (arbitrary parameters) from all agricultural and urban land-ceiling restrictions. If the hill-station cities meet certain requirements, they can be built even within ecologically sensitive areas that the regional plan, prepared by the state government's Urban Development Department, has marked as "no-development zones." Two of the largest developments that have taken shape under the aegis of the Hill Station Regulation are Lavasa Lake City and Amby Valley City. Like Lavasa, Amby Valley is steeped in litigation, and its promoter was in jail on charges of investor fraud.

From the get-go, Lavasa Lake City was geared not toward local residents but toward foreign investors. The IPO prospectus states that 75 percent of its shares will be allotted to Qualified Institutional Buyers (QIBs), with 30 percent of the QIB allotments reserved for Anchor Investors, making it clear that the target market is FIIs.[10] Touting a new city that aspires to be built entirely from private capital, the company promoters knew they would be competing with other privately financed cities around the world. The creation of a strong brand image thus became an important way of differentiating their city from others—city branding is part of the wider urban shift that Harvey has referred to as "managerialism to entrepreneurialism."[11] Before the 1970s, Harvey argues, when capital mobility was more restricted, the main function of local governments was to provide public services to their citizens and residents. Now, with freer capital flows across jurisdictional boundaries, investors can park their capital in any real-estate development that promises the highest rate of return. City branding is an essential ingredient of the city-as-IPO, and Lavasa's branding strategy started with its name. The Paris- and Geneva-based branding company, Landor, invented the name "Lavasa" to make the project more evocative: "The name 'Lake Town' is rational and descriptive, describing a town near a lake. If I told you, 'I bought a house in Lake Town, come for the summer,' I'm sure your brain would react in a very different way than if I told you, 'I bought a house in Lavasa, come for the summer.'"[12] Lavasa Lake City's logo shows the image of a "person evolving and transforming into a bird, which represents freedom, which is fulfillment."[13]

Branding Lavasa has also meant planning the new city in a way that will make it legible even to those investors who have never set foot in the development but need to be assured of the quality of their investment. LCL is planning a Manchester City football academy, a Steve Redgrave rowing club, and a Nick Faldo golf course, as these are globally recognizable brands that will in turn enhance Lavasa's image. The hill city was master-planned by the globally recognizable design firm HOK, and LCL's construction partner is Steiner AG, a Switzerland-headquartered construction firm that has built global landmarks like the headquarters of Nestlé in Switzerland, Terminal T3 at the Geneva Airport, and the World Economic Forum in Geneva. International awards add to the brand image; Lavasa's IPO prospectus highlights the international urban and landscape awards it has won: "the Best Master Plan in 2005 by the Congress for the New Urbanism, based in the USA," the "Award of Excellence for the Dasve Master Plan in 2005, the Honor Award for the Mugaon Valley Master Plan in 2009 and the Merit Award for Lavasa

Landscape Guidelines in 2010 . . . by the American Society of Landscape Architects."[14]

As LCL was promoting Brand Lavasa and soaring high with design accolades and bullish market interest, trouble started brewing for the company. In 2009, the NAPM brought together other oppositional groups and organized a People's Commission of Inquiry.[15] In a report, the commission published the social and environmental irregularities surrounding Lavasa that had emerged through the course of public consultations. Among these charges are the failure of LCL to get an environmental clearance from the central government's MoEF, which is needed for projects of this size; the violation of existing planning regulations; the improper delegation of planning authority to LCL; and irregular water diversions from the Mose River to the hill city. As opposition to the development mounted, the MoEF intervened in November 2010 and issued a show-cause notice to LCL, which required it to stop all construction immediately and maintain the status quo on the project. Shortly afterward, in its 2011 audit, the CAG—the constitutionally charged body that audits government expenditures—harshly indicted LCL on numerous charges.[16]

Table 2 provides the sequence of events in LCL's planning process. Note how the market movement to redevelop the forest lands for speculative urbanization is knotted with countermovements to slow down or reverse the process. Also see how fraught and strategically timed these market movements and countermovements were: in 2009, for instance, the year that the NAPM published its interim report indicting Lavasa, the award from the American Society of Landscape Architects for Mugaon's master plan helped enhance the investment's brand value. Also significant are the connections between politicians and the firms involved, particularly those between LCL and Sharad Pawar's family. Supriya Sule is Pawar's daughter, and she is married to Sadanand Sule; both of them merged their company, Yashomala Leasing and Finance Private Limited, with HCC in 2003 to gain equity shares in LCL. Sharad Pawar's nephew, Ajit Pawar, was the Irrigation Minister for Maharashtra from 1999 to 2003, when LCL got approval for the construction of eight private dams in the catchment area of the Varasgaon Dam.

As can be seen here, a web of public, private, and hybrid institutions was involved in the sequence of events that led to the making of Lavasa Lake City. At the local level, there is the firm itself, LCL, which was given land-use planning powers by the state government; LCL as a public authority has overlapping jurisdictional powers with existing local governments. At the level of

Table 2. Planning Sequence for Lavasa Lake City

1996	The government of Maharashtra enacts the "Special Regulations for the Development of Tourist Resorts/Holiday Homes/Townships in Hill Station Type Areas," also referred to as the Hill Station Regulation.
2000	Incorporation of the company Pearly Blue Lake Resorts Private Limited, with an authorized share capital of 20 million rupees.
June 2001	Maharashtra's Urban Development Department declares eighteen villages as a hill station.
Sept. 2002	The company enters an agreement with the Maharashtra Krishna Valley Development Corporation for the construction of eight private dams in the catchment area of the Varasgaon Dam.
Sept. 2003	Hindustan Construction Company (HCC) acquires shares in the company.
Dec. 2003	The company enters an agreement with the Irrigation Department of Maharashtra for the construction of two additional private dams in the Varasgaon catchment area.
Oct. 2003	Sadanand and Supriya Sule join HCC by merging their company, Yashomala Leasing and Finance Private Limited, with HCC.
Mar. 2004	The company's name is changed to Lavasa Corporation Limited (LCL).
	Maharashtra's Environment Department grants clearance to develop a hill station.
2005	The Congress for New Urbanism, in the United States, awards LCL with the Charter Award of excellence for Dasve village. The American Society of Landscape Architects gives an award for the Dasve township master plan.
2006	A consortium of banks lends 8,000 million rupees to LCL.
2008	The Government of Maharashtra appoints LCL as a Special Planning Authority.
2009	The People's Commission of Inquiry, led by the National Alliance for People's Movements, makes public its interim report.
	The American Society of Landscape Architects gives an award for the Mugaon Valley master plan.
Jan. 2010	The American Society of Landscape Architects gives an award for the Lavasa landscape guidelines.
Sept. 2010	The Securities and Exchange Board of India grants approval for an initial public offering of 8,000 million rupees.
Nov. 2010	The Ministry of Environment and Forests (MoEF) orders LCL to stop construction in light of environmental damages.
Mar. 2011	The Comptroller and Auditor General report indicts LCL of irregularities.

Table 2 (Continued)

Nov. 2011	The MoEF grants conditional environmental clearance to the first phase of the hill-station project for a land area of 2,048 hectares, for the townships of Dasve, Mugaon, and Bhoini, subject to specified conditions.
Mar. 2012	LCL defaults on 1,786 million rupees.
	LCL launches its second township, Mugaon.
Feb. 2013	A consortium of banks disburses a second round of loans for 5,000 million rupees.
2014	LCL's long-term liabilities shoot up, from 8,000 million rupees in 2006 to 23,800 million rupees in 2014.

Source: Lavasa Lake City's Draft Red Herring Prospectus (June 30, 2014).

the state government, there is the Maharashtra Krishna Valley Development Corporation (MKVDC), a parastatal responsible for the governance of the Krishna River basin, from which Lavasa Lake City draws its water supply. At the level of the central government, there are the MoEF, the Securities and Exchange Board of India, and the CAG; the latter two are regulatory institutions with oversight powers over financial markets and public accounts, respectively.

LCL has been charged with a slew of irregularities by these authorities. I will focus here on the charges of water misallocation and tie this misallocation to the wider themes of the book, namely biased routing of infrastructural networks and uneven development. Water is a key valorizer of Lavasa Lake City's brand value. The property value of the corridor city has been significantly enhanced by the promoter's promise of constant drinking water and power, an elusive dream for the urban middle classes in a country that suffers from acute water shortages and power outages. LCL has formed forty subsidiary companies, of which eight are "city management and infrastructure companies" that provide water, sanitation, electric power, and natural gas. These companies are managed by a professional team of salaried employees, and the city manager, Scott Wrighton, has vast experience in service provision, having worked as a municipal official in such U.S. states as Illinois, Kansas, and Missouri.[17] Offering a privately managed, uninterrupted water supply is a branding strategy for attracting distant shareholders. But to make this supply possible, the private city relies on the public resource of river water.

In its promotional brochures for Lavasa Lake City, LCL shows playful recreational images of young, happy people, jet-skiing on a lake encircled by the Dasve township. The brochures neglect to inform us that the lake is actually the Varasgaon Reservoir, part of the Khadakwasla Dam complex. Lavasa Lake City is located on the Mose River, a tributary of one of the largest rivers in India, the Krishna River, which originates in the Western Ghats. The Mose supplies water to the Pune district, then flows downstream to join the Bhima River, which waters the Solapur district, and eventually reaches the neighboring states of Karnataka and Andhra Pradesh. The water flows of the Mose are controlled by the Khadakwasla Dam complex, comprising the Varasgaon, Panshet, and Temghar dams, which channel the waters of the Mose into canals that flow through nearly 45,000 hectares of agricultural fields in the villages of Haveli and Baramati talukas and into cities such as Pune. The public agency that governs these waters is the MKVDC, which comes under the jurisdiction of the state-level Water Resources Department (WRD). The WRD divides water governance in Maharashtra into five river basins, one of which is the MKVDC. The MKVDC is responsible for the "multi sector planning and management of water resources at a river basin level."[18] The MKVDC's decisions regarding the allocation of water from the Khadakwasla Dam complex have ripple effects not only for Mulshi and Pune but for all of the downstream regions, including the drought-prone Solapur district and the neighboring state of Andhra Pradesh.

The WRD started off as the Irrigation Department when the state of Maharashtra was formed in 1960. The name change, in 2004, was part of a restructuring of the water agency in the postliberalization era, when development priorities shifted from agrarian to urban uses. The portfolio for the WRD is highly coveted politically. The earlier Irrigation Department, and now the WRD, has always been controlled by a state-level politician of sugar origins and has been the linchpin of Congress-Maratha-sugar politics. Since 1999, Sharad Pawar's Nationalist Congress Party (NCP) has had uninterrupted control over the water portfolio, with Ajit Pawar, his nephew, supervising it from 1999 to 2012. The restructuring of the Irrigation Department into the WRD facilitated the diversification of agrarian elites into new real-estate and agro-industrial developments. The bureaucrats in charge of the WRD insist that "urbanization is now inevitable" and that an "integrated water management is essential [so that] we can balance irrigation with industrial development."[19]

As the WRD modified the water allocations of a state-controlled agrarian past to meet the demands of a market-oriented urban present, it introduced procedures for granting "new water entitlements" (i.e., the reallocation of water from existing irrigation use to new nonirrigation uses): in other words, shifting water from agricultural to urban land-uses. The procedure for water reallocation is as follows: when a new urban development, say Lavasa Lake City, wants water, the promoter submits an application to the WRD seeking new water entitlements. The WRD makes its decision based on the priority of water use. Of the three categories of water uses—domestic or drinking water, irrigation, and industrial—domestic water is given the highest priority. The WRD also factors in "tail-to-head" equity, meaning that water should be allocated in such a way that the users at the head of the canal do not deprive the downstream users of their fair share of water.[20]

To learn which developments have benefited from these water reallocations, I filed a Right to Information (RTI) petition with the WRD to look at the recent water entitlements for the Khadakwasla Dam complex. The RTI data revealed that, since 2004, the WRD has received 209 applications for the reallocation of water in the Khadakwasla Dam from irrigation to nonirrigation uses. Of these 209 applications, 90 of them are for large-scale projects, each of which will divert water away from more than 10,000 hectares of currently irrigated land. Among the large-scale industrial applicants are promoters of SEZs, including the Khed SEZ (the focus of Chapter 4), as well as the Venkateshwara Hatcheries, the Venkateshwara Research and Breeding Farm, and other firms belonging to the V. H. Group of Companies, whose chairperson, Anuradha Desai, was one of the earliest equity members of Lavasa Lake City. The large-scale domestic applicants include private urban townships like Lavasa Lake City. Particularly important here is the categorization of Lavasa Lake City as a "domestic" water use. Drinking water is justifiably accorded the highest priority in the WRD criteria, but giving a private city like Lavasa the same status as a public city like Pune affords specious parity to the two cities, one of which is governed by a business corporation that reserves the right to deny access to certain groups and the other by a municipal corporation that remains under democratic control. Smaller applicants in the domestic category include Gram Panchayats in the region, which means that these underresourced rural local governments are now competing with financially powerful urban firms like LCL for drinking water.

Other domestic applicants come from the agro-industrial sector, such as the Four Seasons Winery Roti and Baramati Agro Limited. These companies are located in Baramati, the home constituency of Sharad Pawar. The privileged routing of dam waters to Baramati is not surprising when one realizes that Ajit Pawar was the minister in charge of the WRD during the time of these project clearances. But as the WRD reallocates water to domestic and industrial users in Baramati and other politically powerful talukas, downstream agrarian users face acute water shortages. Farmers' organizations and politicians from Solapur, for instance, have filed petitions with the state government questioning the allocation of water within the Krishna River basin. These petitioners argue that the Khadakwasla Dam and other upstream dams have ample water, and that the inequitable distribution of water from the dams to upstream users is leading to distress migration and animal starvation in downstream areas.

The water shortages faced by current Solapur residents are reminiscent of an earlier time, when this region bore the brunt of another inequitable water-distribution policy. In 1972, a severe drought hit Maharashtra. While peasants in Solapur and other districts were reeling under shortages of all kinds—crops, drinking water, fodder—the only cultivators that were protected from the drought and continued to produce in surplus were the water-rich sugar cultivators. Now, the uneven water allocations that earlier enriched the sugar constituency and impoverished those outside the sugar zones are being reproduced in an urban context. The sugar cooperatives would not have been possible without the generous flows of irrigation canals into the arid lands of western Maharashtra; likewise, the new urban-industrial developments will not be possible without a continuous and reliable water supply.

The "new water entitlements" have largely escaped public scrutiny. But a more visible instance of the private appropriation of a public resource, one that has come under intense public scrutiny, is the building of private dams by LCL to meet its water demands. In 2002, the MKVDC signed a contract with LCL granting LCL permission to build ten weirs on the Mose River. These weirs account for nearly 7 percent of the storage capacity of Varasgaon Dam. Activists argue that LCL's diversion of these upstream waters to the private city will exacerbate Pune's already severe drinking-water problem. Though the water contract obliges LCL to release water from its dams during periods of water shortage and other "extraordinary circumstances as determined by MKVDC,"[21] activists are concerned that the private construction of upstream dams for water-consumptive land uses amounts to the privatization of a public resource.

The construction of private dams on a public river cannot be hidden, and these dam constructions were unequivocally indicted by the CAG in its 2011 report:

Lavasa Corporation had approached Maharashtra Krishna Valley Development Corporation (MKVDC) in October, 2001, to construct ten *bandharas* [weirs], eight on Mose and two on Kal river valleys [Mose and Kal are tributaries of the river Krishna]. In view of requests, Water Resources Department (WRD) Minister, who was also Chairman, MKVDC, had granted approval in May 2002 itself to construct ten *bandharas*. . . . Permission given to LCL for construction of *bandharas* on Mose river valley was not only irregular but has adversely reduced water availability to Pune City and adjoining areas at the cost of public interest. . . . Lavasa Project being purely a commercial venture designed to reap rich dividends for itself from the appreciation of land prices, and the proposed activities of the project catering to the elite, we are of the opinion that the grant of exemptions . . . [is] unwarranted and devoid of subservience of any public interest.[22]

The strong pushback by the CAG against the procedurally irregular and substantively unfair diversion of public water resources, coming in the wake of the MoEF show-cause notice, posed a grave risk for Gulabchand, who was trying to raise capital for LCL via the IPO route. The company's Red Herring Prospectus outlines these risks in full disclosure to potential investors:

Construction and development work in Lavasa was completely stopped for a period of approximately one year pursuant to a show cause notice of the Ministry of Environment and Forests, Government of India (the "MoEF"), which had a significant and material adverse effect on our business, financial condition and results of operations including our ability to repay our loans. Any such regulatory actions in the future which affect our development plan could have a material adverse effect on our business, financial condition and results of operations.[23]

Our purchase of land at Lavasa has been challenged by way of public interest litigation.[24]

There are outstanding civil and criminal proceedings against us, our Directors, our Promoters and our Group Companies. An adverse outcome in any of these proceedings may affect our reputation and standing and impact our future business.[25]

The prospectus details the "outstanding litigations" against the company, including five public interest litigations (PILs), sixty-two civil proceedings, five criminal proceedings, forty-six revenue proceedings, two arbitration proceedings, two consumer proceedings, six letters from Gram Panchayats, and four notices from statutory and regulatory authorities.[26]

To regain legitimacy among the company's investors, "local support" became crucial for Gulabchand. The IPO prospectus lists the no-objection certificates received from both the MKVDC and the Sarpanches of the eighteen Gram Panchayats as evidence of the "necessary approvals from the Government, various governmental agencies and other statutory and/or regulatory authorities required for carrying out its present hill station development activities."[27] In repeated interviews, Gulabchand has countered the CAG report and emphasized the support LCL has received from the Gram Panchayats:

> Pune gets 11 trillion cubic feet of water per day which makes it the highest consumption per capita of water in the world. Pune was supposed to recycle water and send it down to Indapur [a downstream taluka], which they haven't. As far as Lavasa is concerned, it would require less than 1 per cent of the water that Pune gets. Secondly, the lake, Varasgaon, doesn't meet Pune's water needs; it's an irrigation lake. Under the law, 10 per cent of water from the lake is the entitlement of the people of the villages in Lavasa. As for local support, all the 18 gram panchayats have signed a unanimous resolution to support Lavasa. Ninety per cent of the villagers have actually come out in support, written letters.[28]

Gulabchand knew that the power to allocate land and water resources vests with state-level politicians. It was the state legislature's enactment of the Hill Station Regulation that made Lavasa Lake City legally possible in the first place. It was the state-level politicians controlling the MKVDC who ensured that river waters flow up to the boundary walls of Gulabchand's development. But support from the local Sarpanches would send a signal to institutional investors that the project has received consent from the local community. Gaining legitimacy through subjecting the Lavasa land-use process to the public scrutiny of the Gram Panchayat was important in conveying to future investors that the risk of the project getting delayed, stalled, or even terminated was low.

Unlike the Magarpatta shareholders, Mulshi residents have not captured any of the profits from the land redevelopment in their taluka. Why then did the local elected representatives support the private city? And why did residents who were opposed to the development not convene a Gram Sabha to challenge both their local elected representatives and the company? To understand the local democratic politics, we need to step back from the current conflict and see it as part of a water conflict with a longer historical arc, going back to the early twentieth century. The next two sections show how local support and opposition to the new corridor city have been shaped by fraught histories of dam-induced displacements.

"Bharat v. India": A View from the Underdeveloped Regions

In 2014, an LCL employee connected me to the Sarpanches of some of the Gram Panchayats who supported the development of Lavasa Lake City. These Sarpanches had formed a voluntary organization called the Mose Khore Nagrik Vikas Sangh (Mose Citizens' Development Forum), which has been at the forefront of the "local support" for LCL. When the MoEF issued a show-cause notice and ordered LCL to stop construction, these Sarpanches wrote to the deputy district collector demanding that the project be resumed. I met with five of these Sarpanches over the course of July and August 2015, and I also interviewed some of their family members (fathers, uncles, cousins). During the first couple of weeks, I met with the Sarpanches in a temple in Mugaon village; later, my interviews with their family members were conducted in their homes.

One of the most vocal supporters of Lavasa Lake City is Vittal-ji. He, along with the other Sarpanches, explained to me how their lives and livelihoods had improved with the coming of the corridor city. Before its development, the families used to grow dry-crop millets on their meager two-acre plots of land. Visiting in the peak monsoon season of July and August, I found it hard to believe that this rain- and river-rich region, set amid a verdant mountain range filled with jackfruit, jamun, and mango trees, supports only subsistence agriculture. But the Sarpanches reminded me that, unless the torrential monsoon rains are regulated, the plateau where they live is vulnerable to water run-offs and severe soil erosion. Before the 2000s, when only meager dirt tracks connected their villages to the nearest town, the residents used to stock up on oil and other commodities in May, as the heavy three-month monsoon rains were likely to cut them off entirely. And in the dry summer months that follow the rains, a reverse set of harsh conditions, including scarce drinking water, confronted the villagers.

Vittal-ji listed the benefits of the new corridor city: his village, which was earlier plunged in darkness, now has electricity; long treks of five to six hours through the forest to reach the nearest urban amenities have now been replaced by short drives in his newly purchased Bolera jeep on the paved, LCL-built road; and his daughter studies at the English-medium Cristel House school, run by LCL for children of the Gram Panchayats surrounding the corridor city. The Sarpanches claim that LCL is responsive to their demands and that they interact constantly with LCL's corporate social responsibility (CSR) team. Vittal-ji, referring to the land conflict in Singur over the Tata Nano factory in West Bengal, told me, "We do not want another Singur here." (LCL's CSR program is headed by the person who managed Tata's CSR program at Singur, and it is possible that Vittal-ji drew his references to Singur from his interactions with the company and its CSR team.)

The almost complete neglect of this region before the 2000s—the villages struggling without even the basic amenities of drinking water and electricity—meant that the Mulshi Gram Panchayats, whose primary functions include decision making about public services, were virtually inactive until the coming of the corridor city. Vittal-ji is a member of the Maratha middle peasantry. Why were people like him in Mulshi unable to mobilize their electoral political system to bring water and other basic amenities to their villages? The answer lies in the earlier dam-building projects that forced these petty propertied Marathas to migrate to Bombay from the 1930s onward, to work in the city's then-thriving textile mills. Now, with the closure of the mills in what some are calling a "post-industrial city,"[29] these same Marathas are returning to their home villages, and their reverse migration is producing a new electoral geography.

As shown in Chapter 1, the Mulshi region used to be largely inhabited by petty proprietary classes and unpropertied forest dependents belonging to the poorest Maratha, Kunbi, Dhangar, and Katkari caste groups. Not only is the Maratha-Kunbi caste cluster highly stratified economically, but the Marathas themselves range from wealthy elites to marginal landowners. Scholars like Anand Teltumbde classify Marathas into the *gadhivarcha* (topmost) Marathas, "a tiny but powerful section of elites that came to have control over cooperatives of sugar, banks, educational institutions, factories and politics"; the *wadyavarcha* (well-off) Marathas, who own large tracts of "land, distribution agencies, transportation companies, contracting firms"; and the *wadivarcha* (lower) Marathas, the small and marginal farmers.[30] The Marathas in the Mulshi region belong to the lowest, wadivarcha stratum. And this caste composition, combined with the water resources in this river-rich region, reduced the Mulshi and Mawal talukas to an exploited hinterland that served the sugar-rich areas and the industrial cities.

The first large dam to be built in the Western Ghats region was the Mulshi Dam, constructed by the industrial house of the Tatas in the 1920s. Rajendra Vora, in his meticulous analysis, calls the peasant struggles against the dam the "world's first anti-dam movement."[31] In his book, Vora seeks to answer an important question: because the Mulshi Dam protests were a struggle against an ideology of economic development espoused by Mohandas Gandhi (that of big dams and capitalist-heavy industry), why did Gandhi not support them? Vora argues that, for one thing, the Mulshi struggle was different from the "peasant movements" in other parts of the country (such as the Deccan Riots of the 1870s in the Bombay Deccan region). These other movements were struggles against a colonial power and received strong support from the Indian nationalist movement. The Mulshi struggle, on the other hand, was against a specific model of economic development (big dams). It involved peasant cultivators, but the struggle was spearheaded by Brahmin moneylenders who had lent to the Mulshi peasants. Even nationalist leaders like Gandhi who were opposed to the big-dam model of development felt ambivalent about the Mulshi struggle and did not want to agitate against the dam, both because industrial capitalist firms like the Tatas were the main bankrollers of the nationalist movement and because the Brahmin moneylenders were seen as antinationalists who had aligned with the colonizers; backing them would have undermined the political credibility of the nationalist movement.

Vora gives us a vivid account of the changes in the land that came with the dam. The colonial state deployed its Land Acquisition Act to acquire nearly 20,000 acres of land in forty-eight villages (the colonial state had previously thwarted indigenous capitalists; its changed attitude arose from the shifting priorities of wartime policies). The building of the dam transformed the Mulshi Peta, as the region was called, from a lush site of fruit groves and rice fields to barren islands trapped between the dam waters and the forests. Vora's account shows how colonial-era development policies affected postcolonial electoral politics. By 1951, about thirty years after the dam was completed, dam-affected residents had deserted their villages for the cities. The migration of residents to cities like Bombay weakened the political power of Mulshi village, a weakness that manifested itself in the growing disparities between these dammed hinterlands and the sugarcane regions to which they supplied water. And the plight of the dam-affected villages further deterio- rated in the following decades. In 1983, the journalist Subhan Vaidya visited these villages and recounted the economic backwardness of the region: "A villager who fell sick had to be physically carried to a medical center situated far away. Government officials never bothered to visit the area. With a reser- voir of water before their eyes, the villagers had to go without drinking water. . . . The dam-affected Peta was deprived of the most basic amenities even as late as 1982–3."[32]

Today, the region is still struggling as a result of these earlier deprivations and remains controlled by powerful sugar elites from outside Mulshi. The eighteen villages that now fall within the Lavasa Lake City boundary come under the Baramati Parliamentary constituency, which encompasses a large territory that includes both water-rich and water-parched talukas. It stretches from the villages of Dasve and Mugaon in Mulshi on its west to Daund taluka on its east; in between, it includes Malegaon and other sugar- rich villages in Baramati. Sugar elites have always dominated the Baramati constituency; the current Member of Parliament from this constituency is Supriya Sule, Sharad Pawar's daughter. The Baramati Lok Sabha constituency includes six State Legislative Assembly constituencies: Daund, Indapur, Bara- mati, Purandar, Khadakwasla, and Bhor. Dasve and its neighboring Mulshi villages come under the Bhor assembly constituency. Since the 1970s, the Bhor constituency has been represented in the state legislature by Congress politicians of sugar origins. Anantrao Thopte, a member of one of Bhor's most dominant families, enjoyed an uninterrupted stint as the constituency's Member of the Legistative Assembly from 1972 to 1995. From 1999 to the present, the constituency has been represented by Thopte's son, Sangram An- antrao Thopte. His family controls a web of cooperative institutions, includ- ing a sugar cooperative in the irrigated zones of Bhor. Represented in both the State Legislative Assembly and the Parliament by sugar elites, the resi- dents of Dasve, Mugaon, and the surrounding villages were electorally mar- ginalized.

Recently, however, the reverse migration of the petty-propertied Marathas to Mulshi has been changing the electoral dynamics of the region. The Con- gress and NCP stronghold over the region is weakening with the rise of the Shiv Sena party, which, as of 2004, has fielded strong runner-up contenders to Sangram Anantrao Thopte in the state assembly elections. Of the five Lavasa-supporting Sarpanches that I spoke to, all of them had family members—fathers, uncles, cousins—who had left their Mulshi villages during earlier decades to work in Mumbai's textile mills. Even before it became a political party, the Shiv Sena started its nativist organizing in the Maratha-dominated working-class unions of Mumbai, including the textile workers' union. Claiming to be the voice of the Marathi-speaking *manoos* (people), the Shiv Sena rallied the working-class job seekers around a "sons of the soil" identity that was militantly anti-immigrant and anti-outsider.[33] With the closure of the mills, many of these workers started migrating back to their villages, mainly in the western Maharashtra and Konkan regions. The closure of the mills marks an important shift in Mumbai's political economy from "mill hands to mill lands"[34]—the advantageously located mill lands, once the site of a thriving industrial working class, are now prized assets in a hyper-commodified real-estate market. Meanwhile, the former industrial workers are returning to reap the profits of postliberalization land commodification in their own villages, and through these reverse migrations the Shiv Sena is expanding its electoral base beyond urban working-class Mumbai to the hinterland. The seeds of support for the nativist Shiv Sena, sown in the industrial neighborhoods of Mumbai, are now spreading to the villages that the ex-industrial Maratha workers are returning to.

When I asked the Mulshi Sarpanches about their political affiliations, they were evasive: "There is no question of party here. We have been working together for a long time. There are new parties that have started now; the Shiv Sena, the MNS. Earlier, *sabhi log Sharad Pawar ko maanthe the* [everyone accepted Sharad Pawar]." Gram Panchayat elections, unlike those of state assemblies and even urban local governments, are supposed to be contested on an apolitical basis, meaning that candidates should not represent political parties and Sarpanches do not openly campaign on a political platform. With their strong support of the Pawar-linked Lavasa Lake City, however, one may assume that the Mulshi Sarpanches are NCP supporters. Nevertheless, the rise of Shiv Sena candidates as close runners-up to the winning, Congress candidates in the state assembly elections of 2004, 2009, and 2014 makes for a more ambivalent electoral geography.[35] The Lavasa case reminds us that many Mulshi residents are undertaking strategic maneuvers within the circumscribed options available to them, and these maneuvers make their electoral affiliations difficult to pin down. The Mulshi Sarpanches' economic support for Lavasa Lake City does not necessarily translate into political support for the NCP. It may, in fact, be in the residents' interest to forge strategic alliances with both of the two oppositional parties.

The rise of the Shiv Sena in Mulshi can be seen as a new form of "Bharat v. India" politics, shaped by the context of an underdeveloped region. In former developed agrarian regions, this political stance, exemplified in the new farmers' movement of the 1980s, was triggered by the inability of the agrarian propertied class to invest their surpluses in an urban economy. Now it is giving rise to a new electoral politics, with politicians like Raju Shetti organizing the middle peasants to capture some of the profits from land redevelopment. In underdeveloped regions like Mulshi, the Maratha middle peasantry lacked the resources to produce any surplus, either agrarian or urban.

These subsistence Maratha peasants migrated to cities in search of industrial work but lost their jobs with the closing of the textile mills in the 1980s. Their declining economic prospects are being exacerbated by the rising power of formerly subordinate caste groups, the Dalits and Adivasis.[36] Decentralization reforms mandate that the Marathas share political power with Dalits and Adivasis (categorized as Schedule Castes and Schedule Tribes in the Indian Census) through policies like the reserving of a third of local-government seats for excluded groups. As I show in the next chapter, the re-valuation of agricultural land is further unsettling agrarian land-based social power, with advantageously located waste land relegated to Adivasis now fetching a higher market price than some of the most irrigated lands owned by Marathas.

A tiny fraction of these poor Marathas, like the Mulshi Sarpanches, are benefiting from the speculative redevelopment of former waste lands. But the majority of them, mainly the younger generation, feel "trapped between agrarian distress and the future of nowhere."[37] Nativist political parties like the Shiv Sena and the MNS are capitalizing on this "politics of frustration, anxiety and outrage" to fuel a brittle identity politics that depicts non-Marathi-speaking migrants as outsiders who steal jobs from Marathas, and the fragmentation of the Bhor state assembly is one expression of its effects within the Golden Triangle. In other parts of the country, similarly retrenched dominant-caste industrial workers have been mobilized by nativist politics. In the neighboring state of Gujarat, the dominant-caste Kanbi Patels started deserting the Congress party in the 1990s for the BJP's Hindutva politics.[38] The movement bears some semblance to wider global trends like Donald Trump's presidential victory and Brexit; social groups that earlier benefited economically from their ethnic or racial identity are now feeling disfranchised and alienated, both by the loss of jobs in a globalizing economy and by the rise in power of formerly oppressed groups. In under-developed regions like Mulshi, where militant and chauvinistic parties are mobilizing excluded Marathas, the role of oppositional social movements like the NAPM is becoming crucial in offering an antidote to an opportunistic politics of hate. I focus on this movement in the next section.

Splintered Voice and Unactivated Gram Sabhas

The Mulshi Sarpanches offered me a supportive view of Lavasa Lake City. Trying to find Mulshi residents opposed to the development turned out to be a greater challenge. The CAG report emphasized that excess ceiling land controlled by the MKVDC for redistribution to the landless had instead been leased by the water parastatal to the Lavasa firm.[39] The landless residents in question had already been displaced by the time I started fieldwork, and it was almost impossible to track them.

Decades after the Mulshi Dam was built, the Mulshi villages suffered from the development-induced displacement of another dam, the Varasgaon Dam, in 1976. This dam submerged large tracts of low-lying rice fields owned largely by petty propertied classes, who had eked out a living as honey gatherers or cattle grazers on the public forest lands of the Sahyadris. For the loss of their fields, the state government gave the villagers a monetary compensation and relocated them to various sites, most of them in Daund. Large families were splintered, with some members moving to relocation sites and others continuing to stay in Mulshi but moving their subsistence activities to higher-elevation forest land. Many of the displaced residents continued to co-own marginal plots of land that were subsequently purchased by LCL, but since they did not reside in Mulshi, it was, again, difficult for me to find them.

In this context of dam-induced displacement, the NAPM has played a key role in providing an alternative citizens' forum for relocated and excluded residents. NAPM activists in Pune and Mumbai have been consistently active in organizing forest dependents and marginal landowners to reclaim their lands from LCL. In 2008, the NAPM, along with four other organizations, initiated the People's Commission of Inquiry.[40] Four members—two advocates, an activist who later entered politics and became the chief minister of Delhi, and a retired inspector general of police—conducted a two-month investigation into the Lavasa deal. This commission was one

Table 3. Distribution of Dams and Irrigation Water in Various Talukas

	Number of dams	Percentage of net sown area (1981)	Percentage of net sown area (1991)	Percentage of net sown area (2001)	Percentage of net sown area (2011)
Haweli	4	58.4	58.8	61.6	61.5
Baramati	5	67.9	80.7	75.3	75.3
Mulshi	31	60.7	62.4	39.3	39.3
Daund	5	67.1	75.7	68.2	68.2
Khed	10	47.1	61.5	64.7	64.7

Sources: Data on the dams are from *National Registry of Large Dams 2009* (New Delhi: Dam Safety Organization, Government of India, 2009). The data for the net sown areas are calculated by the author from the *Pune District Census Handbook,* Government of Maharashtra, for the years 1981, 1991, 2001, and 2011.

of the few means by which Mulshi residents opposed to the corridor city but lacking the democratic channels to express their opposition could make their voices heard.

Through one of the Pune-based NAPM activists, I was introduced to three citizens opposed to the Lavasa development. I conducted open-ended interviews with these residents over the course of three months, from June to August 2015, and through them I also met other splintered Mulshi families. Some of these interviews were conducted in Pune, in the homes of the displaced Mulshi residents. Even fifty years after Varasgaon Dam was completed, not all the displaced residents have received rehabilitation. The voluntary organization that many of them have formed, the Mulshi Dharan Vibhag Vikas Mandal (Mulshi Dam Regional Development Committee), is located not in a Mulshi village but in Pune city, where a critical mass of dam-affected families have moved for work.

Table 3 juxtaposes the location of dams with areas of irrigated land for some of the talukas in the Pune district. For the table, I selected Haweli and Baramati because of their Maratha-sugar politics; Mulshi because it has a high density of dams; Daund because it was the main taluka for dam resettlement; and Khed because it is the site of Khed City, the focus of the next chapter.

Between 1981 and 2011, we see that 75–80% of Baramati's lands constituted its net sown area, despite the taluka having only five dams. Between 1981 and 1991, the percentage of its net sown area increases; soil, rainfall, and other conditions remained constant during this period, and the increase thus indicates new irrigation canals: areas that received fresh doses of irrigation were converted from waste to cultivable land. Mulshi, on the other hand, saw a steep decline in the percentage of its net sown area, from around 61 percent in 1981 to less than 40 percent in 2001. These costs and benefits of the dams are especially striking when we consider that Mulshi has the highest number of dams not only in the Pune district but also in the country (Maharashtra has the highest number of dams in India at 1,845, of which 31 large dams are in Mulshi). Ironically, the building of the dams itself contributed to the depletion of cultivable land in Mulshi. The displaced residents were relocated to Daund, which has some irrigated sugar-rich areas but also bypassed drought-prone areas.

In short, the Varasgaon Dam not only deprived Mulshi residents of their cultivable lands and displaced them to scattered relocation sites, but also undermined the residents' democratic capabilities to exercise their voice and stake their claims on the re-valued Mulshi lands and the future of their villages. One of these displaced residents is Shinde-ji, a vocal critic of Lavasa Lake City and an active NAPM member. Shinde-ji gave me a tour brimming with local knowledge about the repercussions of the private dam construction on the region; he showed me the dams, the receding water levels in the river, and the water-rich tourist spots within Lavasa that benefit from these public rivers. A wadivarcha Maratha, Shinde-ji was displaced from his Mugaon village by the Varasgaon Dam. His family had owned some fertile rice-cultivating land near the river, which he describes as *nature ka khazana* (nature's gift).[41] In the mid-1970s, the state government compensated the family for the loss of this land with a two-acre plot in Daund; Shinde-ji was forcibly relocated there with his parents, wife, and children. The family continued to own a higher-elevation five-acre plot of land that they left unused (it could, in any case, support only subsistence dry crops).

Twelve years ago, after the death of his parents, Shinde-ji decided to move to Pune, where he has been working as a security guard monitoring the closed-circuit cameras in an ice-cream factory. He has been active in local democratic politics in his Pune neighborhood. Shinde-ji told me that he had been cheated out of his family's remaining land by "the company," LCL. Every weekend after being relocated, he used to visit his Mugaon village to check in on this land. He alleges that during one of these visits, in the 1990s, he found that his name was no longer on the official land records at the local revenue office. Having obtained the name and address of the person now listed as the legal title holder, Shinde-ji tracked him down in Pune. After a confrontation, the present owner said he had purchased the land from someone whose name Shinde-ji did not even recognize. He now believes that his plot of land went through multiple transactions without his knowledge. To avoid further trouble, the present owner offered Shinde-ji a check for 200,000 rupees. But when Shinde-ji tried to cash it (he emphasized that this was his first visit to a bank, as he did not have a bank account before that time), the check bounced. Since then, Shinde-ji has been at the forefront of the NAPM-backed opposition to Lavasa Lake City.

I asked Shinde-ji if he would return to Mulshi if he got his land back. In a revealing insight, he immediately said, "Yes," and then added, "But if I have land, that is not enough. Only if I have water can I farm."[42] Petty-propertied Marathas like Shinde-ji have titles to marginal plots of land, but even in an urbanizing context, such plots matter. Landownership is a marker of status, social power, and citizenship; it differentiates the wadivarcha Marathas from the landless Katkari forest dependents who live in the low-lying valleys by the river. Nevertheless, Shinde-ji's decision-making calculus reminds us that control over land is not enough, if one does not have some control over the infrastructural network, like water and roads, that valorize it. And this is where Gram Sabhas become important. Through participation in Gram Sabhas, citizens like Shinde-ji can apply pressure on their local representatives to demand that water and road connections reach the disconnected villages. The new Forest Rights Act recognizes the rights of occupants and dependents on forest lands as well, which means that the Gram Sabhas could serve as forums for the owners, occupants, and dependents of the forest lands in the Sahyadri ranges to stake claims to these lands.

Yet not a single Gram Sabha has been convened in the past fifteen years of protracted conflict over Lavasa Lake City. Displaced citizens like Shinde-ji are active in local democratic politics in their new relocated sites, but, though they continue to be concerned about the future of their Mulshi villages, weekend visits are not enough for deep democratic practice. The plight of these villages recalls what Steve Graham and Simon Marvin call "splintering urbanism."[43] Standing near the unfinished private dam at Mugaon during the lush monsoons, one sees a deceptively sumptuous landscape: the waters in the Mose River are full, an Airtel telecommunication tower runs parallel to its banks, and the forests are ripe with overloaded jackfruit and mango trees. But these river waters and cellphone airwaves are flowing in the direction of the corridor city, leaving the forest dependents disconnected. The phenomenon of splintering urbanism here arises partly from the splintering of the Mulshi residents' collective voice, wrought by earlier dam displacement. The 1992–93 national decentralization laws that mandated the setting up of Gram Sabhas are not enough to ensure the functioning of democratic practices; instead, social transformation depends on the ability of previously excluded groups to translate these laws to practice. In Mulshi, the possibility of activating local democratic politics was eroded by successive rounds of dam displacement, which prevented the residents from re-organizing as a polity and deliberating on the collective future of their own lands. In these institutional vacuums, social movements like the NAPM are crucial in convening alternative public forums for deprived citizens and forging collective action among splintered communities.

CHAPTER 4

From Waste Land to SEZ

Kanersar is a Gram Panchayat of 3,580 households, located around 60 kilometers from Pune in the Khed district. The Pune-Khed Industrial Area is one of the proposed investment regions in the Delhi-Mumbai Industrial Corridor (DMIC) Influence Area. Khed has a patchy landscape, with irrigated plains interspersed by outcroppings of rocky hills. The region grows hardly any sugarcane—only 450 hectares of cane, as compared to 7,027 hectares in Haweli and 12,159 hectares in Baramati[1]—but it is rich in cabbage cultivation and is one of the main suppliers of vegetables to Pune, Mumbai, and other nearby cities. The vegetables are cultivated in the plains, and the more affluent cabbage cultivators belong to the dominant-caste Maratha-Kunbi groups. An Adivasi group called the Thakkars live in segregated settlements on the hills. Because only meager cultivation of dry-land crops like millet is possible on these hills, the Adivasis grow subsistence crops and raise livestock. For their economic livelihoods, they work as agricultural laborers on the lands of the dominant-caste landowners.

A thick boundary wall meanders through this landscape of cabbage fields and dry hills. The wall, built in 2008, demarcates the perimeter of a new Special Economic Zone (SEZ) called Khed City, the first phase of which cuts across the jurisdictional boundaries of four Gram Panchayats: Kanersar, Nimgaon, and Dhawadi in Khed taluka, and Shirur in Shirur taluka. Phase 1 of the SEZ covers an area of 4,213 acres. Khed City is a multiproduct SEZ. The SEZ firms specialize in automotive exports, auto components, engineering, information technology, biotechnology, food and agro processing, electrical and electronics components, and plastics and pharmaceuticals. Also located in it are a domestic industrial park and amenities with housing, commercial, and recreational uses. It was master-planned by the international design firm HOK International, whose website offers seductive images

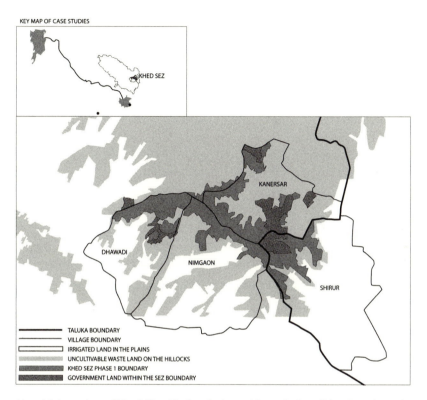

KEY MAP OF CASE STUDIES

KHED SEZ

KANERSAR

DHAWADI

NIMGAON

SHIRUR

TALUKA BOUNDARY
VILLAGE BOUNDARY
IRRIGATED LAND IN THE PLAINS
UNCULTIVABLE WASTE LAND ON THE HILLOCKS
KHED SEZ PHASE 1 BOUNDARY
GOVERNMENT LAND WITHIN THE SEZ BOUNDARY

Map 10. Location of Khed City. Notice the jagged boundaries of the SEZ, drawn in such a way as to encompass only uncultivable waste land in the hillocks and to leave the irrigated land in the plains untouched. Source: Details on the various categories of land acquired by the Maharashtra Industrial Development Corporation (MIDC) for the SEZ are from a land-acquisition file obtained by the author from the MIDC office, Pune.

of the proposed new city: buildings with angular steel frames and large plate-glass windows offering glimpses of open workspaces, lush green foliage hanging down and shading cantilevered roofs, and aerodynamic cars cruising along the smooth roads. HOK claims that "nature's principles [are] driving the design of this new industrial city, which will house 2 million people in an area the size of Manhattan."[2] By 2014, all that existed of this new urban fantasy were walls with billboards that promised a new industrial future: "Khed City: India's Smart Emerging Industrial City."

The jarring presence of the SEZ walls amid the cabbage fields is representative of the emerging built environment in this part of western Maharashtra. The region started seeing industrial changes in the 1980s, as small and medium-scale enterprises starting clustering along the highway that connects the industrialized cities of Pune and Nashik. These clusters formed part of the thriving automotive industry that had been developing in Pune since the 1950s. Some of the biggest domestic firms in automobile manufacturing are Pune-based industrial houses, such as Kirloskar and Mahindra & Mahindra. To spur industrialization further in this region, the industrial parastatal of the state, the Maharashtra Industrial Development Corporation (MIDC), set up two industrial estates in Talegaon and Chakan, about 30 kilometers from Pune, soon after the Mumbai-Pune Expressway was announced. The main advantage of these MIDC-developed industrial estates is that the parastatal assumes full responsibility for the necessary land acquisition and, in many cases, for the provision of services such as water and power. The parastatal then either sells or leases the land to industrial firms. Talegaon is now home to heavy industrial firms as well as new agro-based industries, including export-oriented floriculture firms. In 2006, another Pune-based industrial house, Bharat Forge, proposed the setting up of a new SEZ in this region.

The Khed SEZ is part of a postliberalization wave of SEZs that has attracted much scholarly attention. Some analyses situate the SEZs within the current era of neoliberal globalization. Influential among these is Aihwa Ong's analysis of SEZs as a manifestation of "neoliberalism as exception," in which she argues that nation-states are carving up their territories into a "pattern of graduated or variegated sovereignty" so that they can "better engage and compete in global markets."[3] Disagreeing with Ong in the Indian context, Jamie Cross characterizes SEZs with the phrase "neoliberalism as unexceptional," arguing that the flexible labor regimes within SEZs simply formalize the already-existing and rampant conditions of informality and precariousness that characterize much of India.[4] Michael Levien, taking another perspective, characterizes India's SEZs as a new regime of dispossession under neoliberal globalization.[5] He historicizes SEZs within postcolonial development politics and argues that, unlike an earlier regime of dispossession when the Nehruvian state expropriated land for a "state-driven, productive, employment-generating form of national development," the SEZs are positioned within "the onset of India's neoliberal reforms . . . in which land was increasingly expropriated for any private purpose that represented a higher-value land use than agriculture—no matter how immaterial, consumptive or speculative."[6] The shift from "land for production" to "land for the market," he argues, has generated widespread "land wars" because the former, even though it involved massive dispossession, enjoyed greater ideological legitimacy among the broader public.

Other scholars have analyzed the wave of SEZs in the context of the decentralization reforms. K. C. Sivaramakrishnan argues that the SEZ law, which permits a manufacturing firm to take over the responsibilities of municipalities, contravenes the democratic intent of the new decentralization laws.[7] Each SEZ is built and serviced by a "developer"—a joint venture between the private-sector firm that promotes the project and the industrial parastatal of the state. The private-sector firm takes on the responsibility of raising capital for the SEZ, as well as of providing and maintaining services for it; the industrial parastatal is responsible for land acquisition. Once the SEZ construction is completed, the SEZ Authority—a committee nominated by both the Board of Approval (a new single-window agency that approves SEZ applications) and the developer—replaces the local government as the public authority for that zone. To make it legal for a private corporation to take over the functions of a municipal corporation, the jurisdictional concept of the "Notified Area Committee" was institutionalized in the Indian Constitution through a Proviso to Article 243Q.[8] This provision was introduced in the early decades of post-Independence, when India was struggling to establish itself as a self-sufficient industrial economy in the wake of colonialism; it was the legal basis for the Nehruvian-era steel towns. The municipal acts of that period authorized the setting up of autonomous company towns, or Notified Areas, where manufacturing firms would take over the functions of local governments and become the sole public authorities for those carved-out areas. In 1992–93, the 73rd and 74th Constitutional Amendments (the decentralization laws) mandated the setting up of municipalities and Panchayats for the democratic governance of urban and rural jurisdictions, respectively. Article 243Q, which goes against the spirit of democratic local governance, was reinserted in the new decentralization law. One possible reason for the inclusion of the proviso may have been the involvement of the Tata company, which, "anticipating problems in the future, might have suggested to the Government of India that a special dispensation should be made in regard to Jamshedpur [the Tata company's steel town]."[9]

While Sivaramakrishnan sees the SEZs as contravening the decentralization laws, Rob Jenkins takes another stance, arguing that the explosion of SEZs is a capitulation to the success of the decentralization reforms.[10] As local politics becomes more inclusive, firms and developers are seeking to secede from democratic politics into hyperliberalized enclaves such as the SEZs. Jenkins adds that the SEZ Act marked the culmination of a market-oriented economic policy and, at the same time, catalyzed a widespread protest movement, which became the basis for the state's generous rollout of rights-based legislation (including the ongoing debates over the Right to Fair Compensation and Transparency in Land Acquisition, Rehabilitation and Resettlement Act [LARRA]).

I am interested in situating the SEZs at the intersection of the liberalization and decentralization reforms, and in asking how the market and democratic imperatives of these almost simultaneously enacted institutional reforms collide within the new jurisdictional spaces of the SEZs. Their location is another instance of the overlap of the new corridor cities with former Green Revolution regions.[11] Khed was not the epicenter of western Maharashtra's Green Revolution policies, but it is adjacent to the sugarcane-rich talukas that were the epicenter, and the critical mass of Khed Maratha-Kunbis was strong enough to pull irrigation waters toward their taluka to support vegetable cultivation. The collision between new influxes of urban private capital and existing agrarian propertied capital in the making of Khed City resembles the agrarian-urban collisions in other former Green Revolution regions.

When Khed City was first announced in 2006, the region's agrarian landowners reacted to the proposal with protests that were widely publicized by India's news media channels. Faced with a vociferous backlash from an organized agrarian constituency, the local bureaucrats decided to negotiate with the protesters. Their negotiated solution was the formation of a joint-venture company, which includes among its shareholders not only the private-sector firm and the industrial parastatal (something common to all SEZs) but also a farmers' land cooperative—a solution unique to Khed City. This model has since become popular in the region, and many surrounding villagers have approached the local bureaucrats to mediate similar joint-venture companies, transforming more and more landowners into shareholders in the new corridor cities. But the amicable solution of the joint-venture company is now embroiled in fresh protests: political parties like the Swabhimani Paksha are capitalizing on the anxieties of the landowners-turned-shareholders and demanding that the shareholder model be dissolved and the acquired lands returned to the landowners.

In the rest of this chapter, I track this agrarian-urban encounter, which started in protests, was resolved in a market-oriented shareholding arrangement, and is now again entangled in conflict. A central focus for the chapter is how the shareholder model of land-conflict resolution has unsettled existing land-based caste relations and produced a new politics of recognition for the Khed Adivasis.

Eminent Domain, Inc.

In 2006, the private-sector firm Bharat Forge received an approval from the Board of Approval to set up an SEZ in the Khed region. The new SEZ was to be developed by the shareholding company Khed Economic Infrastructure Private Limited (KEIPL), which is jointly owned by Bharat Forge and the industrial parastatal, the MIDC. In a newly liberalizing economy, firms like Bharat Forge that are expanding into the countryside confront a major risk of encumbered land. Agricultural land in India is highly fragmented, both in size and in tenure, due to intergenerational transfers within large families, and these fragmented landholdings pose a serious collective-action problem, due to the huge transaction costs involved in bringing a large number of small landowners together. Agricultural land is also fractionated—one plot of land may have multiple co-owners and more often than not has an ambiguous ownership history. In the Khed region, the average size of operational landholdings varies from 2 to 5 acres, with more than 25 percent of landowners classified as marginal and less than 5 percent classified as large. Not only are they small, but these landholdings are also fractionated. For example, a 1.68-hectare plot in Kanersar Gram Panchayat is co-owned by seventy-eight landowners, many of whom do not even reside in the region and have migrated to Mumbai or other neighboring cities.[12]

These conditions pose the legal risk of encumbrance (i.e., legal or financial liabilities in land that are undisclosed at the time of purchase and may come to light at a future date). For this reason, private-sector firms tend to insist that the state acquire land for them for infrastructural, industrial, and other uses. When the state acquires land and transfers it to the private sector, the transferred land is delivered free of encumbrance, and this claims-clearing power has become a crucial form of title insurance for the private sector. It is important to remember that, in India, it is possible for development to continue in the absence of clear titles. Ananya Roy argues that ambiguous property regimes are the very basis of Indian state power: when multiple claims on land are kept alive, only the state retains the power to allocate it arbitrarily among multiple "territorial claims in the unmapped city"—and it is in these ambiguous claims that the source of accumulation and authority for the state resides.[13]

Though some of India's most affluent hotels, sports complexes, and religious ashrams are built on encumbered land,[14] most industrial firms do not want to deal with the risks of encumbrance. When the contentious LARRA was being debated in Parliament in the mid-2000s, one of the proposals was for the state to withdraw completely from land acquisition and allow the private sector to transact directly with landowners. The strongest opposition to this suggestion came from the corporate and business lobbies, which insisted on state mediation in their land transactions. Among its many benefits for industrialists, the SEZ policy ensures that the state will acquire land for the SEZ promoter, thereby indemnifying the urban/industrial class against any uncertainties or liabilities related to land tenure. Industrial parastatals like the MIDC, therefore, are invaluable partners in SEZ development. For Khed City, the encumbrance-free nature of the land is featured as a key selling point in the city's promotional brochure: "The land in Khed City has been acquired by MIDC under the MID Act and leased to KEIPL, the developer of Khed City. Therefore, you [potential industrial firms] have no worries about the title of the land. You are free from any concerns of future litigations on the title of the land."[15]

In 2006, MIDC issued the first notice of land acquisition to seventeen villages in the Khed region. The condemnees, many of whom belonged to the organized Maratha-Kunbi landed constituency, reacted swiftly and vehemently. In July 2006, thousands of them staged a protest outside the Khed Revenue Department office, demanding the scrapping of the SEZ. The protest received nationwide media attention when the eminent social activist and leader of the National Alliance for People's Movements (NAPM), Medha Patkar, joined the protest in October 2006.

The composition of the agrarian propertied class in Khed differs from the other two cases discussed in this book. Here, the agrarian landowners are not as powerful as the Magarpatta sugar elites. In 2006, though the Integrated Township Policy had already been enacted as a state-level policy, the Khed landowners were unable to foster collective action among themselves and consolidate their lands for an urban development of their own. They also lacked the political networks needed to ensure the flow of water to any urban development they might have wanted to build. On the other hand, unlike Lavasa, there are enough electorally organized Maratha-Kunbi landowners in the region to make their lack of consent and possible alienation a grave risk for politicians seeking reelection.

MIDC thus found itself caught in the crossfire of two powerful groups: Bharat Forge was applying pressure to acquire the land through eminent domain, while the organized agrarian constituency was expressing wrath at the threatened exercise of these coercive powers. MIDC, as a state-level agency, lacked the expertise to negotiate with the landowners; it turned instead to the district collector (DC) of Pune to mediate the negotiations on its behalf. The DC delegated the power to acquire lands for Bharat Forge to his Revenue Department bureaucrat at the subdistrict level, Shyam Patil. Subdivisional officers (SDOs) like Patil spend long periods of time in one place, and they have an intimate knowledge of local power structures and politics. The negotiations between Patil and the protesting landowners took nearly a year. During the negotiations, Patil learned that the landowners were not opposed to the new corridor city itself, only to the perceived unfairness in the allocation of the new urban land profits from Khed City. Therefore, the Revenue Department and MIDC bureaucrats decided to resolve the conflict with a clever twist: they decoupled takings from compensation. To ensure that the land was delivered encumbrance-free to KEIPL, they consolidated it through an involuntary, nonmarket acquisition. But they arranged for the compensation for the land to be based on a voluntary, market-driven basis.

Determining the "fair market value" of expropriated land is a contentious issue, even in countries like the United States that have a longer history of real-estate markets.[16] In India, the compensation issue is all the more fraught because agricultural land markets, until recently, have been tightly regulated by the state. The bureaucratic solution to the Khed conflict resembles what Amnon Lehavi and Amir Licht have called "Eminent Domain, Inc."[17] Just as a firm is a solution devised to overcome the high transaction costs of collective action by pooling assets in a hierarchical organization,[18] Lehavi and Licht argue that "the takings [or eminent domain] phase resembles a notional incorporation of a firm."[19] The crucial difference, of course, is that the incorporation of a firm is voluntary, while eminent domain is not. In order to "restore market mechanisms to the extent possible" to a coercive eminent-domain procedure, Lehavi and Licht recommend allocating to landowners ad valorem publicly traded shares in the new development. This arrangement can "harness the market's powerful price system to generate better signals about the true economic value of the condemned land."[20] In Khed, the bureaucrats did not want to get stuck in negotiations about fair compensation prices. Instead, the landowners-turned-shareholders model gave landowners a chance to reap some of the long-term appreciation in land price. This model of conflict resolution resembles the arrangement in Magarpatta, in that both models are variations of land readjustment: instead of returning a smaller but higher-priced plot of land to the landowners, they are given pro rata shares in a real-estate company.

At the end of the year, the bureaucrats and protesting landowners arrived at a final solution—a joint-venture company, KEIPL. The bureaucrats mediated the formation of a farmers' land cooperative, Khed Developers' Limited (KDL), which owns 15 percent of the KEIPL shares, while Bharat Forge owns 51 percent and MIDC, 34 percent. The landowners thus receive 15 percent of the compensation for their land as shares, while the remaining 85 percent is monetary. In addition to this shareholding agreement, the SEZ deal included guaranteed admission for one member from each affected landholding family to the Khed Industrial Training Institute (ITI), a public-sector vocational training center. These institutes are in high demand among the younger-generation workforce, which is eager for industrial employment. The Khed ITI has the corporate sponsorship of Bharat Forge, whose employees have played an active role in designing the Khed ITI syllabus, ensuring that the training will produce a workforce with the appropriate skill-set for the region's industrial economy. Lastly, the landowners demanded that the boundaries of the SEZ be redrawn to include only the waste land on the hills, excluding all their fertile land on the plains. I will return to this demand in the next section, as it was a key countermovement for the agrarian propertied classes to mitigate their risks in a nascent real-estate market.

The most innovative part of the SEZ deal was its inclusion of the agrarian landowners as shareholders. Most importantly, though the terms of the deal were decided during the negotiations, the allocation of shares among the three joint-venture partners—the industrial firm, the parastatal, and the farmers' cooperative—was decided at a Gram Sabha. These Gram Sabha negotiations were completed between 2006 and 2008, three years before I started my fieldwork in Khed. Patil, the Revenue Department bureaucrat who had been involved in the negotiations, and the Sarpanches of the Kanersar Gram Panchayat described for me the major points of discussion. During the Gram Sabhas, the KDL share of 15 percent was arrived at; Patil explained that the landowners' contribution in land amounted to 15 percent of the project cost at that time. The landowners preferred that a large percentage of the compensation be in monetary form, as that would give them some short-term liquid benefits from their illiquid assets.

I attended the Kanersar Gram Sabha and other public meetings in 2011, at which the Sarpanches, the MIDC and Revenue Department bureaucrats, and Kanersar residents were in attendance. At these public meetings, the topic being debated was the new risks for the landowners posed by their status as shareholders. The land for Khed City had been acquired in 2006, but the project was facing considerable delays, largely because Bharat Forge was unable to raise additional capital in the wake of the 2008 global financial crisis. The lack of visible construction on the site was a source of anxiety for the Maratha-Kunbi landowners:

> If the company's share dividend had started, that would have been good for us. We gave up their land four years back. I gave up 15 acres of land, but have not received the dividend on my 2.25 acres [15 percent of those 15 acres]. For my 2.25 acres, I should have received 120,000 rupees [in] interest. But for four years now, I have not received anything.[21]

> What assurance do we have that the SEZ will be completed? Will they give us jobs or not?[22]

A heated exchange ensued between one of the Maratha landowners and the DC:

> *Maratha landowner:* We don't have any use of the shares. We want back 15 percent of the land, but they're not giving it.
> *DC:* No one has lost anything. If your land is now worth 10 rupees [a hypothetical price], then with the infrastructure, it will go up to 50.
> *Maratha landowner:* There's no point in adding value to our land. Why don't they [Bharat Forge] use the 5,000 acres that they have? They are all *bade bade log* [rich men]. Why are they not using their own land? They have the 5,000 acres, and now they have their eyes on our 500 acres.
> *Another Maratha landowner:* Give us back our 15 percent lands. If you want to build a 600-crore [6,000,000,000-rupee] company,

do it on your land. We know our lands will not remain unused, someone will come and rent the place. On our land, we can do something for our children. We can build a hotel, a lodge, something. . . . But it is lying idle.[23]

Phase One of Khed City has a spatial footprint of 4,213 acres of dongarpad, that is, waste land, on the hillocks. Of this, around half the acquired waste lands are "government land" and the other half are privately owned. Around 50 percent of these waste lands are owned by the Maratha-Kunbis; the Thakkars own another 30 percent; and the remaining lands are owned by other "backward-class" groups. A long history of sociospatial segregation has relegated the Thakkars to the *dongarpad* waste lands on the hills. They have historically worked as agricultural laborers on the irrigated lands in the plains, but with the new market demand for their land, they have found themselves owners of a high-value market asset. They were not part of the 2006–8 negotiations, but they were included nevertheless as shareholders in the new SEZ deal.

At the 2011 Gram Sabha, while the Maratha-Kunbi landowners were anxious about the delayed status of the SEZ project, the Thakkars voiced a different set of concerns. Shantaram-ji, a Thakkar elected to the Gram Panchayat in a reserved seat for Scheduled Tribes, brought up the issue of caste certificates. In the 2006–8 Gram Sabhas, the bureaucrats had promised the Thakkars both water connection and caste certificates, which are issued to Scheduled Castes and Scheduled Tribes as identity documents to gain access to affirmative-action quotas in government jobs, educational institutions, and poverty-alleviation programs. Shantaram-ji's family already had their caste certificates, but other Thakkar residents did not. As a Scheduled Tribe representative, Shantaram-ji spoke on behalf of the most marginalized members of the community. For the poorest Thakkar shareholders, the perceived benefit of joining the SEZ deal was not the promise of sharing in the urban land profits but rather the increased negotiating power to gain water, caste certificates, and other resources that they are entitled to as citizens but had not received so far.

The Khed joint-venture company has thus brought together historically antagonistic groups—agrarian landowners and an industrial firm, Maratha-Kunbi landowners and Thakkar laborers—as shareholders in a company. The Gram Sabha became the site of negotiations among these oppositional groups. Mohanseth Kelkar, the Sarpanch of Kanersar Gram Panchayat, was one of the first Sarpanches to agree to a negotiation. When I interviewed him, he explained the sequence of events and the need to include the Gram Sabha for political legitimacy:

> Earlier, even we had protested against the industry. Sarpanches of the seventeen villages got together, formed an organization, and in that protest we went to the district collector's office. We went there asking them to close it [the SEZ]. With Patil *sahib* [Shyam Patil], we discussed what will happen if the SEZ comes here. Because of this discussion, four villages immediately agreed to the SEZ. Kanersar was the first village to agree.... Patil sahib told us, "You prepare your people, we will arrange whatever you need." We went around all the farmlands in the village, what to keep and what to remove, we underlined that. We had a Gram Sabha and convinced the people.[24]

As noted earlier, the nature of the agrarian propertied class in Khed differs from that in Magarpatta. The Magarpatta sugar elites had state-level political connections and could facilitate the transition of their constituents from sugar to real estate. The small and marginal sugarcane growers reposed trust in their powerful Maratha elites. As shown in Chapter 2, despite the risks involved in making the transition from sugar to real estate, caste affinities and past experiences of benefiting from the sugar cooperatives produced what Charles Tilly calls "interpersonal relationships," in which "people set valued, consequential, long-term resources and enterprises at risk to the malfeasance of [trusted] others."[25] The absence of a sugar-cooperative history in Khed meant that the Marathas there had to earn their constituents' trust (and support for future elections) through their performances in formal democratic institutions, as well as by providing public services and administering welfare programs. In this context of functioning Gram Sabhas, it was crucial for Kanersar's elected representatives to convince their constituents of the SEZ benefits in that public forum; otherwise, the SEZ deal would have lost legitimacy among the villagers and met vocal opposition.

However, by arriving at a shareholder model of conflict resolution even before the Gram Sabhas were held, the bureaucrats had already framed the public negotiations in a market-oriented language of shares and financial interests. I want to highlight two exclusions from the Gram Sabha negotiations. First, there was no discussion of how much of the new profits from the land redevelopment would be captured by the Gram Panchayats for public services and social welfare programs. Though the landowners obtained 15 percent of the urban land profits in the form of shares, and though marginalized Thakkar landowners were included as shareholders, the framing of the Gram Sabha negotiation as a shareholder model resulted in the privatization of the profits from land redevelopment. Second, when the SEZ boundary was redrawn to exclude irrigated lands, in the process, it enclosed and privatized common grazing lands. Two of the main reasons that the MIDC bureaucrats selected this cluster of seventeen Khed villages for the new SEZ were that they were close to existing water, roads, and other infrastructural networks, and that they contained a significant proportion of what is classified as "government" land. These lands, owned by government agencies such as the Gram Panchayat and the Revenue Department, include common grazing lands, and in the ensuing conflict, these common lands become the least politically contentious areas for acquisition or purchase, leading to a rampant and unchecked enclosure of the commons. Just as the shareholder model precluded any discussion of the capture of land profits for public services, it also forestalled any debate on this shrinking access to public lands. The bureaucrats mediated the land conflict with the innovative organizational solution of "Eminent Domain, Inc.," but the negotiated solution relied so heavily on the market as the arbiter of competing land claims that it excised any public considerations from the negotiations; not only were public lands privatized, but even the profits from the redevelopment of these lands were privatized.

Mediating Uneven Development

At the 2011 Kanersar Gram Sabha, the landowners were particularly perturbed by the absence of the Revenue Department SDO, Shyam Patil, who had mediated the shareholder negotiations. In 2010, Patil had been transferred to become a personal assistant to Ajit Pawar in Mumbai. The Khed landowners felt that their trust had been broken and that the new SDO did not know the details of the deal well enough to effectively mediate the conflict:

> Patil sahib asked everyone their problems. After knowing the problem, he tried to address it. The MIDC said they will not acquire any *bagayat* [irrigated] land, but during the acquisition 200 acres of bagayat land was acquired. We had a meeting with Patil sahib and the

collector, and the bagayat land was removed and returned to farmers. We liked that. Patil sahib did all of this for us. Since he has left for Mantralaya [the Maharashtra State Legislative Assembly], it has become slow here. There is no work going on now. If he were here, the company would have started by now.[26]

The role of the SDO in mediating the Khed conflict merits some analysis. The SDO forms the bureaucratic link between the village accountants and the DC, who comes from the highly regarded Indian Administrative Service (IAS) and heads the Revenue Department at the district level. The SDO—also from the IAS—is in charge of a particular subdivision, which is made up of a group of talukas; the *tahsildar* is in charge of a particular taluk; the circle inspector is responsible for a particular revenue circle, the administrative unit just below the taluk and the bureaucratic equivalent of the Gram Panchayat (though, due to the differing histories of local governments and the revenue bureaucracy, the boundaries of the Gram Panchayat do not coincide with those of the revenue circle); and, lastly, the village accountant, also called the Talathi or Patwari, is a public official who deals with the land records, revenue accounts, and cash books for the revenue circle.

Unlike the DCs, the SDOs have the time to embed themselves in local power structures. At the same time, bureaucratic rules are in place to prevent them from being influenced by local elites. On passing the highly competitive IAS examinations, bureaucrats are assigned to different districts or states according to strict rules: the top candidates are assigned to districts of their choice, while others are assigned by a "quasi-random" procedure to ensure that the bureaucratic talent is more or less evenly distributed across the states.[27] Unless they are at the top of their cohort, bureaucrats are never assigned to their home states. The officers start off as SDOs and are expected to serve a three- to five-year tenure in each post. It takes six to ten years to reach the rank of DC. Though the DC is governed by similar rules for tenure in each place, state-level politicians often apply pressure on the chief minister to get the DCs "transferred" if the latter do not advance the short-term interests of the elected representatives. In their analysis of bureaucratic transfers, Lakshmi Iyer and Anandi Mani find that "the average tenure of IAS officers in a given post is 16 months and only 56% of District Officers spend more than one year in their post. . . . [T]he average rate of bureaucratic transfers in a state increases significantly when there is a new Chief Minister in that state."[28]

Being lower in the bureaucratic hierarchy, the SDOs are protected from these politicized transfers, giving them the time to develop relations of trust with the residents of their jurisdiction and enhancing their capacity for conflict mediation. At the same time, since they belong to the elite technocratic ranks of the Administrative Services, the SDOs have the authority to exercise what Judith Tendler and Sara Freedheim have called "bureaucratic discretion."[29] In coming up with the idea of a market-based, nonmonetary form of compensation, Patil was deviating from existing bureaucratic rules, but he had the authority to convince his bureaucratic superiors at the Revenue Department and the MIDC of the merits of the idea. Sharad Pawar and the sugar elites before him built their political careers on ensuring that the profits from uneven development were shared with their constituents; the agro-industrial and Integrated Township policies are examples. It is fitting, then, that the Nationalist Congress Party recognized and rewarded Patil's conflict-mediating skills by promoting him to be Ajit Pawar's personal assistant. Patil was further promoted: he is now a bureaucrat in charge of land acquisition for the segment of the DMIC that passes through the state of Maharashtra. But with Patil's transfer to Mumbai, the Khed region lost a skilled bureaucratic mediator—and, to make matters worse, the SEZ development is now being further delayed by a fresh round of landowner protests.

For more than a decade, the state government of Maharashtra has tried to find a site for the Pune International Airport. The airport was initially planned for Chakan, but, following attempts at land acquisition that failed due to landowner protests, the airport parastatal—the Maharashtra Airport Development Corporation—decided instead to requisition 850 hectares of land from KEIPL. Both Bharat Forge and the agrarian landowners put up stiff opposition to this plan, as land taken from Khed City will negatively affect their shareholder profits.[30] As a result, the airport location remains in limbo, and political parties have now entered the fray. The interminable delay in getting the SEZ off the ground has heightened the anxieties of the Maratha-Kunbi landowners, and many now want their land back. Raju Shetti—the leader of the Swabhimani Paksha political party—has thrown his weight behind these landowners. In March 2015, he led a 50-kilometer protest march from Khed to Pune, demanding that the SEZ Authority return the acquired land to the aggrieved landowners.[31] Combining forces with Shetti is Shivajirao Adhalrao-Patil, the Member of Parliament for this region, representing the Shiv Sena.[32]

It remains to be seen how the politics of Khed City will play out. However, regardless of any future changes to the shareholder arrangement, the land negotiations so far have spurred the formation of new land-based social relations, which is the focus of the next section.

Antagonistic Cooperation

Khed City has a complex cast of characters. As I have said, KEIPL is an innovative experiment that brings together historically antagonistic groups: agrarian landowners and industrial firms, dominant-caste and subordinate-caste agrarian landowners. Electoral compulsions and the balance of class/caste power among these constituencies force them to accommodate each other's interests. Their coming together thus has less to do with democratic ideals and more to do with the electoral realities of competitive politics. Bishwapriya Sanyal calls such collaborations "antagonistic cooperation,"[33] a fitting description of the ties that underpin the Khed joint-venture company.

The negotiations with the agrarian landowners and the sharing of land profits with them are strategic moves by Bharat Forge. Its chairman and managing director, Baba Kalyani, is the brother-in-law of the managing director of the private-sector consortium Nandi Infrastructure Corridor Enterprises (NICE), which in 1994 attempted to build an economic corridor connecting the southern Indian city Bangalore to a neighboring city, Mysore. That economic corridor has been mired in litigation until now, with the region's dominant-caste agrarian elites effectively blocking the project because they did not receive what they viewed as a fair compensation package. The litigation has been accompanied by successful street protests with slogans such as "NICE: The not-so-nice highway." This experience was a harsh eye-opener to industrialists and developers, forcing them to realize that coercive land acquisition can lead to interminable delays or even terminations at a later stage. The negative publicity can also hurt the images and undermine the reputational capitals of these firms.

Baba Kalyani learned from the mistakes of his brother-in-law and took a more conciliatory route for the Khed SEZ. Among other measures, he promised the four Gram Panchayat Sarpanches construction contracts as additional incentives to gain their consent (similar to the inducements to Sarpanches in the Lavasa case). Accordingly, Mohanseth Kelkar, the Sarpanch of Kanersar Gram Panchayat, started a construction company in 2009 with five of his cousins, all of whom lacked prior experience in construction. A Bharat Forge employee supervising one of their construction sites conceded that the Kelkars' construction company was slow and its quality not up to the mark, but, he said, these "concessions have to be made as confidence-building measures."[34]

These land-use changes have exposed the Maratha-Kunbi landowners to new opportunities and risks. Like the sugar elites in the Magarpatta case, the Khed landowners were eager to make the transition to an urban economy, for two reasons—the push factor of agricultural labor shortages and the pull factor of urban aspirations. The former is evident in the common refrain among Maratha-Kunbi landowners in the Khed region: "*Mazdoor nahi milte*" (workers cannot be not found). The Thakkars who had earlier worked on their agricultural lands are now finding alternative work in the urban informal economy. A Maratha landowner in Kanersar summed up the problem as follows: "Earlier, the villagers used to come for work—Thakkars, others. Once the [SEZ] land payment was made, people work less. Earlier, the Thakkars used to work from morning to night, now they do not. The nearby places— Chakan, Rajgurunagar—there is *chota-mota* [small] factory and construction work there, people have gone to work there. Earlier, we used to pay 60 rupees, now no one comes for less than 100. And they come at 11 and leave at 5, take a break for lunch. This is everywhere. Here [in Khed], because of the land money, it is more."[35]

Besides the agricultural labor shortage, there is the aspiration among agrarian landowners to be part of the "India Shining" growth story.[36] The Maratha Sarpanches of all four consenting Gram Panchayats have educated their children in private, not government, schools, and they are unanimous in wanting their children to leave agriculture and join industry. For these households, one of the most attractive inducements of the SEZ compensation package was the guarantee that one household member would be entitled to admission in the Khed ITI. Getting a permanent, secure job in the Pune-Nashik factories is a coveted prize, and an ITI certificate is one of the filtering devices that separates the few formal and permanent factory jobs from the many informal, contract ones.

The Maratha-Kunbi landowners have urban aspirations for themselves and their children, but they are also aware of the risks of an urban transition. Unanticipated changes—in interest rates, material costs, demand for the industrial products and services of the SEZ—could seriously affect project returns. In the case of such losses, the agrarian landowners will pay the high price of losing their landed assets in an unprofitable industrial venture. It was in anticipation of these risks that the Maratha-Kunbi agrarian landowners demanded that the SEZ boundaries be redrawn. Most of them owned multiple plots of land, often in joint ownership with others, at geographically dispersed sites.[37] Some plots were cabbage-cultivating lands on the plains, others waste land on the hills. The landowners parted with their waste land for the SEZ, but they continue to farm their well-watered agricultural lands. In that way, if the Khed industrial development does not do well, they will have cultivable lands to fall back on. If the SEZ does do well, their waste lands, which would otherwise have been left unused, will become a new source of profit. It must be emphasized that the agrarian landed dominant castes are not holding on to their cultivable lands in anticipation of agricultural profits; instead, the demand to exclude fertile agricultural land from the SEZ development is a protective countermovement. The protected fertile lands are a crucial safety net during a precarious transition, and this preference among the Maratha-Kunbi landowners has been institutionalized in the new LARRA, which mandates that, as far as possible, only "dry-crop land" and "waste land" be acquired for infrastructural development.

The waste-land clause is justified as necessary for ensuring food security, but its advantages to the agrarian propertied classes cannot be ignored. At the same time, the Khed landowners' demand that the MIDC acquire only waste land indirectly targeted the lands of Adivasis, who owned around 30 percent of the land within the new SEZ boundary. Recall from the land-price maps in Chapter 1 that the village of Shiroli, located about 50 kilometers from Kanersar, has seen a skyrocketing increase in the price of its waste land, from 24,000 rupees in 1996 to 3,217,000 rupees in 2016. These waste lands now fetch a higher market price than even the most irrigated lands in Baramati. The re-valuation of their former waste land has combined with the democratic fixes of the decentralization reforms (like the reserved quotas for Scheduled Tribes as elected representatives in local government) to produce a new politics of recognition for the Thakkars.

A New Politics of Recognition

My first visits to the Kanersar Thakkar settlement took place in 2010, two years after the Khed negotiations had been completed. The settlement lay within the proposed SEZ boundary, and Bharat Forge was in the process of building a new resettlement colony (for which the Kanersar Sarpanch and his cousins had the construction contract). At sundown, the scattered cluster of one-room houses, made of rammed mud walls and thatched roofs, was plunged into darkness. The Thakkar settlements on the hills had no access to water or electricity. Two or three cows were tethered outside the houses, and a row of steel pots lined the external plinths. With these pots, the women would fetch water from public taps located in the *gaothan* (village center), trekking forty-five minutes each way, every day, to the only water source.

However, though the settlement lacked basic amenities, parked in front of the Thakkar homes were jeeps that some of the households had purchased with their 85-percent compensation money. The use of this money to buy jeeps and jeans and to conduct lavish weddings with menus as grand as any at Maratha festivities had a severe opportunity cost, depriving many households of, for example, nutritional food. But, as theorists of justice remind us, egalitarian societies require both the redistribution of resources and a cultural politics of recognition.[38] When the Thakkars mimic the consumption patterns of the Marathas, they are engaging in consumerism as an act of defiance and as a mode of expressing their new social status.[39]

By early 2012, the Kanersar Thakkars had been relocated to a new resettlement site housing eighty-five families from the four Gram Panchayats. In accordance with one of the demands from the Thakkars in the 2006–8 Gram Sabhas, the settlement is closer to the Kanersar gaothan, now a fifteen-minute walk for the women fetching water. Laid out in two rows of 12-foot-by-12-foot concrete squares, the new settlement has acquired more bikes and jeeps but lost the livestock that guarded the entryways of the earlier houses. The extended family of Shantaram-ji, the former Adivasi elected representative in the Kanersar Gram Panchayat, owns five houses in the settlement. When I visited Shantaram-ji's sister's house, I found wrought-iron chairs with upholstered cushions lining the living room, a sign of upward mobility in an area where squatting on the floor is common. The granite slabs, steel sink, and tiled walls in the kitchen were a far cry from the earlier settlement, where cooking took place outside on a chulha, a stove heated by burning charcoal.

But these outward semblances of modern living are revealed to be deceptive when one learns that the kitchen and bathroom taps still lack running water. Shantaram-ji confided in me that the "Thakkars wanted to be in a settlement with drinking water; they do not like this location because the

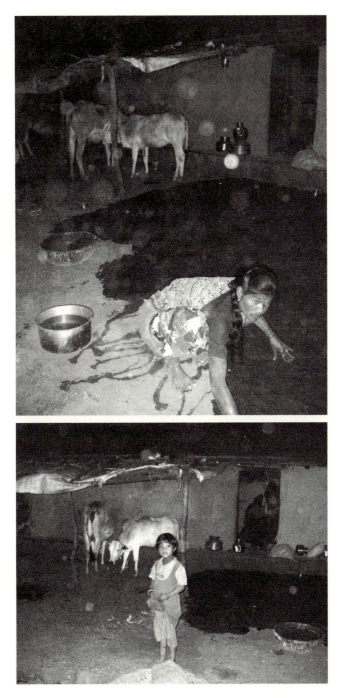

Figure 7. The Thakkar settlement before the SEZ.

Figure 8. The new Thakkar resettlement site.

Marathas are not sharing water with us." Before the relocation, the Thakkars
were promised water supply to their houses: water from the gaothan well was
supposed to be connected to the overhead tank at the edge of the resettlement site, and from this tank water would be supplied to the individual
households. But, here again, the bureaucrats faced a challenge: this water supply depended on the gaothan well, and the well's supply was controlled by
the Marathas. When the Marathas refused to share their water with the resettlement site, alternative arrangements had to be made.

Besides me, the other daily visitor to the resettlement site was a Bharat
Forge employee, who could generally be found sitting on the front steps of
the Thakkar houses and chatting with the young men of the colony. He explained the alternative water arrangement in this way:

> I am from Kharpudi [a village 15 kilometers away]. I work for the
> [Bharat Forge] company, for the water supply. The overhead tank
> water is from the Gram Panchayat. But I work for the SEZ water sup-
> ply. There's not too much water in the well, so the tank cannot be
> filled that way. Since two months, the tank has been filled with
> water from tankers. The company will pay for the tankers for an-
> other six months. After that, there is no guarantee. My work is to
> start the machine pump and release the water. I come every morning
> to start the machine. I come here, and then sit here.[40]

In the Khed region, the combination of democratic fixes and revalued land markets has produced, in the terminology of Albert Hirschman, new "exit-voice relations"[41] that enable the Thakkars to demand entitlements, like water, from the state. During the Green Revolution period, when agricultural work was the main source of employment in agrarian regions, it was common for dominant-caste landowners to quell caste assertions with the threat of economic sanctions.[42] Now, the new demand for their waste land and the availability of industrial work (albeit informal) in the factories are giving the younger-generation Thakkars more ways to break away from their ties of dependency on the Maratha-Kunbi landowners. And these new economic opportunities intersect with the decentralization reforms: previously, a public sphere such as the Gram Sabhas did not exist; now, by contrast, the Khed Thakkars, newly empowered by the increasing economic opportunities in the corridor region, are asserting their claims in the new democratic forums with a diminished threat of economic sanctions. In the 2006–8 Gram Sabhas, the Thakkars gave their consent to the new SEZ deal not just for the profits to be made as SEZ shareholders but for the new market power that would enable them to demand entitlements like water—entitlements, as I have noted, that they should already have been receiving but that had been denied them due to caste discrimination. These Adivasis are now leveraging their status as landowners and shareholders to change the geography of water access, which was previously skewed toward the fields of the middle peasantry.

Because the Thakkars live in concentrated settlements, they can negotiate with the bureaucrats and the Gram Panchayats not as individual landowners but as collectives. This ability has increased their negotiating power, but it has also reinforced existing power relations within the Thakkar settlement. Take, for instance, the guaranteed enrollment in the ITI for one member of every shareholding family. A majority of the Thakkars lack a high-school degree and so could not avail themselves of this benefit. I conducted twenty-five semistructured interviews with Thakkar households in the new resettlement colony. Their literacy rates are a sample of the average educational levels of the Khed Adivasis. Even among the Thakkars who have graduated from high school, not all gained admission to the ITI—and this was one of the reasons for their strong demand later for caste certificates. The exceptions were the Thakkars who are well connected to the Gram Panchayat politicians.

Though Khed City functions as an autonomous jurisdiction outside the authority of the Gram Panchayat, the Gram Panchayat representatives continue to exert some influence on the SEZ labor decisions. The culture of *sifarish*—

Table 4. Literacy Levels of Thakkar Adults Older Than Eighteen Years, from Twenty-Five Households

	Men	*Women*
Primary school (1st–4th grade)	16	42
Middle school (5th–7th grade)	22	6
High school (8th–12th grade)	18	4
Diploma (Industrial Training Institute)	3	2
College	—	—

access to jobs mediated through networks and whom you know—is common in India. It takes a specific form in these agrarian regions, where the elected members of the Gram Panchayat frequently recommend local residents for ITI admission, the stepping-stone to permanent factory jobs. The ITI administration generally obliges, as they do not want any trouble from the local representatives. Out of the eighty-five families in the new resettlement site, only four men—one of whom is Shantaram-ji's nephew—gained admission to the ITI and then secured permanent jobs in the SEZ factories. The other Thakkars work as informal laborers, mainly as helpers, in the surrounding factories that form the strong automobile cluster of Pune. Most of the Thakkars, in other words, do not have the new factory jobs in the SEZ for which they gave up their lands. But unlike workers in the SEZ, within which labor unions are prohibited, the Thakkars working as informal helpers can still aspire to become permanent union staff, after picking up some skills like machine-fitting and welding.

Even within a given Thakkar household, the re-valuation of their waste lands is often experienced unevenly. The land titles in these households are controlled by the male Thakkars in their late thirties and forties. But it is the younger-generation Thakkars, in their twenties and early thirties, who are most eager to leave agricultural labor and enter the urban economy. The Thakkar men in their forties are less enthusiastic about joining the informal industrial economy; indeed, one of the Thakkars from this age group whom I interviewed, Nandu, tried industrial work for some time but has now come back to agricultural work. His experience reflects the riskiness of unprotected, informal factory jobs:

> In the 1980s, I used to work on the Marathas' lands. Five years back, I stopped doing this. The factories here were giving us contract work.

I was ready to do any work. They give the contractor 10,000 rupees [$200] per month; he will give us 4,000 rupees [$80] per month. The contractor got me work in the auto-parts factory. I had to assemble all the auto parts in a line, lots of heat involved in the work. No *surety*. No *safety*. [He said the italicized words in English.] Even if I die or have some injury, there's no surety. I can break my arm, and they will not do anything. That is why I left a year back. Now, I get 150 rupees [$3] per day for agricultural work.[43]

The Thakkars in their forties and fifties, like Nandu, are wary of mechanization. Thakkars in their sixties and older simply lack the physical strength to work in the factories. Most of them expressed dissatisfaction over their sons' decisions to give up their lands for the SEZ. Dairy farming has been a common supplemental occupation in the region since the 1970s. Before liberalization reforms, the Thakkars used the village common lands for grazing their cattle. The past decade has seen rampant privatization of these common lands for urban development, including the enclosure of the "government" land in Kanersar and the surrounding villages for the new corridor city. Around half of the interviewed households had recently sold their cows, thus depriving the older Adivasis of the only livelihood they had. The women in the households were also unhappy with the loss of their waste lands. They complained that their goats had provided their children with a daily dose of milk, but now, with no cows or goats and with the high price of milk in the market, they had been forced to remove milk from their children's diets.

One can see from these varying perspectives that the re-valuation of waste land is not a clean black-and-white narrative of winners and losers. Instead, it is a Janus-faced process of social change that simultaneously empowers and disempowers, enfranchises and disfranchises formerly excluded groups. What we see emerging in the Khed region is a new politics of recognition: the Thakkars, armed by political and economic changes, are becoming more assertive in expressing themselves and imagining a new, caste-equal future. They are breaking away from the old social relations of the moral economy, which were exploitative but also came with a system of reciprocal obligations, and are instead entering an urban informal economy that leaves them unmoored, without any obligations on the part of the state or their new employers. Not only the Adivasis but even the Maratha-Kunbi landowners, who in the Khed region lack the political influence of the Magarpatta sugar elites, are facing new risks during this transition. Without an urban welfare state to shield them from the volatilities of the real-estate market, the Maratha-Kunbi landowners have demanded that their fertile lands be protected as a form of safety net.

Even though the risk is differentially calibrated in each case, with the poor Adivasis exposed to the highest degree of potential loss, both the local politicians and the revenue bureaucrats in Khed felt the need to conduct their land negotiations at least in part within the public sphere of the Gram Sabha. This public sphere may not be the idealized Habermasian space of deliberative democracy, but it is still a public and politicized site of negotiation, where institutional mediation among antagonistic groups can take place not through informal channels but through a formal and recognized democratic institution. As the history of great transformations reminds us, the shift from one social order to another can be brutally dislocating. In India today, with its transitional land markets, the democratic fixes of the decentralization laws and the amendments to land-acquisition laws are necessary countermovements, slowing down and at times altering the course of change to make it socially acceptable. A valuable countermovement institution within these laws is the functioning Gram Sabha.

CHAPTER 5

Shareholder Cities

The slow pace at which public decisions are made in India once led a bureaucrat to quip that the Indian system has the engine of a bullock cart and the brakes of a Rolls Royce.[1] Framers and supporters of recent infrastructure and urban policies, including the Hill Station Regulation, the Integrated Township Policy, and the Special Economic Zone (SEZ) Act, argue that the land regulations enacted during the state-controlled agrarian era have become anachronistic in a country growing with a GDP rate of almost 8 percent. The new pieces of urban legislation are intended to oil the accelerators and dull the brakes of India's land system. Any land regulation that might slow down the pace of urban land-use change, such as restrictions on the sale of agricultural land to nonagriculturalists, finds no place within these new policies. Policy-makers also argue that the multiplicity of public agencies involved in land regulation are a drag on the land-conversion process. They advocate for new policies with centralized decision making and with single-window agencies that can expeditiously approve land-use changes.

These regulatory changes are efforts to produce a new form of fictitious commodity in land. The formation of a new type of market in land is being resisted by various constituents, not least by the agrarian propertied classes. The production of the new corridor cities—integrated townships, hill station cities, SEZs—and their related land conflicts have a discernible geography: most have taken root in former Green Revolution regions. Such geographies of postliberalization private capital affirm a tenet of economic geography, that firms cluster in regions with prior market linkages.[2] In India, the Green Revolution subsidies of water-seeds-fertilizer helped develop certain market linkages in the beneficiary regions, and it is these regions that are now being leveraged by private capital. A few instances of land conflicts, however, have erupted outside former Green Revolution regions; a case in point is the

Singur conflict in West Bengal, where farmers protested the acquisition of their agricultural land for the building of a manufacturing factory for the world's cheapest car, Tata Nano. Kolkata (formerly Calcutta), the largest city in this region, was bypassed by the Green Revolution.[3] Why then did the Tata company decide to set up its factory in Singur? In his interviews, the chairman of the Tata group of companies, Ratan Tata, has reiterated that many considered his choice to be "strange" and "mad," but that he stuck to his choice for patriotic reasons, to give the lagging eastern state a chance to catch up with the rest of the country.[4] It is telling that the subsidy package offered by the West Bengal government to the Tata company was compara-ble to the incentive packages offered by other "economically backward" states.[5] The Singur case affirms the argument that, among formerly agricul-tural regions, new private capital does not flow to regions bypassed by the Green Revolution, except when accompanied by larger and more direct state subsidies.

Just as some conflicts over agricultural land fall outside the former Green Revolution regions, not all Green Revolution regions are smoothly making the transition from agrarian to urban capitalism. Consider, for instance, the variations between Magarpatta in western Maharashtra and Mandya in southern Karnataka. Both regions were the epicenters of the Green Revolu-tion in their respective states. Both were the beneficiaries of uneven flows of irrigation canals that contributed to their becoming the sugar-producing growth centers of their regions. Both saw the emergence of electorally for-midable agrarian elites in the form of the Marathas and Vokkaligas, respec-tively. Both regions have new economic corridors cutting through their sugarcane-rich fields—the Mumbai-Pune Expressway in the former case and the Bangalore-Mysore Infrastructure Corridor (the NICE corridor) in the latter. As this book shows, Magarpatta's sugar elites made a smooth tran-sition from sugar to real estate. But Mandya's agrarian elites remain mired in conflict. As I argue later in this chapter, the Magarpatta region benefited from having sugar cooperatives, something the Mandya region lacked. These agricultural-commodity cooperatives, which fit the "mixed-economy" ideology of the newly Independent socialist state, are now the ba-sis for leveraging the benefits of a liberalizing real-estate economy.

In short, and keeping these variations in mind, the contemporary con-flicts in the corridor regions over agrarian-urban land transformations can be said to have a specific geography. The development fantasies of new eco-nomic corridors are being built on the histories of past agricultural-modernization programs. But as each new economic corridor settles onto older forms of agrarian capitalism, it also unsettles them, most visibly in the re-valuation of waste land, and disrupts traditional land-based social and power relations. In this concluding chapter, I bring the three corridor cities together to answer the questions raised at the start of the book. What new narratives of urbanization arise when older histories of agrarian capitalism and caste/class formation collide, collude, and recombine with the new economic corridors and corridor cities? And how does the entry of agrarian elites into urban real estate force us to rethink conventional theories of urban property relations?

In foregrounding agrarian propertied constituents as key protagonists in urban real-estate markets, the next section uses the category of the Maratha-Kunbi sugarcane landowners both to examine the dynamics of caste/class/space in the Indian context and to situate this social category within western histories of capitalist development.

Agrarian-Urban Uneven Development

The corridor cities in the Mumbai-Pune region have varied distributional outcomes, depending on the caste/class relations of prior agrarian property regimes. These variations in agrarian regions are commonly analyzed in two different ways. One mode of analysis focuses on political regimes. Atul Kohli, for instance, argues that divergences in regional development in India can be explained by the nature of the states in question.[6] Social democratic states, like West Bengal and Kerala, where the political system has a broader social base, have been more successful in land reforms and other redistributive programs than either the developmental states, like Gujarat, which prioritize growth without redistribution, or the neopatrimonial states, like Uttar Pradesh, where growth and redistribution are stifled by patron-client relationships. In this view, a region is defined by the jurisdictional boundaries that define state governments (i.e., West Bengal vis-à-vis Uttar Pradesh).[7]

From another perspective, Barbara Harriss-White redefines India's regions by bringing the country's agrarian capitalist development into conversation with spatial theories of uneven development. Harriss-White and Deepak Mishra map out India's agrarian regions by using production relations, arguing that agrarian regions are "the regions of agrarian accumulation."[8] In this view, which borrows from Henri Lefebvre, the heterogeneity in agrarian modes of surplus extraction is not captured by state governments and their associated political regimes. Take, for instance, one of the prominent cases of capitalist agriculture that benefited from the Green Revolution program, that of the Punjab–Haryana–western Uttar Pradesh region, which is not coterminous with, and which extends beyond, state government boundaries. The broader arc of the surplus-producing Green Revolution region stretches from the northwest (i.e., Punjab–Haryana–western Uttar Pradesh) to the southeast of the country, cutting across the boundaries of several state governments. Most important, the arc of Green Revolution prosperity is in a combined but uneven relationship with the arc of impoverishment that serves the prosperous region.

This book analyzes uneven development not across but within the boundaries of a single state government, Maharashtra. To make for a tighter natural experiment, this book further focuses on the western Maharashtra region, which falls within the formerly developed Green Revolution arc but which is itself highly differentiated and uneven. The western Maharashtra region, drawing on spatial theories of capitalism, was itself produced by the technology packages of seeds-water-fertilizer of the Green Revolution period. In other words, the production of uneven agrarian development in the form of differentiated regions relied on the making of land-use categories such as multicrop and waste land. In a liberalizing and urbanizing society, the re-valuation and the remaking of these land-use categories is the source of conflict, as any restructuring of agrarian land markets also unsettles agrarian land-based forms of power. By focusing on two development moments—the Green Revolution and postliberalization urbanization—the comparative cases track the making and unmaking of agrarian dominant castes through the commodification of agricultural and then urban land. The story of agrarian-urban capitalism can be narrated as one of struggles over land, with political regimes mediating the flows of water and other subsidies to certain lands at the expense of others, while always being alert to managing the political costs of such uneven development.

In a functioning electoral democracy, the potential threat of a backlash from constituents of the bypassed regions and devalued lands forces the state to manage uneven development within socially acceptable thresholds. In western Maharashtra, the costs of uneven agrarian development were borne by marginal owners and occupants of the dammed and bypassed lands who were forcibly relocated or were forced to migrate in distress to urban informal economies (exemplified by the experiences of Shankar-ji in Chapter 2 and

Shinde-ji in Chapter 3). But these constituents have the power of the vote, and caste here becomes a crucial bonding link in mobilizing electoral constituents across class divides. The dominant castes are heterogeneous in their class composition. The Maratha-Kunbi caste cluster composes a tiny fraction of sugar elites, the majority are marginal landowners with less than 1 hectare of land, and the caste cluster also includes landless laborers. The more well-off agrarian landowners were able to build a broad mass-based movement by appealing to the sense of belonging to a dominant caste.[9] Even though poor Maratha laborers have more in common economically with Adivasi laborers, the former still aligned with the Maratha landowners, prioritizing caste identity over economic interests. At times of crisis, the Congress party and the agrarian elites, with their monopoly over resources and capital in a state-controlled society, could divert agrarian surpluses toward welfare programs that could keep inequality at socially acceptable thresholds and avert an electoral backlash.[10]

The new farmers' movement was a critical juncture in India's agrarian-urban development politics, and it was the earliest symptom of the unraveling of the carefully constructed dominant caste constituency of a prior agrarian period. The geography and timing of the new farmers' movement is indicative of the market- and urban-oriented shifts to which the movement was a response. The movement took root in specific regions within the states of Maharashtra, Gujarat, Tamil Nadu, Karnataka, Haryana, and Uttar Pradesh. These regions, *pace* Michael Lipton, were not impoverished sites bypassed by state-led capitalism, nor were they passive, exploited sites of cheap food production for the urban classes. Instead, these regions had been transformed by the Green Revolution subsidies into commoditized, surplus-producing economies. Moreover, as K. Balagopal reminds us, the movement did not erupt in all former Green Revolution regions, but only in those regions where the industrial capitalists belonged to a different caste/ethnicity from that of the agrarian dominant castes.[11] Andhra Pradesh, for instance, remained unaffected because the dominant-caste Kammas had uninterrupted access to move from crops to cities; by contrast, the Maratha-Kunbis in western Maharashtra were unable to invest their agrarian surpluses in cities, blocked as they were by industrial capitalists of a different ethnicity. The movement exploded in the 1980s, in the wake of Green Revolution prosperity and as the Indian state was slowly inching toward liberalizing its state-controlled economy. The slogan "Bharat v. India" was not about the countryside getting impoverished by urban elites, but about "conservative rural

coalitions" of landed castes seeking new terms of entry into India's liberalizing and urbanizing economy.[12]

Since the 1980s, the transformation of the developmental state into a
liberalizing state has further unraveled the dominant caste cluster, with new
class cleavages creating wider rifts between the agrarian elites and the rest of
the peasantry. With economic liberalization reforms, the Central Government now allows external private capital to cross India's national boundaries into agricultural land, but the state governments still retain regulatory
power over land-use and property changes. As new private capital enters
agricultural land, it is transforming land from being one of the least fungible commodities in India to an emerging transnational real-estate market.[13]
As agricultural land is remade into transnational property, agrarian elites
are deploying their regulatory control over land-use and resource allocation
to stake their claims on the new surpluses of a liberalizing economy. Policies
such as the Integrated Township Policy are deliberate strategies by agrarian
elites to form new alliances across the urban-rural divide.

This rift within the agrarian dominant caste, however, has not gone un-
challenged. The politics of Raju Shetti, Shiv Sena, and the Maharashtra
Navnirman Sena can be seen as variations of a new "Bharat v. India" narrative, in which the excluded dominant-caste constituents are opposing the
monopoly of elites on the profits of postliberalization land commodification
and its attendant uneven development. With the decline of the Congress-
Maratha-sugar political economy, a new electoral geography is taking shape
around the "politics of frustration, anxiety and outrage"[14] of this excluded
agrarian constituency that earlier benefited from the privileges of belonging
to a dominant caste but that is now being left behind in a liberalizing economy. These electoral tactics verge on the violent. In 2014, the Shiv Sena and
MNS leaders incited their party workers to vandalize the state's toll booths,
including those along the Mumbai-Pune economic corridor.[15] The two parties competed with one another to see who could create more havoc along
the tolled expressways. Both parties promised their constituents that they
would make the state toll-free. These violent tactics appeal to the excluded
Marathas, who have been prevented from using the world-class corridors by
their inability to pay the high user charges.

In short, the relationship between former Green Revolution regions and
the new economic corridors is not that of capital linkages, as suggested by
earlier debates over the urban-rural divide. These debates analyzed the role
of agriculture within capitalism, and in the context of the newly postcolo-

nial nations in the 1950s and 1960s, they chiefly revolved around the contribution of agriculture to industrialization by producing surpluses necessary for capital formation in the nascent industrial sector.[16] In keeping with these theories, Dani Rodrik and Arvind Subramanian conclude that the transition from "Hindu growth" to India's "productivity surge" after the 1980s had little to do with the Green Revolution, because agricultural productivity in the 1980s was too low to explain any sectoral reallocations of resources from agriculture to industry.[17] However, India's agrarian elites are important protagonists in contemporary urbanization, not just for the surpluses they generate but also for the regulatory power they wield in the state legislatures over subjects like land. Economic liberalization reforms severed the linkages between national agriculture and national industry,[18] and the formerly state-controlled agricultural land markets are now getting linked to global circuits of capital. Policies such as the Integrated Township Policy have to be seen as clever maneuvers by agrarian elites to adjust to the newly liberalizing economy.

As agrarian elites form alliances with urban capitalists (or themselves become urban capitalists, as in the case of the Magarpatta City sugarcane shareholders), these new forms of uneven development have to be politically managed. The politicization of caste and other seemingly noneconomic identities in the Bharat v. India narrative, then, are not extraneous to capitalist accumulation, but are fundamental to overcoming class antagonisms and constraining the backlash to uneven development.[19] The charges of the new farmers' movement of an "urban bias"—of pitting "the rural," "the village," and "the farmers" against exploiting urban elites—were necessary political tactics by agrarian elites to reinforce their land-based forms of power in a liberalizing context while also simultaneously consolidating support among the electorally vital middle peasantry by appealing to them via caste identities.[20] The experiences of the dominant-caste middle peasantry to postliberalization land commodification, however, varies depending on their prior agrarian property regime. The same economic corridor can provoke varied responses from the same class of agrarian constituents, namely, the Maratha-Kunbi middle peasants, and the Mumbai-Pune corridor region analyzed in this book is an attempt to capture the complexities of these agrarian-urban capitalist transformations.

Of the three corridor cities, the dominant-caste middle peasantry in Magarpatta voluntarily transformed their sugarcane fields into an urban township. The risks in this transition are immense: for a landowner to join a real-estate company as a shareholder means exchanging a piece of paper (title) that represents ownership of a physical asset for one that represents purely financial interests in the land. The risks are exacerbated in a real-estate market that is yet in the making. What if the state makes new laws that change market regulations in these transitional regions? What are the safety nets for shareholders in this deregulated (or reregulated) market? Yet, despite these risks, the Maratha middle peasantry in Magarpatta gave up their landed assets for purely financial interests in the form of shares in a real-estate company.

In contrast to the Magarpatta middle peasantry, their counterparts in Khed negotiated to have their fertile lands protected from the SEZ development. The dominant-caste middle peasants in Khed were willing to have their waste land exposed to new market relations but not their fertile lands, as the latter would serve as a safety net in the midst of a precarious transition. The presence of an agrarian elite in Magarpatta explains this differing response to land-use change: the Magarpatta middle peasantry placed their trust in the sugar elites, who had the regulatory power to mobilize the state to mitigate their risks and maximize their returns from land-use change; the absence of equivalent sugar elites in the Khed region meant that the middle peasantry had to rely on local, ad hoc coping tactics and to choose to protect certain lands as their safety net.

For the dominant-caste middle peasantry in Lavasa, the crucial question was not whether or not certain lands be redeveloped into urban real estate, but whether they have voice over the allocation of resources that are needed for the valorization of land. In the past, the region's middle peasantry had suffered the costs of the construction of large dams, which remade drought-prone regions elsewhere into fertile, surplus-producing lands but reduced their own fertile lands to waste lands. Marginal Maratha landowners like Shinde-ji now want to know if water will flow to their lands with the construction of Lavasa Lake City; in other words, will they have control over the flow of resources and capital that unevenly valorize certain lands but not others?

Given that the middle peasantry in all of these regions are entering the debate from unevenly positioned agrarian pasts, to search for a blanket law on land acquisition and land-use change would be futile. A national land law such as the LARRA which mandates that "multicrop" land be safeguarded but "waste" land be acquired for urban expansion depoliticizes these land categories and misses the fact that the decisions on the new forms of landed property must be deliberated within the contexts of their specific agrarian property regimes.

The new economic corridors and corridor cities, then, settle onto older forms of agrarian capitalism and uneven agrarian land markets, but in doing so, they also unsettle agrarian land-based power. As the new forms of urban uneven development are contested by new electoral formations, the political parties that mobilize alienated Marathas often exclude nonpropertied constituents. In that sense, the new electoral formations are not unlike the new farmers' movement that preceded them. As Neil Smith argues, to challenge uneven development does not mean advocating for "some rigidly conceived even development."[21] Rather, he suggests that the politics of uneven development should not be driven by the "logic of capital"[22] or, I might add, in the Indian case, the exclusive electoral politics of propertied constituents.

The Mumbai-Pune corridor region, which is made up of census towns and large villages, all governed by Gram Panchayats,[23] has the potential of making land-use change political, so that informal residents, landless laborers, and various other nonpropertied constituents can also stake their claims on the future of their urbanizing countryside. If the Gram Sabhas, with their new democratic fixes, can be reclaimed as sites of decision making, they will open new views on land and urbanization that hinge on the needs and aspirations of nonpropertied constituents. The next two sections turn to this local democratic institution, and analyzes it in the context of a Polanyian narrative of market movements and counter-movements.

Market Movements: Shareholders over Publics

In his analysis of the political economy of development in postcolonial India, Pranab Bardhan argues that India's democracy is a fragile balance of powers among three dominant proprietary classes: the urban industrialists, the rich farmers, and the bureaucratic elites. Indian democracy, particularly under the Congress system, which lasted until the early 1970s, survived because of its dispersed power among these classes: "In a country where the elements in the dominant (though tacit) coalition are diverse, each sufficiently strong to exert pressures and pulls in different directions, political democracy may have a slightly better chance than elsewhere, particularly in view of the procedural usefulness of democracy as an impersonal (or least arbitrary) rule of negotiation, demand articulation, and bargaining within the coalition, and as a device for one partner to keep the other partners at the bargaining table within some moderate bounds."[24] Indian democracy at that time was thus a transactional model, with the Indian state mediating the allocation of public resources, subsidies, and grants among this "loose and uneasy coalition."[25]

The recent liberalization reforms have transformed these dominant proprietary classes. The rich farmers (agrarian elites) now form class alliances that straddle and blur the agrarian-urban divide, cases in point being Sharad Pawar's new agro-industrial policy and the Magars' Integrated Township Policy. These elites have the regulatory power to make a smooth transition from sugar to wine, real estate, and other commodities in high demand in a liberalizing economy. The experiences of the middle peasantry have been less smooth: in most cases, they possess declining economic power but retain sufficient electoral power to avoid being alienated or neglected. In other words, an agitated middle peasantry that controls some of the most desirable lands in the corridor regions now needs to be placated. Increasingly, the Indian state is turning toward the price system as an arbiter for these land conflicts, relying on the belief that individuals express their preferences through price. In this theory, individual price signals result in an optimal allocation of resources, with the market arbitrating supply and demand to arrive at an equilibrium. As a mode of resolving land conflicts, the price system has taken various forms in the corridor regions.

In some cases, as in the Yamuna Expressway conflict, bureaucrats resolved the conflict between incoming infrastructural firms and the protesting (Jat) middle peasantry by arriving at a compensation price that was considered fair by the landowners. The earlier system of land acquisition had left landowners with little recourse but to accept the low compensation prices set by the government. The new system of arriving at the "right market price of land" has found its way into the new LARRA via the marked-up compensation clause. To get prices right, the Act mandates that, for all future acquisitions, landowners will be compensated at twice the market rate for urban land and four times the market rate for rural land. The search for the right compensation price sometimes reaches absurd levels: in a recent land-compensation conflict in Ludhiana, an agrarian landowner sued the Indian Railways for taking his land; since the Indian Railways is fiscally strapped, the court ordered the public railways to compensate the landowner with a train valued at 1.5 million rupees.[26]

In market transactions, the price system is increasingly taking the form of land readjustment, as in the Magarpatta case, where fragmented plots of land were reassembled into developable plots, and the landowners received shares in lieu of reassembled plots. Land readjustment has gained traction in other parts of the country too; it is now being used for the building of the capital city of Amravathi in the newly bifurcated state of Andhra Pradesh.[27] Under its former entrepreneurial chief minister, Chandrababu Naidu, Amravathi is going to be the largest land-adjustment experiment in India, with 33,000 acres of privately owned, fertile, agricultural land reassembled into a twenty-first-century capital city. The other large-scale land-readjustment experiment currently taking place is the first "Smart City" along the Delhi-Mumbai Industrial Corridor, the Dholera Special Investment Region.[28] The land-readjustment system is gaining popularity among entrepreneurial politicians and bureaucrats who prefer it to land acquisition. However, though as a policy of "property rights exchange" it aims to gain consent among propertied constituents, land readjustment excludes nonpropertied groups from its purview. As I will show in the next section, democratic contestation has led to progressive clauses being inserted in the LARRA, protecting poor and landless groups; but efficiency-driven promoters (be they state governments or firms) are increasingly turning to land readjustment as a way of circumventing these hard-fought clauses.

The most extreme form of the price system is unfolding in the western Maharashtra corridor region, where the new corridor cities are incorporated not as municipalities but as firms, with landowners enlisted in these new real-estate companies as shareholders. Transforming landowners into shareholders may be the most efficient mode of resolving a seemingly intractable conflict between urban firms and the middle peasantry; it may ensure expedient and even efficient regulation of land, water, and other urban services. But the privileging of the shareholders in shareholder cities introduces not only new market relations in land but also new values in urban governance. What is at stake when groups engage with their city not as citizens but as shareholders? How will these new private values in public institutions affect land-use change and urbanization?

Before I outline the adverse effects of this new mode of managing land conflicts in the corridor regions, I want to situate shareholder participation within the wider political ideology of New Public Management (NPM). NPM is a normative set of ideas premised on the assumption that the public sector, exemplified by the bureaucracy, is sluggish, slow, and inefficient, and that public-sector performance could be greatly improved if the government became market-oriented. In their influential book *Reinventing Government*, David Osborne and Ted Gaebler portray cities as marketplaces, "vast, com-

plex aggregations of people and institutions, each constantly making decisions and each adjusting to the other's behavior based on the incentives and
information available to them."[29] NPM introduced a new vocabulary for restructuring government: stakeholders, public managers, public entrepreneurs,
competitive government, entrepreneurial government, result-oriented government, customer-driven government, contract cities. The term "stakeholder" is
now in such wide circulation within public processes that its provenance in
business management has been almost, if not entirely, forgotten. Stakeholder
democracy was popularized in the 1980s in business management, as a reaction against the rise of shareholder values as the guiding rationale for the
governance of firms. The stakeholder approach called for redistributing
power and profits among a wider range of stakeholders, including workers
and consumers.

The point of concern here is not that a term now ubiquitous in public processes may have originated in the business world but that an uncritical bor-
rowing of such terms brings the values of corporate firms into public
institutions. I want to outline two criticisms of the shareholder cities, related
to this increasing overlap of public and private: first, the price system in the
form of shareholder cities is not achieving the purported efficiency goal of
making India a globally competitive manufacturing society; second, it poses
the threat of grave negative distributional consequences, in that it silences
the claims of nonpropertied constituents.

On the efficiency front, the various forms of the price system—marked-up
compensation, land readjustment, shareholder cities—undermine the very intent of building economic corridors: to create spines along which labor-
intensive manufacturing nodes can emerge. The price system locks the
state into certain land-use decisions that go against the touted manufacturing aspirations of the "Make in India" policy. These negotiations, by using
market modes of conflict resolution, in effect trigger "speculative urbanism."[30]
Keeping land prices high benefits some members of the propertied classes,
but it works against the interests not only of the nonpropertied constituents
who rent from the landed classes but of industrial players whose profits are
reduced by the high land rents.[31] With the liberalization push toward creating transnational real-estate markets, industrial firms whose core business
until now was manufacturing are diversifying into the more lucrative sector
of real estate. This trend toward "speculative urbanism" is particularly evident in the corridor regions, where the high cost of land acquisition has been
passed on to the users, increasing the cost of the export-oriented commodi-

ties that will purportedly be conveyed along these corridors. The tolls along the Mumbai-Pune Expressway are so high that only private cars can afford them. Along the Yamuna Expressway, the public authority earlier promised the creation of manufacturing industries and affordable housing along the economic corridor but is now prioritizing high-end luxury housing as a way of recovering the money spent in land acquisition. If the Central Government is serious in its intent to spur labor-intensive manufacturing, what is needed for these prosperous agrarian regions is not unrestrained private property rights and world-class, high-cost economic corridors but socialized land and low-cost bundles of roads, water supplies, and other networked infrastructures.

A deeper concern with the price system is that it silences the claims of nonpropertied constituents. The institution of agricultural-commodity cooperatives is instructive here. In the regions with strong sugar cooperatives, the agrarian elites reworked their cooperatives, which had earlier served to cultivate networks of trust between the Maratha-Kunbi middle peasantry and the agrarian elites, into new real-estate companies, with the former sugarcane growers enlisted as shareholders. But to be a member of a sugar cooperative, one had to be a landowner. This ownership, however marginal, created an important social distinction between even the smallest sugarcane grower in Magarpatta, who owned 0.12 acres of land and is now the owner of two apartments as well as shares in the real-estate company, and the agricultural laborers, who now live in an informal settlement. These laborers used to share their meals with the sugarcane growers, but they are being left out of all the benefits from land redevelopment.

The argument that the price system locks the state into certain development choices is pertinent here. Not all of the laborers in the Magarpatta region are landless: some own plots of land in a drought-prone region that did not receive any irrigation waters. Earlier electoral politics pulled irrigation waters into certain regions and not others, and the price system reinforces these exclusions by forcing the state to prioritize economic corridors with high-cost recovery rather than focusing on low-cost recovery water networks with positive social improvements for the poor.

Older agricultural cooperatives are now using the price system, which reinforces past exclusions. But not all agricultural cooperatives are being mobilized for postliberalization urbanization; the milk cooperatives, as discussed in Chapter 2, are not. Many clusters of villages in the western Maharashtra corridor region have milk cooperatives, and a few of the more well-off Adivasi households in Khed used to be members. But they are not being used in land negotiations because milk cooperatives, unlike sugar cooperatives, do not require landownership as a criterion for membership. The milk-cooperative experiment of Gujarat, which was later scaled up into a national program, was a self-selected poverty-alleviation program. The barrier to entry was extremely low because membership was not premised on landownership, and this meant that the landless, as well as senior citizens who did not control the titles to their families' land, were the main beneficiaries. In this program, waste lands, viewed as economically worthless by the landed cultivating classes, became grazing grounds for the livestock of the nonlanded constituents. The milk cooperatives thus challenge private property rights as a necessary condition for economic growth. If they had been chosen as the institutional route for land negotiations, a very different set of land-use changes would have emerged, in which lands would have been protected from market incursions and the livelihoods of nonpropertied constituents guaranteed.

The current price system is generating new exclusions, but it is also being fiercely contested on the streets, in the courtrooms, and within the laws themselves. A single law, the LARRA, has within it elements of both market movements and countermovements, and it is to the latter that I turn in the next section.

Countermovements: Publics over Shareholders

The LARRA is a disjointed piece of legislation. On the one hand, it privileges the price system as a mode of negotiating among competing property claims. On the other, it deepens democracy by mandating that all land acquisitions undergo a Social Impact Assessment (SIA), which must then be approved by the local Gram Sabha.[32] The LARRA mandates that an appropriate government agency carry out this SIA, taking the following elements into consideration:

> the impact that the project is likely to have on various components such as livelihood of affected families, public and community properties, assets and infrastructure, particularly roads, public transport, drainage, sanitation, sources of drinking water, sources of water for cattle, community ponds, grazing land, plantations, public utilities

such as post offices, fair price shops, food storage godowns, electricity supply, health care facilities, schools and educational or training facilities, anganwadis, children parks, places of worship, land for traditional tribal institutions and burial and cremation grounds.[33]

According to the LARRA, the SIA should include the "views of the affected families," as expressed in Gram Sabhas; moreover, an "independent, multidisciplinary Expert Group," including representatives from the Gram Panchayat and the Gram Sabha, should evaluate the SIA.[34] Crucially, the SIA must include an examination of whether the land acquisition constitutes a legitimate public purpose, thus opening up the "public purpose" clause to democratic debate.

The new LARRA also mandates "rehabilitation and resettlement" (R&R) entitlements for landowners and "landless whose livelihoods are primarily dependent on the lands being acquired."[35] In this way the new land-acquisition act, for the first time in its colonial or postcolonial history, provides safeguards for the landless. Both the SIA and the R&R clauses of the LARRA are the work of a cadre of public-spirited bureaucrats-turned-activists—including Harsh Mander and Aruna Roy—who were part of the formal consultative process and also played a key role in the legal drafting of the bill. The hard-fought SIA clause ensures that the consent of the Gram Sabhas is required for any land-use change. In Polanyian terms, the Gram Sabhas can thus serve as a much-needed countermovement, slowing down the breakneck speed of urban expansion and keeping these normatively freighted decisions on land use and social change open to vigorous contestation.

Yet consent by Gram Sabhas in law does not necessarily translate into consent by Gram Sabhas in practice. In the western Maharashtra corridor region, the role and influence of the Gram Sabha varies across the three property regimes. For one thing, the processes examined in this book began before the 2013 LARRA was enacted. The decentralization laws had already been put in place, however, and the varying mobilization of the Gram Sabha that resulted demonstrates which agrarian regions possessed the balance-of-power relations needed to activate the SIA provisions of the new LARRA.

To return to an earlier point on the concept of the shareholder city, the reconfigurations of territory, authority, and polity in the corridor regions are producing new formations of the local state. The twin institutional reforms of liberalization and decentralization define new territories, such as integrated townships, hill station cities, and SEZs. These laws also authorize

competing public authorities—corporate companies and the Gram Sabhas—
to make and enforce rules for the governance of these territories. The polities
within these territories, which have the power to hold the public authorities accountable, are being redefined by the price system into conflicting
identities of citizens and shareholders. But the glue that binds authority and
polity together is the concept of legitimacy, reaching back to Rousseau's idea
of the "social contract": the authority can exercise coercive power to ensure
that the polity obeys the former's rules, but the exercise of coercive power by
the rule makers must be seen as legitimate by the rule takers.[36] As the promoters of the corridor cities attempt to make new rules for transacting in
agricultural land, the existing agrarian property regimes are influencing the
promoters' decisions on whether or not to activate the local democratic institutions to legitimatize their authority.

What are the conditions that enable the activation of the Gram Sabha?
Which agrarian property regimes have the balance of power relations
needed to translate the Gram Sabhas from law to practice? Table 5 articu-
lates some answers to these questions, based on the three cases examined
in this book.

Magarpatta City

Magarpatta City is being built in some of the most developed agrarian regions
from the Green Revolution period. Regions like Magarpatta and Baramati
are the home constituencies of the wealthiest Maratha elites, who wield immense political power in the state legislature and even in national politics.
Within the Green Revolution regions, these property regimes are nodes of
concentrated electoral and economic power, characterized by consolidated
holdings of irrigated land owned by an economically stratified dominant
caste, which ranges from elites to marginal landowners but whose class disparities are subsumed under a shared caste identity. These attributes cannot
be disconnected from the region's history of sugar cooperatives. Had the
state been involved in the recent large-scale acquisition of irrigated agricultural land for real-estate development, its interference would have incited
resistance on the charge of state actions going against the interests of farmers and food security. But the Magarpatta sugar-to-real-estate transition
sparked no protests. It involved no visible external mediation (though it did
involve behind-the-scenes state support in land exemptions), and this ab-

Table 5. Summary of the Mumbai-Pune Corridor Cities

Case	Existing property regime	Market movements and countermovements in land	Role of the Gram Sabha in the land-use decision-making process
Magarpatta City, a case of agrarian privileges reproduced in an urbanizing context	Fertile sugarcane fields owned by Maratha sugar elites and Maratha-Kunbi middle peasantry.	Agrarian elites voluntarily transformed their sugarcane fields into urban real estate. They included the middle peasantry as shareholders in the new company.	Gram Sabha not formed. Liberalization bypasses decentralization.
Lavasa Lake City, a case of agrarian exclusions reproduced in an urbanizing context	Forest lands owned and occupied by the poorest propertied middle peasantry and other nonpropertied forest dependents.	The urban promoter commodified the forest lands, captured all the profits from redevelopment, and dispossessed the forest dependents.	Gram Sabha not formed. Decentralization legitimates liberalization.
Khed City, a case of agrarian-urban recombination	A mixed landscape of irrigated fields in the plains owned by Maratha-Kunbi middle peasantry and waste lands in the hillocks owned by Adivasis.	The middle peasantry negotiated for the protection of their fertile lands from SEZ development. Adivasis are using the re-valuation of their waste land to forge a new politics of recognition.	Gram Sabha became a site of market transactions. Liberalization combines with decentralization.

sence of coercion has made Magarpatta City attractive to policy-makers as an example of "inclusive capitalism."

However, the agrarian property regime that made Magarpatta City possible was built on the foundations of an uneven sugar economy, and it is the beneficiaries of an uneven agrarian past that are now reaping the benefits of urban real estate. The agrarian elites mobilized past networks of trust to gain legitimacy for the new corridor city, relying on their connections with state-level politicians to create favorable regulatory policies, thus precluding the need to go to the Gram Panchayats or Gram Sabhas for the citizens' consent. In bypassing the Gram Sabha, the corridor city reproduced the region's agrarian caste/class privileges and exclusions in a liberalizing context. The agrarian elites continue to retain material control over the region, and the middle peasants are included in the profits by virtue of their caste privileges, but the landless laborers who used to work on the sugarcane fields have been entirely excluded from the gains of postliberalization land commodification and urbanization. These landless laborers, belonging to the nondominant Sudra, Dalit, and Adivasi caste groups, migrated to these surplus-producing regions during the Green Revolution from drought-prone regions that had not been given irrigation waters. If the land-use negotiations had taken place in the Gram Sabha, they would have had a voice in the process. But the bypassing of the Gram Sabha further reinforced and reproduced agrarian-era exclusions. In Magarpatta, the twin institutional reforms thus intersected in the following way: liberalization bypassed decentralization.

Lavasa Lake City

If the Magarpatta case represents the most developed regions of an uneven agrarian past, the Lavasa case represents the most underdeveloped regions. This forested region served as the dammed hinterland for the sugar-rich core. The Western Ghats lacked a critical mass of Maratha agrarian elites, and the middle peasantry in the region make up the poorest stratum of Marathas, who in the 1940s began a distress migration out of the region to Bombay, in search of urban industrial work. The migration was fueled by the first round of dam-induced displacement, after the building of the Mulshi Dam in the 1920s, and exacerbated by another round of displacement after the building of the Varasgaon Dam in the 1970s. Both dams contributed to the making of an uneven agrarian land market: the middle peasantry and tribal forest dependents bore the cost of cash-crop capitalism, watching their cultivable land become submerged so that the dam waters could transform other, drought-prone regions, occupied by more powerful Marathas, into surplus-producing regions.

With the building of the Mumbai-Pune Expressway, an urban promoter saw a "rent gap" for the redevelopment of these forest regions. As the firm started purchasing the lands from the politically unorganized forest dependents in allegedly fraudulent transactions, the Comptroller and Auditor General (CAG) and the National Alliance for People's Movements (NAPM) launched a countermovement for the protection of these ecologically fragile and socially beneficial lands. Faced with a legitimacy crisis that threatened to decrease the share value of the IPO, the promoter sought the consent of the Gram Panchayats, both to gain the trust of future investors and to convince them that the risk of the project being delayed, stalled, or even terminated by local opposition was low. In the meantime, also triggered by the revaluation of their former waste land, the middle peasantry who had migrated to Bombay started a reverse migration back to the region. Some of the former industrial workers are now running in local elections and entering the Gram Panchayat, thus emerging as local elites. To gain legitimacy among foreign investors, the promoter offered attractive inducements to these local elites and gained the consent of the Gram Panchayat for the new real-estate development.

The intent for the Gram Sabha was to shift political power from such elites to the citizens themselves, but in the Lavasa case this transfer of power never happened because the past history of dam-induced displacement had dispersed the middle peasantry to scattered relocation sites, thus undermining their collective ability to form Gram Sabhas. The case is thus one of liberalization co-opting decentralization, in which the elected local government consolidated power and legitimated the new enclosures without granting any power to the other local democratic institution, the Gram Sabha. The NAPM has played a crucial role in this context by stepping into the democratic vacuum and providing alternate "citizen juries" that can help displaced citizens exercise their collective voice in these processes of land-use change.

Khed City

In between these privileged and excluded regions of uneven agrarian development are the mixed lands of Khed City. Of the three corridor cities, Khed is the only one in which the land-use negotiations took place in the already-activated public sphere of the Gram Sabha. Citizens in the region use the regularly convened Gram Sabhas to demand transparency from their elected representatives in the allocation of development subsidies and grants from higher levels of government. The middle peasantry in the Khed region is neither entrenched nor dispersed. This region is an example of former Green Revolution regions that were not the home constituencies of the most powerful agrarian elites but still had a critical mass of politically organized middle peasantry who could not be alienated without grave losses at the ballot boxes.

The sequence of events in the Khed land negotiations is important. Caught between two powerful interests, the electorally organized middle peasantry and the industrial firm, both of which were staking their claims on the same land, the bureaucrats held informal negotiations with the elected representatives of the Gram Panchayat. During these negotiations, the middle peasants demanded that their fertile lands remain protected from the new SEZ development. In the absence of any guaranteed social obligations from either the state or the firm, the protected fertile lands would be their safety nets as they made this precarious agrarion-to-urban transition. As it turned out, their anxiety was justified: the delays in the SEZ project have led the middle peasantry to demand the return of their lands, with Raja Shetti joining their protests.

The informally negotiated solution to redraw the boundaries of the SEZ, including only waste land, indirectly targeted the lands of the Adivasis. The Gram Panchayat members had their political tenures to think about; they or members of their extended family would be seeking reelection. So, to gain legitimacy, the representatives decided that the allocation of shares would take place in the open forum of the Gram Sabha—but only after they had redrawn the SEZ boundaries. In other words, having secured a safety net for themselves by deleting their fertile lands from within the SEZ boundary, they then opened up to public debate the redevelopment of the waste lands. Such informal framing of a supposedly open debate is far from ideal, but it still allowed the Gram Sabha a role and some power in the negotiations. The need for the Gram Sabha as a site of legitimacy reflects a process of democratization, in which, to quote Charles Tilly, the trust networks shift "from asymmetrical interpersonal relations to formal public institutions."[37]

Nevertheless, the shareholder model vitiates the political power of these new public spheres. As emphasized earlier, it silences the claims of nonpropertied constituents; the preferences of women and older-generation Thakkars to protect their waste land from new market relations found no place in these negotiations. But the decisions of the Thakkar male heads-of-household might have been different if the Gram Sabha negotiations had focused on the forms of public infrastructure needed for these villages. The Khed Thakkars were eager for the new corridor city, not because they wanted profits from land redevelopment but because they wanted to live closer to the village wells. If the Thakkars had had a voice in deciding whether or not a new economic corridor or a subsidized irrigation canal should be routed through their waste lands—if, in other words, the Gram Sabha negotiations had been framed differently and constituents had entered these negotiations without the a priori status of shareholders—we probably would have seen a different set of public infrastructures and land uses emerge in lieu of the Khed corridor city. But these alternate, and hopefully radical, possibilities were bypassed through the shareholding model of land-conflict resolution. The shareholder negotiations also imposed the gravest risk on groups that have the least resources to manage risk: the Thakkars have now agreed to part with their only landed asset for an SEZ and they possess no safety nets to fall back on.

The Khed region is most representative of the former Green Revolution regions. In similar agrarian regions—those that are not the home constituencies of powerful agrarian elites but have a critical mass of politically organized middle peasantry, like the Jats along the Yamuna Expressway—there exist the conditions necessary for the mobilization of the Gram Sabha. Still, as the Khed case makes clear, it is not only the activation of the Gram Sabha but also the terms of its activation that will determine the democratic potential of this public sphere.

Reclaiming the "City" in Shareholder Cities

According to the 2011 Census of India, India is 31.16 percent urban.[38] These census definitions do not consider the vast range of jurisdictions within the Mumbai-Pune corridor region—including the Hadapsar, Mugaon, and Kanersar Gram Panchayats—which exhibit varying characteristics of the urban but are yet governed by Gram Panchayats. Outside the census definition of the urban are 3,894 census towns[39] where agriculture is not the mainstay of the economy, giving rise to the oxymoronic phenomenon of nonagrarian villages. Also not categorized as urban are 3,961 villages that have a population of over 10,000,[40] far exceeding the demographic criterion of 5,000 persons for an urban settlement. It is these ambiguous definitions that led Ananya Roy to "suggest that we take up the question of whether the urban is a particular way of being political as precisely this, a question, rather than an ontological truth."[41] Here, I foreground the "shareholder city" as a concept for analyzing the transformation of the local state at these agrarian-urban junctures. The institutional reforms of decentralization and liberalization articulate as public-private collisions in the corridor regions, with the Gram Sabha and the company colliding as jurisdictional authorities. Of importance here are the institutional arrangements that can enable the Gram Sabha to prevail over the company in these tussles. The commitment to privilege the democratic city in these democratic-market encounters recalls Polanyi's double movement.

As this chapter shows, the contested debates around a single law—LARRA—reveals the tussle between market movements and countermovements in the making of a new market in land. The new market-oriented urban policies such as the Integrated Township Policy, the Hill Station Regulation, and the SEZ Act are focused on expediting the redevelopment of agricultural land, stripping it of layers of approval needed from local democratic institutions. The democratic safeguard of embedding land-use change in the Gram Sabha is a countermovement to these economic reforms; the land-readjustment policies in turn are a market movement to circumvent these democratic safeguards. In this fraught terrain, it is imperative that land in the corridor regions remain open to contestation, so that various constituents, including nonpropertied groups, have a voice in staking their "moral claims, arguments about justice, and forms of entitlement" on the new land relations.[42] The Gram Sabhas are one viable democratic institution within which these land-use changes can, and should, be embedded.

In liberalizing India, the billion-dollar question (an unfitting metaphor for a book that critiques the limits of the price system as a mode of political negotiation) is this: which types of democratic institutions can most effectively regulate land-use change in a liberalizing economy and a decentralizing polity? The planning questions confronting contemporary India are not technical ones for which the market has easy answers. Instead, to be answered fairly, they require the voices of all members of the polity. What types of public infrastructure—economic corridors or rural roads—should the Indian state prioritize for development? How should these infrastructures be routed? Whose lands should be acquired or purchased for the building of these infrastructures? Which lands should be protected and retained in the commons, and what institutional arrangements will protect these lands from market incursions? These are difficult planning questions, complicated further by the different meanings attached to the ideas of land and land use.

Currently, instead of seeking answers to these questions in local democratic institutions, the new shareholder cities are situating them in the seemingly neutral sphere of the market. But doing so silences the claims and desires of the most vulnerable members of the polity.

To suggest that the Gram Sabha be a central institution of democratic decision making is not to offer it as a magic bullet for managing complex processes of social change. As scholars of decentralization have shown, the effectiveness of local governments requires the recentralization of certain functions.[43] It is also not enough for public processes to take place in a Gram Sabha; the assembly must be pervaded by public values, underpinned not least by language that does not reduce citizens to individual market actors or shareholders. In other words, the Gram Sabha by itself cannot assure more democratic decision-making for large-scale infrastures that cut across multiple political jurisdictions. Nevertheless, it can help reclaim the "public" nature of public infrastructure and the "city" in shareholder cities. Only by entrenching land-use change in public spheres like the Gram Sabha can these processes of change be kept public in the fullest sense of the term, so that the poorest and most marginalized residents can stake claims on land and the state through the everyday practice of *takleef dena*. If the Indian state is committed to its normative obligation of democratic problem solving, it must ensure that its land-use changes are firmly entrenched in the public domain, where they belong.

Agrarian to Urban Land-Use Change

The term "conversion" does not adequately capture the multiple stages involved in changing land use from agricultural to urban. Instead, the process includes the following steps.

1. Consolidation: Assembling multiple landowners of agricultural land is an exercise in collective action. Landowners can be assembled either through voluntary negotiations or through coercion (i.e., the exercise of eminent-domain powers by the state). Consolidation also includes arranging the fragmented plots of agricultural land, which are generally of irregular dimensions, into gridded developable plots.

2. Conversion: In India, the public agencies and the regulations vary, depending on whether the land is forest or agriculture and on whether the proposed urban land use is residential/commercial or industrial.

3. Incorporation: The consolidated, converted land has to be incorporated within a jurisdiction so that infrastructural services—such as water supply, sanitation, electricity, and roads—can be extended to it. Incorporation generally takes the form of annexation, whereby existing municipal boundaries are redrawn to include surrounding cities and villages within the new city limits. At other times, it takes the form of parastatals or special-purpose governments, whereby the jurisdictional boundaries of public agencies that perform specialized functions, such as providing water supply and sanitation, or public transportation, are flexibly redrawn to incorporate the new urban areas. At yet other times, the new development is carved out from existing local governments and set up as a separate legal entity with its own public authority and laws (the new hill cities and the Special Economic Zones are examples).

4. Building permits: Once the land is legally ready for urban use, separate permission is needed for individual buildings to ensure that the new buildings comply with safe planning standards.

Each of these successive steps in land-use change—consolidation, conversion, incorporation, and building permits—increases the price of land.

Consolidation allows for plot boundaries to be redrawn so that they can accommodate higher-density, urban uses. This is particularly important for the agrarian context, where the intergenerational transfer of land within large joint families has led to agricultural land plots of small size and irregular dimensions. The assembly of these fragmented plots into larger, more regularly dimensioned plots amenable for serviced, urban development increases their land price.

Conversion from agricultural to urban land use further increases the land price, particularly in real-estate markets like India where the supply of serviced urban land was earlier under tight state control.

With incorporation, infrastructural services are extended into the new urban areas. Land prices are positively affected by different types of urban infrastructure: studies, for instance, estimate that the introduction of sanitation infrastructure increases land value by 3.03 times, road infrastructure increases value by 2.58 times, and a piped water supply increases value by 1.02 times.[1] In other words, the benefits of urban infrastructure are capitalized into the land prices, leading to a multiplier effect in land-value gains.

Getting regulatory approval for conforming to building standards further increases the land price. Building regulations evolved in the first place in order to eliminate negative externalities and to minimize transaction costs.[2] A building is, after all, a complex matrix of structural, mechanical, and electrical systems, which can be dangerous if the quality and method of construction is unregulated. As laypersons, most consumers do not have the relevant information or technical know-how to ascertain the quality of the building they wish to purchase. Government regulations, then, set minimum building standards to ensure safety and public health, which removes the burden off of consumers for assaying building quality. Buildings with the necessary approvals from the regulatory authorities—in this case, local governments—then fetch a higher price than those that do not adhere to government-prescribed building regulations.

Figures 9 through 12 map out the process of land-use change both pre- and postliberalization.

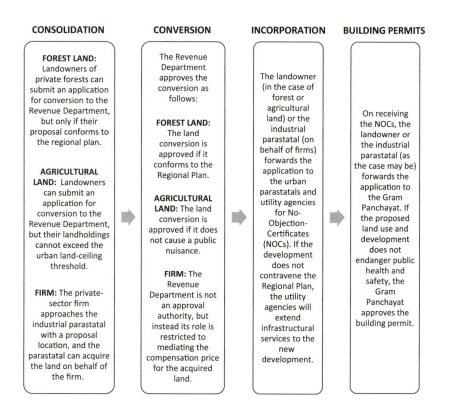

Figure 9. Land-use change before liberalization.

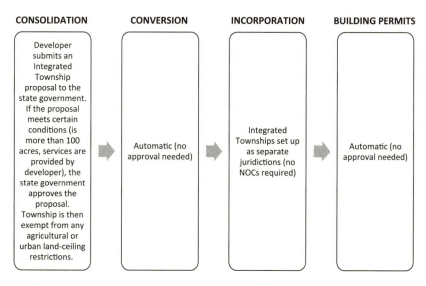

Figure 10. Land-use change after liberalization: Integrated Township Policy.

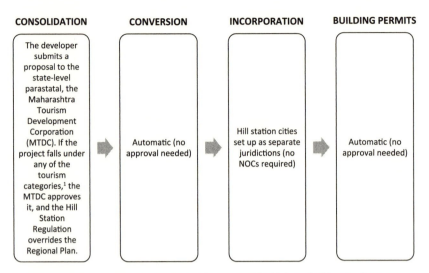

CONSOLIDATION	CONVERSION	INCORPORATION	BUILDING PERMITS
The developer submits a proposal to the state-level parastatal, the Maharashtra Tourism Development Corporation (MTDC). If the project falls under any of the tourism categories,[1] the MTDC approves it, and the Hill Station Regulation overrides the Regional Plan.	Automatic (no approval needed)	Hill station cities set up as separate juridictions (no NOCs required)	Automatic (no approval needed)

1. Tourism categories include hotels, heritage hotels, resorts and health farms, health and wellness spas, water sports and amusement parks, arts and crafts villages, golf courses convention centers, adventure tourism projects, eco-tourism projects, museums and aquariums, and, of particular interest to the book, the development of hill stations.

Figure 11. Land-use change after liberalization: Hill Station Regulation.

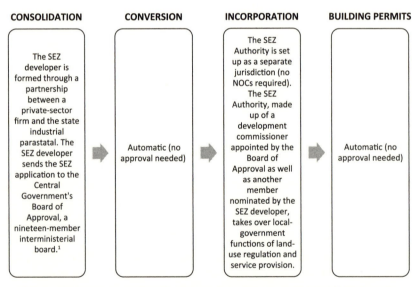

CONSOLIDATION	CONVERSION	INCORPORATION	BUILDING PERMITS
The SEZ developer is formed through a partnership between a private-sector firm and the state industrial parastatal. The SEZ developer sends the SEZ application to the Central Government's Board of Approval, a nineteen-member interministerial board.[1]	Automatic (no approval needed)	The SEZ Authority is set up as a separate jurisdiction (no NOCs required). The SEZ Authority, made up of a development commissioner appointed by the Board of Approval as well as another member nominated by the SEZ developer, takes over local-government functions of land-use regulation and service provision.	Automatic (no approval needed)

1. Note that the Hill Station Regulation and the Integrated Township Policy centralize land-use decision making with the state government, whereas the SEZ Act centralizes land-use regulatory power with the Central Government.

Figure 12. Land-use change after liberalization: SEZ Act.

Research Methodology

Phase 1

During the period of June to October 2010, I was a research affiliate at the Center for the Study of Regional Development, Jawaharlal Nehru University, New Delhi. I spent these initial months in Delhi so I could interact with policy-makers, nongovernmental organizations (NGOs), and academics who are working on issues of land in India. Starting my research in the national capital gave me a bird's-eye view of the main planning challenges confronting those working on land. I asked all my Delhi interviewees for cases that, to them, exemplified innovative practices in land governance. Most of the examples mentioned were variations of land readjustment, including the Magarpatta township in Pune. The Pune case had received little attention in the scholarship at the time I started my fieldwork, and I decided to focus on the Mumbai-Pune economic corridor region for the fresh research possibilities it offered on urbanization along economic corridors.

Phase 2

During the second phase of fieldwork (which occurred in the following time frames: November 2010–December 2011, June–September 2012, July–December 2014, and June–August 2015), I lived in Pune for most of the time, with frequent visits to Mumbai to interview bureaucrats. Pune was a central site of inquiry for both the Magarpatta and Lavasa cases; for the latter, as mentioned in the Introduction, the National Alliance for People's Movements (NAPM) activists and some of the dam-displaced splintered families lived in Pune. For the Khed research, I lived in Rajgurunagar—the nearest census town to Kanersar village, around 40 kilometers from Pune—from January to April 2011.

Below is a list of the main institutional actors that I interviewed for the Mumbai-Pune economic corridor and the three corridor cities. I conducted all the interviews myself in either Hindi or English. Many of the Thakkars speak only Marathi. For the interviews with the Thakkars in the Khed settlement, I had a translator for three months. Suvarna worked for the NGO Chaitanya in Rajgurunagar; Suvarna and I conducted the Khed interviews from June to August 2012.

List of Interviews for the Mumbai-Pune Economic Corridor

- Anil Diggikar, vice chairman and managing director of the Maharashtra State Road Development Corporation (MSRDC), July 2014
- MSRDC bureaucrats, Mumbai, July and August 2014
- R. N. Kawale, deputy inspector general of registration, Mumbai
- For data on the land prices along the Mumbai-Pune Expressway, I visited and followed up with multiple meetings at the sub-registrar offices in Panvel, Khalapur, Mawal, Mulshi, Khed, Haweli, and Baramati; land-price data were collected between July and December 2014

List of Interviews for Magarpatta City

- Satish Magar, managing director of Magarpatta Township Development and Construction Company Limited (MTDCCL), May 2011
- Open-ended interviews with five Magar shareholding families, May to June 2011
- Open-ended interviews with the informal residents of the *basti* (informal settlement) near Magarpatta City, particularly open-ended interviews with the household of Shankar-ji; these interviews occurred from June to September 2012
- Ward councilor, Hadapsar constituency, Pune, July to September 2012

List of Interviews for Lavasa Lake City

- Suniti Suresh, activist for NAPM, June to August 2015
- Bureaucrats at the Regional Training Institute, Comptroller and Auditor General (CAG), Mumbai, October 2014

- Bureaucrats at the Maharashtra Krishna Valley Development Corporation (MKVDC), Water Resources Department (WRD), Pune, October 2014
- Open-ended interviews with five Sarpanches of the Mulshi villages who support the Lavasa development, July to August 2015
- Open-ended interviews with three Mulshi landholding families who support the NAPM, June to August 2015

List of Interviews for Khed City

- *Note: All the bureaucrats held these respective offices in 2011; they have since been transferred to other positions.*
- Prabhakar Deshmukh, district collector, Revenue Department, Pune, January 2011
- Shyam Patil, sub-divisional officer, Revenue Department, Pune District (name changed), May 2011
- Nimbankar, Tahsildar, Khed Revenue Circle (name changed), July 2014
- Bhushan Gagrani, chairman of Maharashtra Industrial Development Corporation (MIDC), July 2014
- Vishwas Kute, executive engineer, MIDC, Pune, January to May 2011
- Open-ended interviews with the eleven Sarpanches of Kanersar Gram Panchayat and the Sarpanches of Nimgaon, Shirur and Dhawadi Gram Panchayats, January to May 2011
- Open-ended interviews with twenty-five Thakkars in the Khed resettlement site, June to September 2012

Phase 3

The timeline for this phase overlaps with phase 2. Because the focus of the research is on the experiences of agrarian constituents in the process of urbanization, for each of the three corridor cities, I started with a questionnaire of semistructured interviews for the landowners. The questions for the semistructured interviews emerged from the previous rounds of open-ended interviews with the institutional actors interviewed in phase 2. Recognizing the interlocked nature of these agrarian societies—the interconnectedness of land, labor, and credit in structuring social relations and hierarchies—my questionnaire was organized into five modules: education, jobs, land, credit, and politics.

Below is a list of the following caste-stratified interviews. Each of these interviews lasted around sixty minutes. Phases 2 and 3 were iterative processes, and these semistructured interviews were then followed up with specific open-ended interviews in the respective settlements. All interviews were conducted in the agrarian constituents' homes.

List of Caste-Stratified Agrarian Interviews

- Magarpatta shareholding families: five households
- Agricultural laborers who now live in a basti adjacent to Magarpatta City: ten households
- Mulshi residents who supported Lavasa: five households
- Mulshi residents who supported NAPM: three households
- Maratha-Kunbi agrarian landowners in Kanersar (Khed City): twenty households
- Maratha-Kunbi agrarian landowners in Nimgaon (Khed City): ten households
- Thakkar agrarian landowners in Kanersar's resettlement site: twenty-five households

Questionnaire for Semistructured Interview

Introduction

Why don't you tell me a little bit about yourself? Maybe you could start off telling me a little bit about your family.

(Intent: Warm-up to establish rapport, get a sense of family context.)

Probe:
- Your name
- Your age

- Family members living with you—names of adult family members
- How long lived here?

Education

Education of respondent: Never went to school / 5th Standard / 9th Standard / 12th Standard (PUC) / Diploma / Graduate / Post-Graduate

Education levels of all family members (adults and children): Never went to school / 5th Standard / 9th Standard / 12th Standard (PUC) / Diploma / Graduate / Post-Graduate

- What do you want your child to become when they grow up?

Jobs
DOMINANT-CASTE LANDOWNERS

Tell me about your typical workday. For example, describe a typical workday from last week.

If the respondent has a non-agricultural job:

- If working for someone else: If owner of business:
- Name of employer   When started?
- How long worked there?   Number of employees
- Salary   Capital for it
- Type of work   Current projects

Many people around here have been telling me about agricultural labor shortage. Have you been facing any shortages for your field?

- How many workers worked on your fields in the past? 20 years back? 10 years back?
- Form of payment then. If in cash, how much?
- How many workers now?
- Form of payment now. If in cash, how much?

AGRICULTURAL LABORERS

Tell me about your current job. For example, describe your typical workday from last week.

If the respondent has a job:

- Location, distance—how do you get there?
- Pay, hours of work (daily wage, contract labor, others)
- Description of work—what do you do when you're there? (If working on someone's land, details on the landowner's name, acres of land, crop grown, details of work)
- How long have you been working there?
- How did you get this present job?

If the respondent does not have a job:

- What was your last job? Why did you stop working there?
- Are you currently looking for a job? What kind of job (agriculture, industry, others)?
- How are you supporting your family now (food, other expenditures)?

Tell me about your last agricultural job.

- Did you work on others' lands? (details on the landowners' name, acres of land, crop grown, details of work)
- Location, distance—how do you get there?
- Pay, hours of work (daily wage, contract labor, others)
- How long did you work there? Did your father (previous generation) also work with the same landowner?
- When did you stop working there? Why?
- Your relationship with your previous landowner now?

Land

How much land do you own?

- Do you have a 7/12 (*saath barah*) [title] for your land? Any restrictions on use of land?

- If joint ownership of land on 7/12, the names of the other landowners
- Number of acres
- What grown on the land? Who works on the land?
- Is the land irrigated? If yes, what kind of irrigation (public irrigation, wells, others)? Who paid for the irrigation?
- Other uses for your land—cattle grazing, medicinal plants, others? Any revenue from these additional uses of land? How much?

Credit

DOMINANT-CASTE LANDOWNERS

Tell me about the biggest expenditure you've had in your life (wedding, others)?

How did you pay for this expenditure (sold land, borrowed money from landowner, others)?

Probe: If the father/family borrowed money, from whom, what were the terms of repayment; did he/family repay the loan through working on the lenders' lands?

When was the last time your family lent money to someone else?

ADIVASI AGRICULTURAL LABORERS

Tell me about the biggest expenditure you've had in your life (wedding, others)?

How did you pay for this expenditure (sold land, borrowed money from landowner, others)?

Probe: If the father/family borrowed money, from whom, what were the terms of repayment; did he/family repay the loan through working on the lenders' lands?

Do you have daughters/sisters? Yes No

If yes, are they married? Yes No

If yes, how did you/your father/your family pay for your daughter's/sister's wedding (sold land, borrowed money from landowner, others)?

Probe: If the father/family borrowed money, from whom, what were the terms of repayment; did he/family repay the loan through working on the lenders' lands?

Politics

Have you been an elected representative at any level? If yes, details—when, which political party

Have any of your family members been elected representatives? If yes, details

NOTES

Introduction

1. Though economic reforms had started more a decade earlier, the Central Government of India officially announced its economic liberalization policy in 1991.

2. Ajoy Ashirwad Mahaprashasta, "Striking Unity," *Frontline* 27, no. 18 (August–September 2010); Uma Vishnu, "Two Sides of an Expressway," *Indian Express* (May 15, 2011).

3. On the role of Vokkaligas in urban and peri-urban land politics in southern Karnataka, see Narendar Pani, "Globalization, Group Autonomy, and Political Space: Negotiating Globalized Interests in an Indian City" (unpublished mimeo, 2013); Sai Balakrishnan, "Land-Based Financing for Infrastructure: What Is New About India's Land Conflicts?," in *Political Economy of Contemporary India*, ed. R. Nagaraj and Sripad Motiram (Delhi: Cambridge University Press, 2017).

4. An exception to these silos in agrarian and urban studies is the growing niche of scholarship that interrogates agrarian-urban linkages. See, for instance, Michael Levien, *Dispossession Without Development: Land Grabs in Neoliberal India* (New York: Oxford University Press, 2018); and Ananya Roy, "What Is Urban About Critical Urban Theory?" *Urban Geography* 37, no. 6 (2016): 810–23.

5. See www.makeinindia.com/policy/new-initiatives.

6. Steven Graham and Simon Marvin, *Splintering Urbanism: Networked Infrastructures, Technological Mobilities and the Urban Condition* (London: Routledge, 2002).

7. Keller Easterling, *Extrastatecraft: The Power of Infrastructure Space* (Brooklyn, NY: Verso Books, 2014).

8. Deborah Cowen, *The Deadly Life of Logistics: Mapping Violence in Global Trade* (Minneapolis: University of Minnesota Press, 2014).

9. Bent Flyvbjerg, Nils Bruzelius, and Werner Rothengatter, *Megaprojects and Risk: An Anatomy of Ambition* (Cambridge, UK: Cambridge University Press, 2003).

10. The World Bank's Logistics Performance Index, available at lpi.worldbank.org.

11. David Harvey, *The Condition of Postmodernity*, vol. 14 (Oxford: Blackwell, 1989).

12. Bipan Chandra, "Indian Nationalists and the Drain, 1880–1905," *Indian Economic and Social History Review* 2, no. 2 (1965): 103–44.

13. For more on colonial railway policy and uneven development, see Chapter 2.

14. Easterling, *Extrastatecraft*; Saskia Sassen, *Territory, Authority, Rights: From Medieval to Global Assemblages* (Princeton, NJ: Princeton University Press, 2008).

15. Parag Khanna, *The Rise of Hybrid Governance* (n.p.: McKinsey and Company, 2012).

16. The Census of India defines urban settlements as requiring a municipality, corporation, cantonment board, or some form of urban local government; a population of not less than 5,000; a population density of at least 400 persons per square kilometer; and more than 75 percent of the male labor force employed in nonagricultural work (note the gender bias in the economic criterion). The Census definition, therefore, includes demographic, economic, and administrative criteria. Census towns are settlements that meet the demographic and economic criteria but are not notified by the state government, which means that they continue to be governed by rural local governments. The motivations for state governments not to classify settlements as urban varies; for more on this topic, see, for instance, Ram Bhagat, "Rural-Urban Classification and Municipal Governance in India," *Singapore Journal of Tropical Geography* 26, no. 1 (2005): 61–73.

17. Eric Denis, Marie-Hélène Zérah, and Partha Mukhopadhyay, *Subaltern Urbanisation in India* (New Delhi: Springer, 2017).

18. Kanhu Pradhan, "Unacknowledged Urbanisation: New Census Towns of India," *Economic and Political Weekly* 48, no. 36 (2013): 43–51.

19. Tim Bunnell and Anant Maringanti, "Practising Urban and Regional Research Beyond Metrocentricity," *International Journal of Urban and Regional Research* 34, no. 2 (2010): 415–20.

20. Terence McGee, "The Emergence of Desakota Regions in Asia: Expanding a Hypothesis," in *The Extended Metropolis: Settlement Transition in Asia*, ed. N. Ginsburg, B. Koppel, and T. G. McGee (Honolulu: University of Hawaii Press, 1991), 3–25.

21. McGee's argument on prior agroeconomic systems, which are embedded in "socioeconomic systems, export trade and class relations," draws on earlier work by Douglas Dowd, Richard Morse, and others who analyzed divergent patterns of urbanization in the United States and Latin America, depending on differences in settlement patterns—between the American West and South in the case of the former, and between the hacienda and plantation systems in the latter. See Douglas Dowd, "A Comparative Analysis of Economic Development in the American West and South," *Journal of Economic History* 16, no. 4 (1956): 558–74; and Richard M. Morse, "Trends and Patterns of Latin American Urbanization, 1750–1920," *Comparative Studies in Society and History* 16 (1974): 416–47.

22. Derek Hall, *Land* (Cambridge, UK: Polity Press, 2012); Wendy Wolford, *This Land Is Ours Now: Social Mobilization and the Meanings of Land in Brazil* (Durham, NC: Duke University Press, 2010).

23. Hung-Ying Chen, *Cashing in on the Sky: Instrumentation of Air Rights in Taipei Metropolitan Area* (paper presented at the American Association of Geographers conference, 2017; shared with the author).

24. Fiona McCormack, *Private Oceans: The Enclosure and Marketisation of the Seas* (London: Pluto Press, 2017).

25. See, for instance, the Space Law program at Harvard Law School for the development of property rights over outer-space resources, as activities like asteroid mining grow in importance.

26. Ashutosh Varshney, *Democracy, Development, and the Countryside: Urban-Rural Struggles in India* (Cambridge, UK: Cambridge University Press, 1998).

27. Johann Heinrich von Thünen, *Isolated State*, trans. Carla M. Wartenberg, ed. Peter Hall (London: Pergamon, 1966).

28. Homer Hoyt, *One Hundred Years of Land Values in Chicago: The Relationship of the Growth of Chicago to the Rise in Its Land Values, 1830–1933* (1933; Washington, DC: Beard Books, 2000).

29. William Alonso, *Location and Land Use: Toward a General Theory of Land Rent* (Cambridge, MA: Harvard University Press, 1964).

30. Paul Krugman, "The New Economic Geography, Now Middle-Aged," *Regional Studies* 45, no. 1 (2011): 1–7. See also Masahisa Fujita, Paul Krugman, and Anthony Venables, *The Spatial Economy: Cities, Regions and International Trade* (Cambridge, MA: MIT Press, 1999).

31. For an excellent overview of critiques against the economic view of land use and cities, see Allen J. Scott, *The Urban Land Nexus and the State* (London: Pion, 1980), 73–82.

32. David Harvey, "The Spatial Fix: Hegel, von Thünen, and Marx," *Antipode* 13, no. 3 (1981): 2.

33. Ibid., 4.

34. Ibid.

35. See, for instance, William Cronon, *Nature's Metropolis: Chicago and the Great West* (New York: W. W. Norton and Company, 1991); and Richard White, *Railroaded: The Transcontinentals and the Making of Modern America* (New York: W. W. Norton and Company, 2011).

36. Neil Smith, *The New Urban Frontier: Gentrification and the Revanchist City* (London: Routledge, 1996), 58.

37. On whether the rent-gap theory, now framed as "planetary rent gaps," fits the postcolonial context, see Tom Slater, "Planetary Rent Gaps," *Antipode* 49, no. 1 (2017): 114–37; Asher Ghertner, "Why Gentrification Theory Fails in 'Much of the World,'" *City* 19, no. 4 (2015), 552–63.

38. See, for instance, Ben White, Saturnino M. Borras Jr., Ruth Hall, Ian Scoones, Wendy Wolford, eds., *The New Enclosures: Critical Perspectives on Corporate Land Deals, Journal of Peasant Studies* 39, no. 3–4 (2012): 619–47.

39. Ibid., 631.

40. Relatedly, Borras and Franco call for more analytical clarity in the catch-all land grab phrase: Saturnino M. Borras Jr. and Jennifer C. Franco, "Global Land Grabbing and Trajectories of Agrarian Change: A Preliminary Analysis," *Journal of Agrarian Change* 12 no. 1 (2012): 34–59.

41. For the regional agrarian histories of Tamil Nadu, see Sharad Chari, *Fraternal Capital: Peasant-Workers, Self-Made Men, and Globalization in Provincial India* (Stanford, CA: Stanford University Press, 2004); and Barbara Harriss-White, *A Political Economy of Agricultural Markets in South India: Masters of the Countryside* (New Delhi: Sage Publications, 1996). For the Patidars in Gujarat, see Vinay Gidwani, *Capital, Interrupted: Agrarian Development and the Politics of Work in India* (Minneapolis: University of Minnesota Press, 2008). On Punjab, see Meenu Tewari, "Successful Adjustment in Indian Industry: The Case

of Ludhiana's Woolen Knitwear Cluster," *World Development* 27, no. 9 (1999): 1651–71; and Surinder Jodhka, *Caste and Power in the Lands of Agri-Culture: Revisiting Rural North-West India*, available at sas-space.sas.ac.uk/5649/1/AHRC_1_Jodhka_Northwest_Caste_and _Rural_Power._Shimla.pdf. On the Kammas in Andhra Pradesh, see K. Balagopal and G. Haragopal, *Probings in the Political Economy of Agrarian Classes and Conflicts* (Hyderabad: Perspectives, 1988). On the Vokkaligas in Karnataka, see M. N. Srinivas, *The Dominant Caste and Other Essays* (New Delhi: Oxford University Press, 1987); and Scarlett Epstein, "Back to the Village," Seventh Annual M. N. Srinivas Memorial Lecture, NIAS Lecture No. L2-2007 (Bangalore: National Institute of Advanced Studies, 2007). For more countrywide perspectives on caste-based linkages between agrarian and industrial capitalism, see Harish Damodaran, *India's New Capitalists: Caste, Business, and Industry in a Modern Nation* (New Delhi: Springer, 2008); and Barbara Harriss-White, Christine Lutringer, and Elisabetta Basile, eds., *Mapping India's Capitalism: Old and New Regions* (London: Palgrave Macmillan, 2015).

42. In the 1946 Constituent Assembly debates, the Sudras were categorized as a backward caste, along with the Dalits and Adivasis. The backward-caste criterion was then adopted by the Indian Census, with the categories of Other Backward Castes (Sudras), Scheduled Castes (Dalits), and Scheduled Tribes becoming the foundation for positive-discrimination or affirmative-action programs.

43. Yogendra Yadav, "Understanding the Second Democratic Upsurge: Trends of Bahujan Participation in Electoral Politics in the 1990s," in *Transforming India: Social and Political Dynamics of Democracy*, ed. Francine Frankel, Zoya Hasan, Rajeev Bhargava, and Balveer Arora (New York: Oxford University Press, 2002).

44. The concept of the dominant caste was coined by M. N. Srinivas; see M. N. Srinivas, "The Dominant Caste in Rampura," *American Anthropologist* 61, no. 1 (1959): 1–16.

45. For an overview of Maharashtra politics, see Jayant Lele, *Elite Pluralism and Class Rule: Political Development in Maharashtra, India* (Toronto: University of Toronto Press, 1981); Rajendra Vora, "Shift of Power from Rural to Urban Sector," *Economic and Political Weekly* 31, no. 2/3 (1996): 171–73; Suhas Palshikar and Rajeshwari Deshpande, "Electoral Competition and Structures of Domination in Maharashtra," *Economic and Political Weekly* (1999): 2409–22; and Rajeshwari Deshpande and Suhas Palshikar, "Political Economy of a Dominant Caste," in *Political Economy of Contemporary India*, ed. R. Nagaraj and Sripad Motiram (New Delhi: Cambridge University Press, 2017), 77–97.

46. Francine Frankel, *India's Green Revolution: Economic Gains and Political Costs* (1971; Princeton, NJ: Princeton University Press, 2015), 3.

47. Ibid., 5.

48. Ibid.

49. Utsa Patnaik, *Agrarian Relations and Accumulation* (published for the Sameeksha Trust by Oxford University Press, 1990). See also a series of conversations in *Economic and Political Weekly* in the 1970s among Ashok Rudra, Utsa Patnaik, Amit Bagchi, and others about how to characterize agrarian capitalism in India during this decade.

50. Lloyd I. Rudolph and Susanne Hoeber Rudolph, *In Pursuit of Lakshmi: The Political Economy of the Indian State* (Chicago: University of Chicago Press, 1987), 2, 333.

51. K. Balagopal, "An Ideology for the Provincial Propertied Class," *Economic and Political Weekly* (1987): 2177.

52. Eric R. Wolf, *Peasant Wars of the Twentieth Century* (Norman: University of Oklahoma Press, 1969), 291.

53. See the chapter "Can the Subaltern Accumulate Capital?" in Chari, *Fraternal Capital,* 182–239.

54. Harriss-White et al.'s *Mapping India's Capitalism* is one of the few works attentive to uneven spatial development. The edited chapters map out first India's old regions of uneven agrarian capitalism and then the new regions of growth, such as regions of Dalit economic participation and luxury consumption (for instance, along the Delhi-Mumbai Industrial Corridor). But the central question I am interested in remains unanswered: how do the new luxury-consumption spaces map onto regions of older agrarian capitalism?

55. Ashutosh Varshney, "Mass Politics or Elite Politics? India's Economic Reforms in Comparative Perspective," *Journal of Policy Reform* 2, no. 4 (1998): 301–35.

56. Rob Jenkins, "India's SEZ Policy: The Political Implications of 'Permanent Reform,'" in *Power, Policy, and Protest: The Politics of India's Special Economic Zones,* ed. Rob Jenkins, Loraine Kennedy, and Partha Mukhopadhyay (New Delhi: Oxford University Press, 2014).

57. Partha Chatterjee, "Democracy and Economic Transformation in India," *Economic and Political Weekly* 43, no. 16 (2008): 53–62.

58. Nikita Sud, *Liberalization, Hindu Nationalism and the State: A Biography of Gujarat* (New Delhi: Oxford University Press, 2012); Sanjoy Chakravorty, *The Price of Land: Acquisition, Conflict, Consequence* (New Delhi: Oxford University Press, 2013).

59. Chakravorty, *Price of Land*, 15–18.

60. See, for instance, Omar Razzaz, "Contestation and Mutual Adjustment: The Process of Controlling Land in Yajouz, Jordan," *Law and Society Review* 28, no. 1 (1994): 7–39; Solomon Benjamin, "Occupancy Urbanism: Radicalizing Politics and Economy Beyond Policy and Programs," *International Journal of Urban and Regional Research* 32, no. 2 (2008): 719–29.

61. Karl Polanyi, *The Great Transformation: The Political and Economic Origins of Our Time* (1944; Boston: Beacon Press, 2001).

62. Ibid., 3.

63. Ibid., xxv.

64. See, for instance, Jairus Banaji, "The Metamorphoses of Agrarian Capitalism," *Journal of Agrarian Change* 2, no. 1 (2002): 96–119; and Anand Yang, *Bazaar India: Markets, Society, and the Colonial State in Bihar* (Berkeley: University of California Press, 1999).

65. A note on the status of LARRA, which has been the subject of intense and protracted debate: after the Act came into force in 2013, strong opposition from industry players and some state governments resulted in the promulgation of three ordinances for amending the Act. In June 2015, the current Modi government introduced the 2015 LARR Amendment Bill, which significantly dilutes the consent clauses of the 2013 LARRA. This bill was passed by the Lok Sabha (Lower House), but it has been stuck since 2015 in the Rajya Sabha (Upper House), where the incumbent National Democratic Alliance does not have a majority. The difficulty in arriving at a consensus over the Act exemplifies the fraught nature of the land question in contemporary India.

66. See, for instance, Fred Block's introduction to the 2001 edition of Polanyi's *The Great Transformation*: "Although the working-class movement has been a key part of the protective countermovement, Polanyi explicitly states that all groups in society have participated in this project. When periodic economic downturns destroyed the banking system, for example, business groups insisted that central banking be strengthened to insulate the domestic supply of credit from the pressures of the global market. In a word even capitalists periodically resist the uncertainty and fluctuations that market self-regulation produces and participate in efforts to increase stability and predictability through forms of protection" (pp. xxviii). This then leads to the influential Polanyian argument that it was statecraft that shaped the market, i.e., "laissez-faire was planned" (147).

67. Timothy Mitchell, "The Properties of Markets," in *Do Economists Make Markets? On the Performativity of Economics*, ed. Donald MacKenzie, Fabian Muniesa, and Lucia Siu (Princeton, NJ: Princeton University Press, 2007), 244–75.

68. Quoted in Devesh Kapur, "India's Promise?" *Harvard Magazine* (July–August 2005): 36–39, 87.

69. Llerena Searle, *Landscapes of Accumulation: Real Estate and the Neoliberal Imagination in Contemporary India* (Chicago: University of Chicago Press, 2016). On the contemporary making of real-estate markets in other Asian countries, see You-tien Hsing, *The Great Urban Transformation: Politics of Land and Property in China* (New York: Oxford University Press, 2010); Anne Haila, *Urban Land Rent: Singapore as a Property State* (West Sussex, UK: John Wiley, 2015); Gavin Shatkin, *Cities for Profit: The Real Estate Turn in Asia's Urban Politics* (Ithaca, NY: Cornell University Press, 2017).

70. Patrick Heller, "Making Citizens from Below and Above: The Prospects and Challenges of Decentralization in India," in *Understanding India's New Political Economy: A Great Transformation?*, ed. Sanjay Ruparelia, Sanjay Reddy, John Harriss, and Stuart Corbridge (London: Routledge, 2011), 164.

71. Ramya Parthasarathy and Vijayendra Rao, *Deliberative Democracy in India*, Policy Research Working Paper 7995 (World Bank, March 2017).

72. Abdul Aziz, "Democratic Decentralisation: Experience of Karnataka," *Economic and Political Weekly* (2000): 3521–26.

73. For more on the contestability of property regimes, see Katharina Pistor and Olivier De Schutter, *Governing Access to Essential Resources* (New York: Columbia University Press, 2015). The normative concern for democratic contestation also aligns with the urban scholarship of, among others, Susan Fainstein. Fainstein's work urges planners to not uncritically privilege efficiency as the overriding value in urban decision making, but instead to bring social justice values front-and-center in these contested processes. See Susan Fainstein, *The Just City* (Ithaca, NY: Cornell University Press, 2010).

74. Madhav Gadgil et al., "Report of the Western Ghats Ecology Expert Panel," submitted to the Ministry of Environment and Forests, Government of India, August 31, 2011, 9.

75. On the "right to stay put" in the context of the informal residents of Mumbai's Dharavi settlement, see Liza Weinstein, *The Durable Slum: Dharavi and the Right to Stay Put in Globalizing Mumbai* (Minneapolis: University of Minnesota Press, 2014).

76. Henri Lefebvre, *The Urban Revolution* (Minneapolis: University of Minnesota Press, 2003); Neil Brenner and Christian Schmid, "The 'Urban Age' in Question," *International Journal of Urban and Regional Research* 38, no. 3 (2014): 731–55. Also see Janaki Nair, "Indian Urbanism and the Terrain of the Law," *Economic and Political Weekly* 50, no. 36 (2015): 54–63, where she analyzes the Bengaluru-Mysore NICE corridor as a "sign of new urbanism" that resembles what Lefebvre called "urban society."

77. Paul Starr, "The Meaning of Privatization," *Yale Law and Policy Review* 6, no. 1 (1988): 38.

78. See Appendix II for more details on my research methodology.

79. Martha Feldman, Jeannine Bell, and Michele Tracy Berger, *Gaining Access: A Practical and Theoretical Guide for Qualitative Researchers* (Walnut Creek, CA: Rowman Altamira, 2004).

80. Parthasarathy and Rao, *Deliberative Democracy in India.*

Chapter 1

1. Shubhangi Khapre, "First Big Ticket FDI: Tech Major Foxconn Pledges $5 Billion in Maharashtra," *Indian Express* (August 9, 2015); Makarand Gadgil, "How Maharashtra Bagged the $5 Billion Foxconn Deal," *Live Mint* (August 13, 2015).

2. *SUPA, Japanese Industrial Zone* (Mumbai: Maharashtra Industrial Development Corporation). This brochure is part of the "Magnetic Maharashtra" promotional material produced by the MIDC. I received this brochure, along with a CD on "Magnetic Maharashtra," from the CEO of MIDC during my visits to their Mumbai office during my 2010–15 research.

3. *The Right to Fair Compensation and Transparency in Land Acquisition, Rehabilitation and Resettlement Act, 2013*, no. 30 of 2013, *Gazette of India* (Ministry of Law and Justice, Legislative Department, September 27, 2013).

4. Ibid., chap. 3.

5. Dave Donaldson, *Railroads of the Raj: Estimating the Impact of Transportation Infrastructure*, no. 16487 (Cambridge, MA: National Bureau of Economic Research, 2010).

6. S. J. Phansalkar, "Political Economy of Irrigation Development in Vidarbha," *Journal of Indian School of Political Economy* 17, no. 4 (2005): 613.

7. Neil Charlesworth, *Peasants and Imperial Rule: Agriculture and Agrarian Society in the Bombay Presidency 1850–1935*, vol. 32 (Cambridge, UK: Cambridge University Press, 2002), 144.

8. Ibid. For maps and passenger-miles data on colonial-era railway systems in India from 1870 to 1930, see Dan Bogart and Latika Chaudhary, "Railways in Colonial India: An Economic Achievement?" (2012), available at ssrn.com/abstract=2073256; and John Hurd, "A Huge Railway System but No Sustained Economic Development: The Company Perspective, 1884–1939: Some Hypotheses," in *27 Down: New Departures in Indian Railway Studies,* ed. Ian Kerr (New Delhi: Orient Longman, 2007).

9. For an account of the colonial-era railways as part of a wider imperial project of spatial unevenness, see Manu Goswami, *Producing India* (Chicago: University of Chicago Press, 2004).

10. "Shakuntala Railways: India's Only Private Railway Line," *Economic Times* (December 11, 2016).

11. Sven Beckert, "Emancipation and Empire: Reconstructing the Worldwide Web of Cotton Production in the Age of the American Civil War," *American Historical Review* 109, no. 5 (2004): 1405–38.

12. Sharada Dwivedi and Rahul Mehrotra, *Bombay: The Cities Within* (Mumbai: Eminence Designs, 2001); Dwijendra Tripathi, *The Oxford History of Indian Business* (Oxford: Oxford University Press, 2004).

13. Daniel Thorner, ed., *Ecological and Agrarian Regions of South Asia Circa 1930* (Karachi: Oxford University Press, 1996), 122.

14. Ibid.

15. Amartya Sen, *Poverty and Famines: An Essay on Entitlement and Deprivation* (Oxford: Oxford University Press, 1981).

16. Stuart Sweeney, "Indian Railways and Famine 1875–1914: Magic Wheels and Empty Stomachs," *Essays in Economic and Business History* 26, no. 1 (2012): 149. For more on the dissatisfaction of Indian nationalists with the colonial-era railways, see Bipan Chandra, "Indian Nationalists and the Drain, 1880–1905," *Indian Economic and Social History Review* 2, no. 2 (1965): 103–44; Daniel Thorner, *Investment in Empire: British Railways and Steam Shipping Enterprise in India 1825–1949* (Philadelphia: University of Pennsylvania Press, 1977); and Ian Kerr, *Building the Railways of the Raj, 1850–1900* (Oxford: Oxford University Press, 1995).

17. Donald W. Attwood, *Raising Cane: The Political Economy of Sugar in Western India* (Boulder, CO: Westview Press, 1992). For another seminal book on sugar cooperatives in western Maharashtra, see B. S. Baviskar, *The Politics of Development: Sugar Politics in Rural Maharashtra* (Delhi: Oxford University Press, 1980).

18. Neil Smith, *The New Urban Frontier: Gentrification and the Revanchist City* (London: Routledge, 1996).

19. See Attwood, *Raising Cane*. Also see Donald Attwood, "Peasants Versus Capitalists in the Indian Sugar Industry: The Impact of the Irrigation Frontier," *Journal of Asian Studies* 45, no. 1 (1985): 59–80.

20. Harish Damodaran, *India's New Capitalists: Caste, Business, and Industry in a Modern Nation* (Delhi: Permanent Black, 2008).

21. Rajendra Vora, *The World's First Anti-Dam Movement: The Mulshi Satyagraha, 1920–1924* (Delhi: Permanent Black, 2009).

22. Ibid.

23. *Report of Fact Finding Committee on Regional Imbalance in Maharashtra*, under the chairmanship of V. M. Dandekar (Government of Maharashtra, 1984).

24. *Report of the High Level Committee on Balanced Regional Development Issues in Maharashtra* (Government of Maharashtra, October 2013).

25. Suhas Palshikar, *Caste Politics Through the Prism of Region* (2006), available at s3 .amazonaws.com/academia.edu.documents/34764819/Suhas_Palshikar_Caste_Region.pdf. For more on the second democratic upsurge, see Yogendra Yadav, "Understanding the Second Democratic Upsurge: Trends of Bahujan Participation in Electoral Politics in the 1990s," in *Transforming India: Social and Political Dynamics of Democracy*, ed. Francine

R. Frankel, Zoya Hasan, Rajeeva Bhargava, and Balveer Arora (Delhi: Oxford University Press, 2000), 120–45.

26. For more on the making of the Maratha-Kunbi political caste bloc, see Jayant Lele, *Elite Pluralism and Class Rule: Political Development in Maharashtra, India* (Toronto: University of Toronto Press, 1981); and Suhas Palshikar and Rajeshwari Deshpande, "Electoral Competition and Structures of Domination in Maharashtra," *Economic and Political Weekly* (1999): 2409–22.

27. Each state government has a Department of Backward Classes and Most Backward Classes and Minorities Welfare. This department maintains "a list of castes under each category as per the provisions contained in Article 15(4) and 16(4) of the Constitution of India" for the purposes of affirmative-action programs that target social welfare programs to these caste categories. For a list of "backward" caste categories in the state of Maharashtra, see www.bcmbcmw.tn.gov.in/obc/faq/maharashtra.pdf.

28. See, for instance, Govind Pansare, Anirudh Deshpande, and Prabhat Patnaik, *Who Was Shivaji?* (New Delhi: LeftWord Books, 2015).

29. Palshikar, *Caste Politics*, 5.

30. Ashutosh Varshney, "Is This India's Transformative Urban Moment?" *Indian Express* (August 25, 2011).

31. Abhijit Banerjee, Dilip Mookherjee, Kaivan Munshi, and Debraj Ray, "Inequality, Control Rights, and Rent Seeking: Sugar Cooperatives in Maharashtra," *Journal of Political Economy* 109, no. 1 (2001): 138–90; Sandip Sukhtankar, "Sweetening the Deal? Political Connections and Sugar Mills in India," *American Economic Journal: Applied Economics* (2012): 43–63.

32. B. S. Baviskar, *Milk and Sugar: A Comparative Analysis of Cooperative Politics* (Brighton, UK: Institute of Development Studies at the University of Sussex, 1985); Mala Lalvani, "Sugar Co-operatives in Maharashtra: A Political Economy Perspective," *Journal of Development Studies* 44, no. 10 (2008): 1474–1505.

33. Ashutosh Varshney, *Democracy, Development, and the Countryside: Urban-Rural Struggles in India* (Delhi: Cambridge University Press, 1998).

34. For an overview of the Third World political project, see Vijay Prashad, *The Darker Nations: A People's History of the Third World* (New York: New Press, 2008).

35. Amitabh Kundu, Girish Kumar Misra, and Rajkishor Meher, *Location of Public Enterprises and Regional Development* (New Delhi: Concept Publishing Company, 1986).

36. Varshney, *Democracy, Development, and the Countryside*. For more on cooperatives, see D. R. Gadgil, *Towards a Cooperative Commonwealth* (Chandigarh: Punjab University Publication Bureau, 1961); Baviskar, *Politics of Development*; and Attwood, *Raising Cane*.

37. Varshney, *Democracy, Development, and the Countryside*. See also Shiv Visvanathan, *From the Green Revolution to the Evergreen Revolution: Studies in Discourse Analysis* (IDS Seminar on Agriculture Biotechnology and the Developing World, 2003).

38. Baviskar, *Milk and Sugar*.

39. Rajiv Lall, "The Bitter Truth About Sugar Policies," *Business Standard* (December 18, 2013).

40. A. K. D. Jadhav, "Cooperatives in Maharashtra," *Economic and Political Weekly* 43 (2008): 90.

41. Donald Attwood and B. S. Baviskar, "Why Do Some Co-operatives Work but Not Others? A Comparative Analysis of Sugar Co-operatives in India," *Economic and Political Weekly* (1987): A38–A56; Donald Attwood, "Does Competition Help Co-operation?" *Journal of Development Studies* 26, no. 1 (1989): 5–27.

42. The selection of Nagpur as the location for the proposed Multi-Modal International Cargo Hub and Airport has to do with Nitin Gadkari, the current Member of Parliament from that constituency. Nagpur is the headquarters of a Hindutva right-wing organization, the Rashtriya Swayamsevak Sangh (RSS). Politicians from the current ruling government, the Bharatiya Janata Party, including Gadkari and Prime Minister Narendra Modi, have close ties to the RSS. Until 2014, when Gadkari became the first non-Congress MLA to be elected, the Nagpur constituency had been a stronghold of the Congress. The location of the new logistics hub is probably an effort by Gadkari to bring investment into the economically lagging but politically important region.

43. Sanjoy Chakravorty, "Capital Source and the Location of Industrial Investment: A Tale of Divergence from Post-Reform India," *Journal of International Development* 15, no. 3 (2003): 365–83.

44. Sanjoy Chakravorty, *The Price of Land: Acquisition, Conflict, Consequence* (New Delhi: Oxford University Press, 2013), 377.

45. Partha Mukhopadhyay and Kanhu Charan Pradhan, "Location of SEZs and Policy Benefits: What Does the Data Say?" in *Special Economic Zones: Promise, Performance and Pending Issues* (Delhi: Center for Policy Research, 2009).

46. RITES and Scott Wilson Kirkpatrick, *Mumbai-Pune Expressway Feasibility Study*, commissioned by the Maharashtra State Road Development Corporation (1990).

47. National Transport Development Policy Committee, *Trends in Growth and Development of Transport* (Government of India Planning Commission, 2003), available at planningcommission.nic.in/sectors/NTDPC/volume2_p1/trends_v2_p1.pdf; see the Planning Commission reports on infrastructural allocations, for the Government of India, particularly the fourth, fifth, sixth, and seventh Five-Year Plans.

48. Traffic count for the Mumbai-Pune Expressway from October 2013 to April 2015, collected by the author from the Maharashtra State Road Development Corporation (MSRDC).

49. These land categories, used for revenue purposes, do not exactly map onto the land-use categories used by the State Government's Department of Agriculture, which gives rise to jurisdictional overlaps and mismatches. But some equivalences can be drawn across these categories. The Department of Agriculture, for instance, uses the land category of "net sown area," and in a state like Maharashtra, where multicropped land cleanly maps onto irrigated land, we can use the category of "net sown area" interchangeably with "bagayat land." Similarly, the Department of Agriculture uses the category of "barren and uncultivable waste" (i.e., land that is not suitable for cultivation or that has not been cultivated for more than five years). This land category can be interchanged with dongarpad.

50. For administrative land categories in the state of Maharashtra, see the 1966 Maharashtra Land Revenue Code.

51. R. G. Gordon, *The Bombay Survey and Settlement Manual*, vol. 2 (Bombay: Government Central Press, 1917), 315.

52. A note on data collection and analysis: Each taluka has a subregistrar office for registering property and paying stamp duties. I visited seven subregistrar offices in the Pune district and collected copies of the ready reckoner files for each of the talukas in question from 1996 to 2016. The ready reckoner files do not contain land prices for every village within the taluka but rather focus on a few representative villages; for the seven talukas, this came to a total of 242 villages with data on their ready reckoner rates.

I obtained the Geographic Information System (GIS) base maps for these talukas from the Maharashtra Remote Sensing Applications Center (MRSAC) in Nagpur. I digitized the land prices for the 242 villages from the soft-copy files to Microsoft Excel; then I linked the Excel data to the GIS maps. Some of the 242 villages contained both waste and multicrop land in both 1996 and 2016. Most villages lack certain land categories (for instance, the villages in Baramati have no waste lands). In these cases, I have left these villages unshaded to represent the absence of data for that land category.

53. Masalwadi has a category of land called *jirayat* (i.e., rainfed dry-crop land). The price of the dry-crop land in Masalwadi in 1996 was 22,000 rupees; in 2016, it was 958,500 rupees. To make my point about the re-valuation of waste land vis-à-vis irrigated land, I have restricted the maps to the dongarpad and bagayat land categories and have not mapped out the ready reckoner rates for the common grazing land and dry-crop land.

54. Shirish Patel, "Regional Planning for Bombay," *Economic and Political Weekly* (1970): 1011–18; Charles Correa, *Housing and Urbanisation* (Mumbai: Urban Design Research Institute, 1999).

55. *World Development Report 2009: Reshaping Economic Geography* (Washington, DC: World Bank, 2009).

56. Ibid., 129.

57. Ibid., xx–xxi.

58. On path dependence within the historical institutionalist scholarship, see, inter alia, Theda Skocpol and Paul Pierson, "Historical Institutionalism in Contemporary Political Science," in *Political Science: State of the Discipline*, ed. Ira Katznelson and Helen V. Milner (New York: W. W. Norton, 2002), 693–721. See also Abhijit Banerjee and Lakshmi Iyer, "History, Institutions, and Economic Performance: The Legacy of Colonial Land Tenure Systems in India," *American Economic Review* 95, no. 4 (2005): 1190–1213.

59. Francine Frankel, *India's Green Revolution: Economic Gains and Political Costs* (Princeton, NJ: Princeton University Press, 2015). For other criticisms of the Green Revolution program, from ecological and science, technology, and society perspectives, see Shiv Visvanathan, *From the Green Revolution to the Evergreen Revolution: Studies in Discourse Analysis* (IDS Seminar on Agriculture Biotechnology and the Developing World, 2003); and Vandana Shiva, *The Violence of the Green Revolution: Third World Agriculture, Ecology, and Politics* (Lexington: University Press of Kentucky, 2016).

60. Parag Khanna, *The Rise of Hybrid Governance* (McKinsey Center for Government, 2012), available at www.mckinsey.com/industries/public-sector/our-insights/the-rise-of-hybrid-governance.

61. See the Border Roads Organization website at www.bro.gov.in. See also the *Commemorative Issue on the National Conference on Rural Roads and Exposition* (New Delhi: Gra-

meen Sampark, in the newsletter of the National Rural Roads Development Agency, 2007), available at pmgsy.nic.in/downloads/gs_22may07.pdf. The organization in charge of the PMGSY is the state-level Public Works Department, but due to the violence in the Naxalite areas, the work has been delegated to the Border Roads Organization.

62. See www.dmicdc.com/newsdetail.aspx.

63. Harish Damodaran, "Pradhan Mantri Gram Sadak Yojana: How the Programme Impacted Indian Hinterland," *Indian Express* (February 25, 2016).

64. See, for instance, the Expert Group Report to the Planning Commission of India, *Development Challenges in Extremist-Affected Areas* (New Delhi: Government of India, 2008).

65. See, for instance, Topher McDougal, "The Political Economy of Rural-Urban Conflict: Lessons from West Africa and India" (Ph.D. dissertation, Massachusetts Institute of Technology, 2007).

66. For an excellent review of the literature on the Naxalite movement, see John Harriss, *The Naxalite/Maoist Movement in India: A Review of Recent Literature* (Singapore: Institute of South Asian Studies, 2010).

Chapter 2

1. "The Poor as Stakeholders: Can 'Inclusive Capitalism' Thrive in India?" Knowledge@Wharton, Wharton School at the University of Pennsylvania (January 4, 2010), available at knowledge.wharton.upenn.edu/india/article.cfm?articleid=4336.

2. Ranesh Nair, "Magarpatta: Building a City with Rural-Urban Partnership," *Indian Express* (May 26, 2010).

3. Neha Sami, "From Farming to Development: Urban Coalitions in Pune, India," *International Journal of Urban and Regional Research* 37, no. 1 (2013): 151–64.

4. For more on cooperatives and cooperation as alternatives to neoliberal capitalism, see William Foote Whyte and Kathleen King Whyte, *Making Mondragon: The Growth and Dynamics of the Worker Cooperative Complex* (Ithaca, NY: ILR Press, 1991); and Richard Sennett, *Together: The Rituals, Pleasures and Politics of Cooperation* (New Haven, CT: Yale University Press, 2012).

5. Yu-hung Hong, "Assembling Land for Urban Development: Issues and Opportunities," in *Analyzing Land Readjustment: Economics, Law, and Collective Action*, ed. Yu-hung Hong and Barrie Needham (Cambridge, MA: Lincoln Institute of Land Policy, 2007), 3–34. For a more recent overview of land-readjustment experiences around the world, including a chapter on Magarpatta City by the author, see *Global Experiences in Land Readjustment: Urban Legal Case Studies*, vol. 7 (Nairobi: UN-HABITAT, 2018), available at unhabitat.org/books/global-experiences-in-land-readjustment-urban-legal-case-studies-volume-7/.

6. Teresa Caldeira, *City of Walls: Crime, Segregation, and Citizenship in São Paulo* (Berkeley: University of California Press, 2000); Setha Low, *Behind the Gates: Life, Security and the Pursuit of Happiness in Fortress America* (New York: Routledge, 2003).

7. All names have been changed except for Satish Magar.

8. Interview with author (May 14, 2011).

9. Ibid.

10. The source for this information is a file with the details of landholdings for the SEZ project, compiled by the MIDC.

11. Fractionation in land ownership means that the land is not physically divided but rather that multiple owners have undivided interests in the land. Fractionated land ownership in India is the result of large joint families passing on a single plot of land from generation to generation.

12. Interview with the author (May 21, 2011).

13. Trilochan Sastry, "How Commodity Cooperatives Differ from Milk or Sugar Cooperatives" (2011), available at www.techsangam.com/2011/08/01/how-commodity-cooperatives -differ-from-milk-sugarcooperatives.

14. B. S. Baviskar, *Milk and Sugar: A Comparative Analysis of Cooperative Politics* (Brighton, UK: IDS Publications, 1985).

15. Sujatha Patel, "Co-operative Dairying and Rural Development: A Case Study of Amul," in *Co-operatives and Rural Development*, ed. Donald Attwood and B. S. Baviskar (Delhi: Oxford University Press, 1987); Kalpesh Patel and S. J. Phansalkar, *Politics and Relationship with State in Commodity Cooperatives in Gujarat* (unpublished, 1992).

16. Wilfred Candler and Nalini Kumar, *India: The Dairy Revolution: The Impact of Dairy Development in India and the World Bank's Contribution* (Washington, DC: World Bank Operations Evaluation Department, 1998).

17. Interview with the author (May 28, 2011).

18. Press Trust of India, "Water from Khadakwasla Dam Diverted to Nanded at NCP's Behest," *Business Standard* (September 16, 2015).

19. See, for instance, this report, which is based on the state of Karnataka but has relevance for other Indian states: A. Ravindra, B. K. Chandrashekar, V. Govindraj, and P. S. S. Thomas, *The Committee on Urban Management of Bangalore City*, submitted to the Government of Karnataka, Bangalore, Karnataka (1997).

20. Sharad Pawar, *Fast Forward: Reflections on Changing Economic and Social Scenario of India* (Pune: Rohan Prakashan, 2007).

21. Suhas Palshikar and Rajeshwari Deshpande, "Electoral Competition and Structures of Domination in Maharashtra," *Economic and Political Weekly* (1999): 2409–22.

22. Lekha Rattanani, "Raiding Sugar Daddy," *Outlook* (November 24, 1997); Sourish Bhattacharyya, "Maharashtra Policy to Hit Wine Imports," *Delhi Wine Club*, available at www .delhiwineclub.com/news/Maharashtra_Policy.asp.

23. Rob Jenkins, *Democratic Politics and Economic Reform in India* (Cambridge, UK: Cambridge University Press, 1999), 102. See also Venkatesh Kumar, "Governance Issues in State Universities in Maharashtra," *Economic and Political Weekly* 44, no. 50 (2009): 23–25.

24. I borrowed the apt phrase "land, liquor, and learning" from Pratap Bhanu Mehta, "It's Land, Stupid," *Indian Express* (August 19, 2010).

25. For more on the Shetkari Sanghatana, see Gail Omvedt, "Shetkari Sanghatana's New Direction," *Economic and Political Weekly* (1991): 2287–91; Staffan Lindberg, "New Farmers' Movements in India as Structural Response and Collective Identity Formation: The Cases of the

Shetkari Sanghatana and the BKU," *Journal of Peasant Studies* 21, nos. 3–4 (1994): 95–125; and D. N. Dhanagare, "The Class Character and Politics of the Farmers' Movement in Maharashtra During the 1980s," *Journal of Peasant Studies* 21, nos. 3–4 (1994): 72–94. For more on the wider agrarian movement of the 1980s, of which the Shetkari Sanghatana was the regional expression in Maharashtra, see Tom Brass, *New Farmers' Movements in India* (London: Frank Cass, 1995).

26. Sharad Joshi, "The Run-Up to Lavasa," *Hindu Business Line* (March 23, 2011).

27. Michael Lipton, *Why Poor People Stay Poor: A Study of Urban Bias in World Development* (Canberra: Temple Smith; Australian National University Press, 1977).

28. See K. Balagopal and G. Haragopal, *Probings in the Political Economy of Agrarian Classes and Conflicts* (Hyderabad: Perspectives, 1988). The authors ask why the intermediate-caste Kammas in Andhra Pradesh did not join the new farmers' movement while the Maratha-Kunbis in Maharashtra did. In passing, they allude to the agrarian Kammas being unobstructed from entering the urban Hyderabad economy.

29. Rajnarayan Chandavarkar, *The Origins of Industrial Capitalism in India: Business Strategies and the Working Classes in Bombay, 1900–1940* (Cambridge, UK: Cambridge University Press, 2002).

30. Sharad Joshi: "It is just a conspiracy on the part of the Indian elite to try and divide Bharat in terms of the big, the medium and the small farmers. There is no line of contradiction between the big and the small farmers with respect to remunerative prices." Quoted in Mangesh Nadkarni, *Farmers' Movements in India* (New Delhi: Allied Publishers, 1987), 142.

31. Website of Swabhimani Shetkari Sanghatana: www.swabhimani.com.

32. Pune Municipal Corporation, "Slum Details Under Hadapsar Area for the Year 2017 Under PMC."

33. Interview with the author (August 16, 2012).

34. Ibid.

35. Interview with the author (August 22, 2012).

Chapter 3

1. Chaitanya Kalbag, "We Create Entrepreneurship Against Odds: HCC Chief Ajit Gulabchand," *Business Today* (July 31, 2012).

2. Interview with the author (September 3, 2014).

3. Lavasa Lake City's Draft Red Herring Prospectus (June 30, 2014), 76.

4. Ibid.

5. The work on agglomeration can be divided, based on disciplinary distinctions, into (economic) geography and (geographical) economics. You can see some disagreements between these disciplines in, for instance, Jamie Peck and Eric Sheppard, "Worlds Apart? Engaging with the World Development Report 2009: Reshaping Economic Geography," *Economic Geography* 86, no. 4 (2010): 331–40. For more on the (economic) geography views on agglomeration, see Michael Storper, *Keys to the City: How Economics, Institutions, Social Interaction, and Politics Shape Development* (Princeton, NJ: Princeton University Press, 2013); Trevor Barnes and

Eric Sheppard, *A Companion to Economic Geography* (Hoboken, NJ: John Wiley and Sons, 2008); and Allen J. Scott, *Regions and the World Economy: The Coming Shape of Global Production, Competition, and Political Order* (Oxford: Oxford University Press, 1999). For more on the (geographical) economics view, see Paul Krugman, *How the Economy Organizes Itself in Space: A Survey of the New Economic Geography*, Paper No. 96-04-021 (Santa Fe Institute, 1996); and Masahisa Fujita, Paul R. Krugman, and Anthony J. Venables, *The Spatial Economy: Cities, Regions, and International Trade* (Cambridge, MA: MIT Press, 2001).

6. David Harvey, *The New Imperialism* (New York: Oxford University Press, 2003), 158.

7. Asher Ghertner, *Rule by Aesthetics: World-Class City Making in Delhi* (Delhi: Oxford University Press, 2015); Gautam Bhan, *In the Public's Interest: Evictions, Citizenship, and Inequality in Contemporary Delhi* (Athens: University of Georgia Press, 2016). For more on "worlding cities," see Ananya Roy and Aihwa Ong, eds., *Worlding Cities: Asian Experiments and the Art of Being Global* (Hoboken, NJ: John Wiley and Sons, 2011).

8. Anokhi Parikh, "The Private City: Planning, Property, and Protest in the Making of Lavasa New Town, India" (Ph.D. diss., London School of Economics and Political Science, 2015). See also Susan Parnell and Jennifer Robinson, "(Re)theorizing Cities from the Global South: Looking Beyond Neoliberalism," *Urban Geography* 33, no. 4 (2012): 593–617.

9. R. Kamath, "The Hills Are Alive with the Sound of Controversy," *Business Standard* (September 7, 2010).

10. Lavasa Lake City's Draft Red Herring Prospectus (June 30, 2014), 4.

11. David Harvey, "From Managerialism to Entrepreneurialism: The Transformation in Urban Governance in Late Capitalism," *Geografiska Annaler, Series B, Human Geography* 71, no. 1 (1989): 3–17.

12. Landor website, available at landor.com/thinking/interview-with-luc-speisser-the -promise-of-a-city.

13. Ibid.

14. Lavasa Lake City's Draft Red Herring Prospectus (June 30, 2014), 213.

15. *Report of the People's Commission of Inquiry: To Inquire into the Land Deals, Land Transfers and Displacement Due to Dams and Lavasa Project in the Sahyadri (Mountainous) Region of Pune* (Pune: National Alliance for People's Movements, 2009).

16. Comptroller Auditor General (CAG) India, *Report of the Comptroller Auditor General of India: (Revenue Receipts) Government of Maharashtra, 2011* (New Delhi: Comptroller Auditor General India, 2011), available at www.cag.gov.in/sites/default/files/audit_report_files /Maharashtra_Revenue_2011.pdf.

17. Lavasa Lake City's Draft Red Herring Prospectus (June 30, 2014), 77–78.

18. See wrd.maharashtra.gov.in/portal/portal/MKVDC/aboutus.

19. Interview with the author (October 2014).

20. Details on water entitlements are based on the author's interviews with WRD bureaucrats in Pune (from September to December 2014). On the new water entitlements, see also Subodh Wagle, Sachin Wargade, and Mandar Sathe, "Water Reallocation and Grabbing: Processes, Mechanisms, and Contributory Factors," Working Paper No. 2 (Tata Institute of Social Studies, February 2013); and Subodh Wagle, Sachin Wargade, and Mandar Sathe,

"Exploiting Policy Obscurity for Legalising Water Grabbing in the Era of Economic Reform: The Case of Maharashtra, India," *Water Alternatives* 5, no. 2 (2012): 412–30.

21. The MKVDC-LCL water contract was obtained by the author by filing a Right to Information petition with the WRD in Pune.

22. *Report of the Comptroller Auditor General of India: (Revenue Receipts) Government of Maharashtra, 2011* (New Delhi: Comptroller Auditor General India, 2011), available at www .cag.gov.in/sites/default/files/audit_report_files/Maharashtra_Revenue_2011.pdf.

23. Lavasa Lake City's Draft Red Herring Prospectus (June 30, 2014), 19.

24. Ibid., 21.

25. Ibid., 26.

26. Ibid., 27–28.

27. Ibid., 516–19.

28. "The Environment Ministry Does Not Have Measurable Standards. So How Do You Know What and Whom to Deal With," *Financial Express* (January 9, 2011).

29. Sumeet Mhaskar, *Claiming Entitlements in Neo-Liberal India: Mumbai's Ex-Millworkers' Political Mobilisation on the Rehabilitation Question* (QEH Working Paper Series—QEHWPS200, November 2013), available at www.qeh.ox.ac.uk/sites/www.odid.ox.ac .uk/files/www3_docs/qehwps200.pdf.

30. Anand Teltumbde, "Behind the Ire of the Marathas," *Margin Speak* 51 no. 40 (2016). For another, similar analysis of the Maratha caste group, see Keshav Waghmare, "Keshav Waghmare Writes About the Maratha Community," *Divya Marathi* (September 18, 2016).

31. Rajendra Vora, *The World's First Anti-Dam Movement: The Mulshi Satyagraha, 1920–1924* (Delhi: Permanent Black, 2009).

32. Vora, *The World's First Anti-Dam Movement*, 161.

33. For more on the rise of the Shiv Sena and its nativist politics, see Jayant Lele, "Saffronization of the Shiv Sena: The Political Economy of the City, State and Nation," in *Bombay: Metaphor for Modern India*, ed. Sujata Patel and Alice Thorner (New Delhi: Oxford University Press, 1985); Thomas Blom Hansen, *Wages of Violence: Naming and Identity in Postcolonial Bombay* (Princeton, NJ: Princeton University Press, 2001); and Gyan Prakash, "From Red to Saffron," in *Mumbai Fables* (Princeton, NJ: Princeton University Press, 2010), 204–50.

34. Mhaskar, *Claiming Entitlements in Neo-Liberal India*.

35. National Election Watch, Association for Democratic Reforms, myneta.info.

36. Rajeshwari Deshpande, "Politics of Frustrations, Anxieties and Outrage," *Economic and Political Weekly* 41, no. 14 (2006): 1304–7; Sumeet Mhaskar, "The Roots of the Maratha Unrest Lie in Mumbai's Changing Political Economy," *Wire* (December 5, 2016).

37. Suhas Palshikar, "Limits of Dominant Caste Politics," Seminar No. 620 (April 2011); see also Deshpande, "Politics of Frustrations, Anxieties and Outrage."

38. For more on the rise of exclusionary politics among Gujarat's ex-industrial workers, see Supriya Roy Chowdhury, "Industrial Restructuring, Unions and the State: Textile Mill Workers in Ahmedabad," *Economic and Political Weekly* 31, no. 8 (February 24, 1996): L7–L13; and Jan Breman, *The Making and Unmaking of an Industrial Working Class: Sliding Down to the Bottom of the Labour Hierarchy in Ahmedabad, India* (New Delhi: Oxford University Press, 2004).

39. *Report of the Comptroller Auditor General of India: (Revenue Receipts) Government of Maharashtra, 2011* (New Delhi: Comptroller Auditor General India, 2011), available at www .cag.gov.in/sites/default/files/audit_report_files/Maharashtra_Revenue_2011.pdf.

40. *Report of the People's Commission of Inquiry: To Inquire into the Land Deals, Land Transfers and Displacement Due to Dams and Lavasa Project in the Sahyadri (Mountainous) Region of Pune* (Pune: National Alliance for People's Movements, 2009).

41. Interviews with the author (July–August 2014).

42. Ibid.

43. Steve Graham and Simon Marvin, *Splintering Urbanism: Networked Infrastructures, Technological Mobilities and the Urban Condition* (London: Routledge, 2001).

Chapter 4

1. Socio-Economic Abstract of Pune District (Census of India, 2014–15), available at http://censusindia.gov.in/2011census/dchb/2725_PART_B_DCHB_%20PUNE.pdf.

2. See the HOK website, at www.hok.com/design/region/india/khed-special-economic-zone-/.

3. Aihwa Ong, *Neoliberalism as Exception* (Durham, NC: Duke University Press, 2006).

4. Jamie Cross, "Neoliberalism as Unexceptional: Economic Zones and the Everyday Precariousness of Working Life in South India," *Critique of Anthropology* 30, no. 4 (2010): 355–73.

5. Michael Levien, "Regimes of Dispossession: From Steel Towns to Special Economic Zones," *Development and Change* 44, no. 2 (2013): 381–407.

6. Ibid., 403.

7. K. C. Sivaramakrishnan, "Special Economic Zones: Issues of Urban Growth and Management," in *Special Economic Zones: Promise, Performance and Pending Issues* (New Delhi: Center for Policy Research, 2009), 93–114.

8. Ibid., 97–98.

9. Ibid., 98.

10. Rob Jenkins, "Land, Rights and Reform in India," *Pacific Affairs* 86, no. 3 (2013): 591–612.

11. See Chapter 1 for more details on the SEZ location.

12. The information on the landholdings is in a file for the SEZ project, obtained by the author.

13. Ananya Roy, "Why India Cannot Plan Its Cities: Informality, Insurgence and the Idiom of Urbanization," *Planning Theory* 8, no. 1 (2009): 76–87.

14. D. C. Wadhwa, "Guaranteeing Title to Land: The Only Sensible Solution" (World Bank, 2002), available at siteresources.worldbank.org/INTINDIA/Resources/dc_wadhwa_paper.pdf.

15. Khed City brochure (April 2016), available at khedcity.com/wp-content/uploads/2016/04/Khedcity-Booklet-Updated.pdf.

16. See, for instance, Hanoch Dagan, "Takings and Distributive Justice," *Virginia Law Review* (1999): 741–804; Michael Heller and James E. Krier, "Deterrence and Distribution in the Law of Takings," *Harvard Law Review* (1999): 997–1025; Brian Angelo Lee, "Just Undercompensation: The Idiosyncratic Premium in Eminent Domain," *Columbia Law Review* (2013):

593–655; and Lee Anne Fennell, *Just Enough* (University of Chicago, Coase-Sandor Institute for Law and Economics Research, Paper No. 659, 2013), available at ssrn.com/abstract=2341453.

17. Amnon Lehavi and Amir Licht, "Eminent Domain, Inc.," *Columbia Law Review* 107 (2007): 1704–48.

18. Ronald Coase, "The Nature of the Firm," *Economica* 4, no. 16 (1937): 386–405.

19. Lehavi and Licht, "Eminent Domain, Inc.," 1732.

20. Ibid., 1735.

21. Proceedings at a public meeting in Khed attended by author (June 19, 2012).

22. Ibid.

23. Ibid.

24. Interview with the author (March 10, 2011).

25. Charles Tilly, "Trust and Rule," *Theory and Society* 33, no. 1 (2004): 5.

26. Interview with the author (March 10, 2011).

27. Lakshmi Iyer and Anandi Mani, "Traveling Agents: Political Change and Bureaucratic Turnover in India," *Review of Economics and Statistics* 94, no. 3 (2012): 723–39.

28. Ibid., 731.

29. Judith Tendler and Sara Freedheim, "Trust in a Rent-Seeking World: Health and Government Transformed in Northeast Brazil," *World Development* 22, no. 12 (1994): 1771–91.

30. Kaumudi Gurjar, "New Airport Plans Grounded as Baba Kalyani Slices Land Offer by Over 50%," *Pune Mirror* (June 20, 2014); Alka Kshirsagar, "Khed City: A Bitter-Sweet Experiment for Baba Kalyani," *Hindu Business Line* (March 22, 2015).

31. Parthasarathi Biswas, "Raju Shetti on a 50-km March to Seek Return of Land Taken for SEZ to Farmers," *Indian Express* (March 24, 2015).

32. Vijay Chavan, "Khed Wants Its Project Back," *Pune Mirror* (September 29, 2016).

33. Bishwapriya Sanyal, "Antagonistic Cooperation: A Case Study of Nongovernmental Organizations, Government and Donors' Relationships in Income-Generating Projects in Bangladesh," *World Development* 19, no. 10 (1991): 1367–79.

34. Interview with the author (April 6, 2011).

35. Interview with the author (April 23, 2011).

36. This was the campaign slogan of the Bharatiya Janata Party in the run-up to the 2004 national elections; it sought to capture the economic optimism of a liberalizing India.

37. File with the details of landholdings for the SEZ project obtained by the author.

38. See, for instance, Nancy Fraser, *Justice Interruptus: Critical Reflections on the "Postsocialist" Condition* (London: Routledge, 2014).

39. For an analysis of the changing consumer patterns of Dalits as constituting a politics of recognition, see Nivedita Menon and Aditya Nigam, *Power and Contestation: India since 1989* (London: Zed, 2007), 83–102; and Devesh Kapur, Chandra Bhan Prasad, Lant Pritchett, and Shyam Babu, "Rethinking Inequality: Dalits in Uttar Pradesh in the Market Reform Era," *Economic and Political Weekly* (August 28, 2010): 39–49.

40. Interview with the author (July 6, 2012).

41. Albert Hirschman, *Exit, Voice, and Loyalty: Responses to Decline in Firms, Organizations, and States* (Cambridge, MA: Harvard University Press, 1970).

42. See, for instance, Scarlett Epstein, "Back to the Village," Seventh Annual M. N. Srinivas Memorial Lecture, NIAS Lecture No. L2-2007 (Bangalore: National Institute of Advanced Studies, 2007).

43. Interview with the author (July 17, 2012).

Chapter 5

1. Quoted in Devesh Kapur, "India's Promise?" *Harvard Magazine* (July-August 2005): 87.

2. Sanjoy Chakravorty, "Capital Source and the Location of Industrial Investment: A Tale of Divergence from Post-Reform India," *Journal of International Development* 15, no. 3 (2003): 365–83.

3. The common explanation that communist rule led to Kolkata's economic decline falls short as an argument when we realize that the Left Front came to power in West Bengal only in 1977, whereas the first phase of the Green Revolution was launched as early as 1962.

4. Kushan Mitra, "Tata's Options," *Business Standard* (October 19, 2008); Manish Basu, "Singur Brings Sadness That We Couldn't Do Anything, Says Tata," *Live Mint* (August 31, 2012).

5. See "How Tatas Chose Singur as Base for Nano Plans," *Hindu Business Line*, www .thehindubusinessline.com/todays-paper/tp-corporate/how-tatas-chose-singur-as-base-for -nano-plans/article1636538.ece; agreement between Tata Motors and West Bengal's industrial parastatal, the West Bengal Industrial Development Corporation (WBIDC), available at www .wbidc.com/images/pdf/Agreement%20between%20TML,%20WBIDC%20and%20Govern- ment%20of%20West%20Bengal.pdf.

6. Atul Kohli, *Poverty Amid Plenty in the New India* (Delhi: Cambridge University Press, 2012).

7. On this view, see also John Harriss, "Comparing Political Regimes Across Indian States: A Preliminary Essay," *Economic and Political Weekly* (1999): 3367–77.

8. Deepak Mishra and Barbara Harriss-White, "Mapping Regions of Agrarian Capitalism in India," in *Mapping India's Capitalism: Old and New Regions*, ed. Barbara Harriss-White, Christine Lutringer, and Elisabetta Basile (London: Palgrave Macmillan, 2015), 9–42.

9. K. Balagopal, "An Ideology for the Provincial Propertied Class," *Economic and Political Weekly* (1987): 2177; Tom Brass, "Introduction: The New Farmers' Movement in India," in Brass, *New Farmers' Movements in India*, 3–26. On how identity politics deflects class interests, Tom Brass writes, "Any ideological form which proclaims a common identity based on a notion of classlessness (we-are-all-the-same) in a context where this is palpably not the case . . . cannot but reflect the class interests of those whose class position would be revealed (and thus open to attack in the name of class struggle) if such a notion of 'classlessness' was absent. . . . It is precisely this kind of deflecting role that suggests the possibility of identities/ interests now only unconnected with class but also one that can be shared with rich peasants (we-are-all-the-same by virtue of being rural-not-urban, peasants-not-workers, Hindus-not-Muslims, Maharashtrians-not-Gujaratis, Indian-not-'foreigner')." Ibid., 13.

10. Vishal Jadhav, "Elite Politics and Maharashtra's Employment Guarantee Scheme," *Economic and Political Weekly* 41, no. 50 (2006): 5157–62.

11. K. Balagopal and G. Haragopal, *Probings in the Political Economy of Agrarian Classes and Conflicts* (Hyderabad: Perspectives, 1988).

12. Jairus Banaji, "The Farmers Movement: A Critique of Conservative Rural Coalitions," in Brass, *New Farmers' Movements in India*, 228–45; Brass, "Introduction," *New Farmers' Movements in India*.

13. Llerena Searle, *Landscapes of Accumulation: Real Estate and the Neoliberal Imagination in Contemporary India* (Chicago: University of Chicago Press, 2016); R. Nagaraj, "India's Dream Run, 2003–08," *Economic and Political Weekly* 48, no. 20 (2013): 39–51.

14. Rajeshwari Deshpande, "Politics of Frustrations, Anxieties and Outrage," *Economic and Political Weekly* 41, no. 14 (2006): 1304–7.

15. Makarand Gadgil, "MNS Workers Vandalise Toll Booths in Thane," *Live Mint* (January 27, 2014); Chandran Iyer, "Taking Its Toll," *Sunday Indian* (February 16, 2014).

16. For more on the "agrarian question" and capitalist agrarian transitions, see Terence J. Byres, "The Agrarian Question and Differing Forms of Capitalist Agrarian Transition: An Essay with Reference to Asia," in *Rural Transformation in Asia*, ed. Jan Breman and Sudipto Mundle (New Delhi: Oxford University Press, 1991), 3–76. For more on capitalist agrarian transitions viewed more broadly, under contemporary conditions of globalization, see, for instance, Henry Bernstein, "Agrarian Questions Then and Now," *Journal of Peasant Studies* 24, nos. 1–2 (1996): 22–59; and Jens Lerche, Alpa Shah, and Barbara Harriss-White, "Introduction: Agrarian Questions and Left Politics in India," *Journal of Agrarian Change* 13, no. 3 (2013): 337–50.

17. Dani Rodrik and Arvind Subramanian, *From "Hindu Growth" to Productivity Surge: The Mystery of the Indian Growth Transition*, no. w10376 (Cambridge, MA: National Bureau of Economic Research, 2004).

18. Bernstein, "Agrarian Questions Then and Now"; Lerche, Shah, and Harriss-White, "Introduction: Agrarian Questions and Left Politics in India."

19. Brass, "Introduction," *New Farmers' Movements in India*.

20. Ibid.; Balagopal, "An Ideology for the Provincial Propertied Class."

21. Neil Smith, *Uneven Development: Nature, Capital, and the Production of Space* (Athens: University of Georgia Press, 2010), 211.

22. Ibid.

23. Denis, Zérah, and Mukhopadhyay, *Subaltern Urbanisation in India*.

24. Pranab Bardhan, "Dominant Proprietary Classes and India's Democracy," in *India's Democracy: An Analysis of Changing State-Society Relations*, ed. Atul Kohli (Princeton, NJ: Princeton University Press, 2014), 216.

25. Ibid., 218.

26. Aneesha Sareen Kumar, "Express Justice: When a Ludhiana Farmer Became Owner of Swarna Shatabdi Train," *Hindustan Times* (March 16, 2017).

27. Mridula Chari, "Land Pooling Strategy for the New Andhra Capital Could Become a Model for India's Smart Cities," *Scroll.in* (August 12, 2015); Kanchi Kohli, "Andhra Pradesh Wants to Dilute the Central Land Acquisition Law—and That Could Harm Farmers," *Scroll.in* (January 30, 2017); Mridula Chari, "No Place for Flowers and Workers in Andhra Pradesh's New Capital," *Scroll.in* (August 5, 2017).

28. Preeti Sampat and Simi Sunny, "Dholera and the Myth of Voluntary Land Pooling," *Socio-Legal Review* 12, no. 2 (2016): 1–17.

29. David Osborne and Ted Gaebler, *Reinventing Government* (Reading, MA: Addison-Wesley, 1992), 282. For more on NPM, see also David Osborne and Peter Plastrik, *Banishing Bureaucracy: The Five Strategies for Reinventing Government* (Reading, MA: Addison-Wesley, 1997). For critiques of NPM, see, for instance, Janet Denhardt and Robert Denhardt, *The New Public Service: Serving, Not Steering* (Armonk, NY: M. E. Sharpe, 2003).

30. See, for instance, Michael Goldman, "Speculative Urbanism and the Making of the Next World City," *International Journal of Urban and Regional Research* 35, no. 3 (2011): 555–81.

31. The contradiction in capitalist societies between the need to socialize land to benefit the nonpropertied industrial workers and the need to privatize land in order to benefit propertied capital—what Richard Foglesong calls the "property contradiction"—has been an influential framework for theorizing urban property relations in the West. See Richard Foglesong, *Planning the Capitalist City: The Colonial Era to the 1920s* (Princeton, NJ: Princeton University Press, 1986).

32. See Chapter 1, regarding the 2013 LARRA. A major critique of this clause is that only acquisitions on behalf of the private sector are required to go through a SIA, despite the fact that more than 90 percent of infrastructure-induced displacement in postcolonial India has been caused by public projects, such as dams.

33. The Right to Fair Compensation and Transparency in Land Acquisition, Rehabilitation and Resettlement Act, 2013, No. 30 of 2013, Ministry of Law and Justice (Legislative Department), *Gazette of India* (September 2013), chap. 2, 7–8.

34. Ibid.

35. Ibid., chap. 4.

36. Jean-Jacques Rousseau, *The Social Contract and Other Later Political Writings* (1762; Cambridge: Cambridge University Press, 1997).

37. Charles Tilly, "Processes and Mechanisms of Democratization," *Sociological Theory* 18, no. 1 (2000): 1–16; see also Charles Tilly, "Trust and Rule," *Theory and Society* 33, no. 1 (2004): 1–30.

38. Government of India, "Census of India 2011: Urban Agglomerations and Cities," available at http://censusindia.gov.in/2011-prov-results/paper2/data_files/India2/1.%20Data%20Highlight.pdf.

39. Ibid.

40. Ibid.

41. Ananya Roy, "What Is Urban About Critical Urban Theory?" *Urban Geography* 37, no. 6 (2016): 810–23.

42. This follows Timothy Mitchell's argument on conceptualizing "the distinction between market and nonmarket or capitalist and non-capitalist . . . not as a thin line but as a broad terrain, in fact a frontier region that covers the entire territory of what is called capitalism. The region is the scene of political battles, in which new moral claims, arguments about justice, and forms of entitlement are forged." See Timothy Mitchell, "The Properties of Markets," in *Do Economists Make Markets? On the Performativity of Economics*, ed. Donald MacKenzie, Fabian Muniesa, and Lucia Siu (Princeton, NJ: Princeton University Press, 2007), 244–75, quote on p. 247.

43. For more on decentralization requiring some recentralization, see Judith Tendler, *Good Government in the Tropics* (Baltimore: Johns Hopkins University Press, 1997).

Appendix I

1. George Peterson, "Unlocking Land Values to Finance Urban Infrastructure: Land-based Financing Options for Cities," *Gridlines* (PPIAF, World Bank) Note No. 40 (August 2008).

2. Ronald Coase, "The Problem of Social Cost," *Journal of Law and Economics* 3 (1960).

BIBLIOGRAPHY

Alonso, William. *Location and Land Use: Toward a General Theory of Land Rent.* Cambridge, MA: Harvard University Press, 1964.

Arthur, Brian. *Increasing Returns and Path Dependence in the Economy.* Ann Arbor: University of Michigan Press, 1994.

Attwood, Donald. "Does Competition Help Co-operation?" *Journal of Development Studies* 26, no. 1 (1989): 5–27.

———. "Peasants Versus Capitalists in the Indian Sugar Industry: The Impact of the Irrigation Frontier." *Journal of Asian Studies* 45, no. 1 (1985): 59–80.

———. *Raising Cane: The Political Economy of Sugar in Western India.* Boulder, CO: Westview Press, 1992.

Attwood, Donald, and B. S. Baviskar. "Why Do Some Co-operatives Work but Not Others? A Comparative Analysis of Sugar Co-operatives in India." *Economic and Political Weekly* (1987): A38–A56.

Aziz, Abdul. "Democratic Decentralisation: Experience of Karnataka." *Economic and Political Weekly* (2000): 3522–23.

Balagopal, K. "An Ideology for the Provincial Propertied Class." *Economic and Political Weekly* (1987): 2177–78.

Balagopal, K., and G. Haragopal. *Probings in the Political Economy of Agrarian Classes and Conflicts.* Hyderabad: Perspectives, 1988.

Balakrishnan, Sai. "Land-Based Financing for Infrastructure: What Is New About India's Land Conflicts?" In R. Nagaraj and Sripad Motiram, eds., *Political Economy of Contemporary India.* Delhi: Cambridge University Press, 2017: 260–78.

———. "Land Readjustment in Western India: New Conditions and Challenges for the 21st Century." In UN-HABITAT, *Global Experiences in Land Readjustment: Urban Legal Case Studies,* vol. 7. Nairobi: UN-HABITAT, 2018. Available at unhabitat.org/books/global-experiences-in-land-readjustment-urban-legal-case-studies-volume-7/.

Banaji, Jairus. "The Farmers Movement: A Critique of Conservative Rural Coalitions." In Tom Brass, ed., *New Farmers' Movements in India.* London: Frank Cass, 1995: 228–45.

———. "The Metamorphoses of Agrarian Capitalism." *Journal of Agrarian Change* 2, no. 1 (2002): 96–119.

Banerjee, Abhijit, and Lakshmi Iyer. "History, Institutions, and Economic Performance: The Legacy of Colonial Land Tenure Systems in India." *American Economic Review* 95, no. 4 (2005): 1190–213.

Banerjee, Abhijit, Dilip Mookherjee, Kaivan Munshi, and Debraj Ray. "Inequality, Control Rights, and Rent Seeking: Sugar Cooperatives in Maharashtra." *Journal of Political Economy* 109, no. 1 (2001): 138–90.

Bardhan, Pranab. "Dominant Proprietary Classes and India's Democracy." In Atul Kohli, ed., *India's Democracy: An Analysis of Changing State-Society Relations.* Princeton, NJ: Princeton University Press, 2014: 214–24.

Barnes, Trevor, and Eric Sheppard. *A Companion to Economic Geography.* Hoboken, NJ: John Wiley and Sons, 2008.

Basu, Manish. "Singur Brings Sadness That We Couldn't Do Anything, Says Tata." *Live Mint,* August 31, 2012.

Baviskar, B. S. *Milk and Sugar: A Comparative Analysis of Cooperative Politics.* Brighton, UK: Institute of Development Studies at the University of Sussex, 1985.

———. *The Politics of Development: Sugar Politics in Rural Maharashtra.* Delhi: Oxford University Press, 1980.

Beckert, Sven. "Emancipation and Empire: Reconstructing the Worldwide Web of Cotton Production in the Age of the American Civil War." *American Historical Review* 109, no. 5 (2004): 1405–38.

Bernstein, Henry. "Agrarian Questions Then and Now." *Journal of Peasant Studies* 24, nos. 1–2 (1996): 22–59.

Bhagat, Ram. "Rural-Urban Classification and Municipal Governance in India." *Singapore Journal of Tropical Geography* 26, no. 1 (2005): 61–73.

Bhan, Gautam. *In the Public's Interest: Evictions, Citizenship, and Inequality in Contemporary Delhi.* Athens: University of Georgia Press, 2016.

Bhattacharyya, Sourish. "Maharashtra Policy to Hit Wine Imports." *Delhi Wine Club.* Available at www.delhiwineclub.com/news/Maharashtra_Policy.asp; accessed March 21, 2012.

Biswas, Parthasarathi. "Raju Shetti on a 50-km March to Seek Return of Land Taken for SEZ to Farmers." *Indian Express,* March 24, 2015.

Bogart, Dan, and Latika Chaudhary. "Railways in Colonial India: An Economic Achievement?" May 1, 2012. Available at ssrn.com/abstract=2073256.

Brass, Tom. "Introduction: The New Farmers' Movement in India." In Tom Brass, ed., *New Farmers' Movements in India.* London: Frank Cass, 1995: 3–26.

———, ed. *New Farmers' Movements in India.* London: Frank Cass, 1995.

Breman, Jan. *The Making and Unmaking of an Industrial Working Class: Sliding Down to the Bottom of the Labour Hierarchy in Ahmedabad, India.* New Delhi: Oxford University Press, 2004.

Brenner, Neil, and Christian Schmid. "The 'Urban Age' in Question." *International Journal of Urban and Regional Research* 38, no. 3 (2014): 731–55.

Bunnell, Tim, and Anant Maringanti. "Practising Urban and Regional Research Beyond Metrocentricity." *International Journal of Urban and Regional Research* 34, no. 2 (2010): 415–20.

Business Standard. "Maha Farmers Setting Up First 'Cooperative MIDC' in State." September 27, 2017.

———. "Water from Khadakwasla Dam Diverted to Nanded at NCP's Behest." September 16, 2015.

Byres, Terence J. "The Agrarian Question and Differing Forms of Capitalist Agrarian Transition: An Essay with Reference to Asia." In Jan Breman and Sudipto Mundle, eds., *Rural Transformation in Asia*. New Delhi: Oxford University Press, 1991: 3–76.

Caldeira, Teresa. *City of Walls: Crime, Segregation, and Citizenship in São Paulo*. Berkeley: University of California Press, 2000.

Candler, Winfred, and Nalini Kumar. *India: The Dairy Revolution: The Impact of Dairy Development in India and the World Bank's Contribution*. Washington, DC: World Bank Operations Evaluation Department, 1998.

Central Water Commission, *National Registry of Large Dams*. Delhi: Government of India, 2009.

Chakravorty, Sanjoy. "Capital Source and the Location of Industrial Investment: A Tale of Divergence from Post-Reform India." *Journal of International Development* 15, no. 3 (2003): 365–83.

———. *The Price of Land: Acquisition, Conflict, Consequence*. New Delhi: Oxford University Press, 2013.

Chandavarkar, Rajnarayan. *The Origins of Industrial Capitalism in India: Business Strategies and the Working Classes in Bombay, 1900–1940*. Cambridge: Cambridge University Press, 2002.

Chandra, Bipin. "Indian Nationalists and the Drain, 1880–1905." *Indian Economic and Social History Review* 2, no. 2 (1965): 103–44.

Chari, Mridula. "Land Pooling Strategy for the New Andhra Capital Could Become a Model for India's Smart Cities." *Scroll.in*, August 12, 2015.

———. "No Place for Flowers and Workers in Andhra Pradesh's New Capital." *Scroll.in*, August 5, 2017.

Chari, Sharad. *Fraternal Capital: Peasant-Workers, Self-Made Men, and Globalization in Provincial India*. Stanford, CA: Stanford University Press, 2004.

Charlesworth, Neil. *Peasants and Imperial Rule: Agriculture and Agrarian Society in the Bombay Presidency 1850–1935*. Vol. 32. Cambridge: Cambridge University Press, 2002.

Chatterjee, Partha. "Democracy and Economic Transformation in India." *Economic and Political Weekly* 43, no. 16 (2008): 53–62.

Chavan, Vijay. "Khed Wants Its Project Back." *Pune Mirror*, September 29, 2016.

Chen, Hung-Ying. "Cashing in on the Sky: Instrumentation of Air Rights in Taipei Metropolitan Area." Paper presented at the American Association of Geographers conference, 2017.

Chowdhury, Supriya Roy. "Industrial Restructuring, Unions and the State: Textile Mill Workers in Ahmedabad." *Economic and Political Weekly* 31, no. 8 (1996): L7–L13.

Coase, Ronald. "The Nature of the Firm." *Economica* 4, no. 16 (1937): 386–405.

Correa, Charles. *Housing and Urbanisation*. Mumbai: Urban Design Research Institute, 1999.

Cowen, Deborah. *The Deadly Life of Logistics: Mapping Violence in Global Trade*. Minneapolis: University of Minnesota Press, 2014.

Cronon, William. *Nature's Metropolis: Chicago and the Great West*. New York: W. W. Norton, 1991.

Cross, Jamie. "Neoliberalism as Unexceptional: Economic Zones and the Everyday Precariousness of Working Life in South India." *Critique of Anthropology* 30, no. 4 (2010): 355–73.

Dagan, Hanoch. "Takings and Distributive Justice." *Virginia Law Review* (1999): 741–804.

Damodaran, Harish. *India's New Capitalists: Caste, Business, and Industry in a Modern Nation*. New Delhi: Springer, 2008.

———. "Pradhan Mantri Gram Sadak Yojana: How the Programme Impacted Indian Hinterland." *Indian Express*, February 25, 2016.

Denhardt, Janet, and Robert Denhardt. *The New Public Service: Serving, Not Steering*. Armonk, NY: M. E. Sharpe, 2003.

Denis, Eric, Marie-Hélène Zérah, and Partha Mukhopadhyay. *Subaltern Urbanisation in India*. New Delhi: Springer, 2017.

Deshpande, Rajeshwari. "Politics of Frustrations, Anxieties and Outrage." *Economic and Political Weekly* 41, no. 14 (2006): 1304–7.

Deshpande, Rajeshwari, and Suhas Palshikar. "Political Economy of a Dominant Caste." In R. Nagaraj and Sripad Motiram, eds., *Political Economy of Contemporary India*. New Delhi: Cambridge University Press, 2017: 77–97.

Dhanagare, D. N. "The Class Character and Politics of the Farmers' Movement in Maharashtra During the 1980s." *Journal of Peasant Studies* 21, nos. 3–4 (1994): 72–94.

Donaldson, Dave. *Railroads of the Raj: Estimating the Impact of Transportation Infrastructure*. No. 16487. National Bureau of Economic Research, 2010.

Dowd, Douglas. "A Comparative Analysis of Economic Development in the American West and South." *Journal of Economic History* 16, no. 4 (1956): 558–74.

Dwijendra Tripathi. *The Oxford History of Indian Business*. Oxford: Oxford University Press, 2004.

Dwivedi, Sharada, and Rahul Mehrotra. *Bombay: The Cities Within*. Mumbai: Eminence Designs, 2001.

Easterling, Keller. *Extrastatecraft: The Power of Infrastructure Space*. Brooklyn, NY: Verso Books, 2014.

Economic Times. "Shakuntala Railways: India's Only Private Railway Line." December 11, 2016.

Engerman, Stanley, and Kenneth Sokoloff. "Factor Endowments, Institutions and Differential Paths of Growth Among New World Economies: A View from Economic Historians of the United States." In Stephen Haber, ed., *How Latin America Fell Behind: Essays on the Economic Histories of Brazil and Mexico*. Stanford, CA: Stanford University Press, 1997: 260–304.

Epstein, Scarlett. "Back to the Village." Seventh Annual M. N. Srinivas Memorial Lecture, NIAS Lecture No. L2-2007. Bangalore: National Institute of Advanced Studies, 2007.

Fainstein, Susan. *The Just City*. Ithaca, NY: Cornell University Press, 2010.

Feldman, Martha, Jeannine Bell, and Michele Tracy Berger. *Gaining Access: A Practical and Theoretical Guide for Qualitative Researchers*. Walnut Creek, CA: Rowman Altamira, 2004.

Fennell, Lee Anne. *Just Enough*. University of Chicago, Coase-Sandor Institute for Law and Economics Research, Paper No. 659, 2013. Available at ssrn.com/abstract=2341453.

Financial Express. "The Environment Ministry Does Not Have Measurable Standards. So How Do You Know What and Whom to Deal With." January 9, 2011.

Flyvbjerg, Bent, Nils Bruzelius, and Werner Rothengatter. *Megaprojects and Risk: An Anatomy of Ambition*. Cambridge: Cambridge University Press, 2003.

Foglesong, Richard. *Planning the Capitalist City: The Colonial Era to the 1920s*. Princeton, NJ: Princeton University Press, 1986.

Frankel, Francine. *India's Green Revolution: Economic Gains and Political Costs*. Princeton, NJ: Princeton University Press, 2015. Originally published in 1971.

Fraser, Nancy. *Justice Interruptus: Critical Reflections on the "Postsocialist" Condition*. London: Routledge, 2014.

Fujita, Masahisa, Paul R. Krugman, and Anthony J. Venables. *The Spatial Economy: Cities, Regions, and International Trade*. Cambridge, MA: MIT Press, 2001.

Gadgil, D. R. *Towards a Cooperative Commonwealth*. Chandigarh: Punjab University Publication Bureau, 1961.

Gadgil, Makarand. "How Maharashtra Bagged the $5 Billion Foxconn Deal." *Live Mint*, August 13, 2015.

———. "MNS Workers Vandalise Toll Booths in Thane." *Live Mint*, January 27, 2014.

Ghertner, Asher. *Rule by Aesthetics: World-Class City Making in Delhi*. Delhi: Oxford University Press, 2015.

———. "Why Gentrification Theory Fails in 'Much of the World.'" *City* 19, no. 4 (2015): 552–63.

Gidwani, Vinay. *Capital, Interrupted: Agrarian Development and the Politics of Work in India*. Minneapolis: University of Minnesota Press, 2008.

Ginsburg, Norton Sydney, Bruce Koppel, and T. G. McGee, eds. *The Extended Metropolis: Settlement Transition in Asia*. Honolulu: University of Hawaii Press, 1991.

Goldman, Michael. "Speculative Urbanism and the Making of the Next World City." *International Journal of Urban and Regional Research* 35, no. 3 (2011): 555–81.

Gordon, R. G. *The Bombay Survey and Settlement Manual*. Vol. 2. Bombay: Government Central Press, 1917.

Goswami, Manu. *Producing India*. Chicago: University of Chicago Press, 2004.

Government of Maharashtra, *Maharashtra Water and Irrigation Commission Report*, 1999. Available at https://wrd.maharashtra.gov.in/portal/content/default/pdf/contents/home/kc/MWIC_1999_1.pdf.

———. *Report of Fact Finding Committee on Regional Imbalance in Maharashtra*, 2014.

Graham, Steven, and Simon Marvin. *Splintering Urbanism: Networked Infrastructures, Technological Mobilities and the Urban Condition*. London: Routledge, 2001.

Gurjar, Kaumudi. "New Airport Plans Grounded as Baba Kalyani Slices Land Offer by Over 50%." *Pune Mirror*, June 20, 2014.

Hall, Derek. *Land*. Cambridge, UK: Polity Press, 2012.

Hansen, Thomas Blom. *Wages of Violence: Naming and Identity in Postcolonial Bombay*. Princeton, NJ: Princeton University Press, 2001.

Harriss, John. "Comparing Political Regimes Across Indian States: A Preliminary Essay." *Economic and Political Weekly* (1999): 3367–77.

———. *The Naxalite/Maoist Movement in India: A Review of Recent Literature.* Singapore: Institute of South Asian Studies, 2010.

Harriss-White, Barbara. *A Political Economy of Agricultural Markets in South India: Masters of the Countryside.* New Delhi: Sage Publications, 1996.

Harriss-White, Barbara, Christine Lutringer, and Elisabetta Basile, eds. *Mapping India's Capitalism: Old and New Regions.* London: Palgrave Macmillan, 2015.

Harvey, David. *The Condition of Postmodernity.* Vol. 14. Oxford: Blackwell, 1989.

———. "From Managerialism to Entrepreneurialism: The Transformation in Urban Governance in Late Capitalism." *Geografiska Annaler, Series B, Human Geography* 71, no. 1 (1989): 3–17.

———. *The New Imperialism.* New York: Oxford University Press, 2003.

———. "The Spatial Fix: Hegel, von Thünen, and Marx." *Antipode* 13, no. 3 (1981): 1–12.

Heller, Michael, and James E. Krier. "Deterrence and Distribution in the Law of Takings." *Harvard Law Review* (1999): 997–1025.

Heller, Patrick. "Making Citizens from Below and Above: The Prospects and Challenges of Decentralization in India." In Sanjay Ruparelia, Sanjay Reddy, John Harriss, and Stuart Corbridge, eds., *Understanding India's New Political Economy: A Great Transformation?* London: Routledge, 2011: 157–71.

Hirschman, Albert. *Exit, Voice, and Loyalty: Responses to Decline in Firms, Organizations, and States.* Cambridge, MA: Harvard University Press, 1970.

Hong, Yu-hung. "Assembling Land for Urban Development: Issues and Opportunities." In Yu-hung Hong and Barrie Needham, eds., *Analyzing Land Readjustment: Economics, Law, and Collective Action.* Cambridge, MA: Lincoln Institute of Land Policy, 2007: 3–34.

Hoyt, Homer. *One Hundred Years of Land Values in Chicago: The Relationship of the Growth of Chicago to the Rise in Its Land Values, 1830–1933.* Washington, DC: Beard Books, 2000. Originally published in 1933.

Hurd, John. "A Huge Railway System but No Sustained Economic Development: The Company Perspective, 1884–1939: Some Hypotheses." In Ian Kerr, ed., *27 Down: New Departures in Indian Railway Studies.* New Delhi: Orient Longman, 2007: 314–62.

Iyer, Chandran. "Taking Its Toll." *Sunday Indian,* February 16, 2014.

Iyer, Lakshmi, and Anandi Mani. "Traveling Agents: Political Change and Bureaucratic Turnover in India." *Review of Economics and Statistics* 94, no. 3 (2012): 723–39.

Jadhav, A. K. D. "Cooperatives in Maharashtra." *Economic and Political Weekly* 43 (2008): 90.

Jenkins, Rob. *Democratic Politics and Economic Reform in India.* Cambridge, UK: Cambridge University Press, 1999.

———. "India's SEZ Policy: The Political Implications of 'Permanent Reform.'" In Rob Jenkins, Loraine Kennedy, and Partha Mukhopadhyay, eds., *Power, Policy, and Protest: The Politics of India's Special Economic Zones.* New Delhi: Oxford University Press, 2014.

———. "Land, Rights and Reform in India." *Pacific Affairs* 86, no. 3 (2013): 591–612.

Jodhka, Surinder. "Caste and Power in the Lands of Agri-*Culture*: Revisiting Rural North-West India." Available at sas-space.sas.ac.uk/5649/1/AHRC_1_Jodhka_Northwest_Caste_and _Rural_Power._Shimla.pdf.

Joshi, Sharad. "The Run-Up to Lavasa." *Hindu Business Line*, March 23, 2011.

Kalbag, Chaitanya. "We Create Entrepreneurship Against Odds: HCC Chief Ajit Gulabchand." *Business Today*, July 31, 2012.

Kamath, R. "The Hills Are Alive with the Sound of Controversy." *Business Standard*, September 7, 2010.

Kapur, Devesh. "India's Promise?" *Harvard Magazine* (July–August 2005): 36–39, 87.

Kapur, Devesh, Chandra Bhan Prasad, Lant Pritchett, and Shyam Babu. "Rethinking Inequality: Dalits in Uttar Pradesh in the Market Reform Era." *Economic and Political Weekly* (2010): 39–49.

Kerr, Ian. *Building the Railways of the Raj, 1850–1900*. Oxford: Oxford University Press, 1995.

Khanna, Parag. *The Rise of Hybrid Governance*. N.p.: McKinsey & Company, 2012. Available at http://governanceconnect.eu/wp-content/uploads/2012/11/26-RiseofHybridGovernance1 .pdf.

Khapre, Shubhangi. "First Big Ticket FDI: Tech Major Foxconn Pledges $5 Billion in Maharashtra." *Indian Express*, August 9, 2015.

Knowledge@Wharton. "The Poor as Stakeholders: Can 'Inclusive Capitalism' Thrive in India?" Wharton School at the University of Pennsylvania (January 4, 2010). Available at knowledge.wharton.upenn.edu/india/article.cfm?articleid=4336.

Kohli, Atul. *Poverty amid Plenty in the New India*. Delhi: Cambridge University Press, 2012.

Kohli, Kanchi. "Andhra Pradesh Wants to Dilute the Central Land Acquisition Law—and That Could Harm Farmers." *Scroll.in*, January 30, 2017.

Krishnakumar, R. "A Man Behind the Plan." *Frontline*, October–November 2004.

Krugman, Paul. *How the Economy Organizes Itself in Space: A Survey of the New Economic Geography*. Paper No. 96-04-021. Santa Fe, NM: Santa Fe Institute, 1996.

———. "The New Economic Geography, Now Middle-Aged." *Regional Studies* 45, no. 1 (2011): 1–7.

Kshirsagar, Alka. "Khed City: A Bitter-Sweet Experiment for Baba Kalyani." *Hindu Business Line*, March 22, 2015.

Kumar, Aneesha Sareen. "Express Justice: When a Ludhiana Farmer Became Owner of Swarna Shatabdi Train." *Hindustan Times*, March 16, 2017.

Kumar, Venkatesh. "Governance Issues in State Universities in Maharashtra." *Economic and Political Weekly* 44, no. 50 (2009): 23–25.

Kundu, Amitabh, Girish Kumar Misra, and Rajkishor Meher. *Location of Public Enterprises and Regional Development*. New Delhi: Concept Publishing Company, 1986.

Lall, Rajiv. "The Bitter Truth About Sugar Policies." *Business Standard*, December 18, 2013.

Lalvani, Mala. "Sugar Co-operatives in Maharashtra: A Political Economy Perspective." *Journal of Development Studies* 44, no. 10 (2008): 1474–505.

Lee, Brian Angelo. "Just Undercompensation: The Idiosyncratic Premium in Eminent Domain." *Columbia Law Review* (2013): 593–655.

Lehavi, Amnon, and Amir Licht. "Eminent Domain, Inc." *Columbia Law Review* 107 (2007): 1704–48.

Lele, Jayant. *Elite Pluralism and Class Rule: Political Development in Maharashtra, India*. Toronto: University of Toronto Press, 1981.

———. "Saffronization of the Shiv Sena: The Political Economy of the City, State and Nation." In Sujata Patel and Alice Thorner, eds., *Bombay: Metaphor for Modern India*. New Delhi: Oxford University Press, 1985: 185–212.

Lerche, Jens, Alpa Shah, and Barbara Harriss-White. "Introduction: Agrarian Questions and Left Politics in India." *Journal of Agrarian Change* 13, no. 3 (2013): 337–50.

Levien, Michael. "Regimes of Dispossession: From Steel Towns to Special Economic Zones." *Development and Change* 44, no. 2 (2013): 381–407.

Lindberg, Staffan. "New Farmers' Movements in India as Structural Response and Collective Identity Formation: The Cases of the Shetkari Sanghatana and the BKU." *Journal of Peasant Studies* 21, nos. 3–4 (1994): 95–125.

Lipton, Michael. *Why Poor People Stay Poor: A Study of Urban Bias in World Development*. Canberra: Australian National University Press, 1977.

Low, Setha. *Behind the Gates: Life, Security and the Pursuit of Happiness in Fortress America*. New York: Routledge, 2003.

Mahaprashasta, Ajoy Ashirwad. "Striking Unity." *Frontline* 27, no. 18 (August–September 2010).

Maharashtra Water Resources Regulatory Authority. *Major and Medium Irrigation Projects in Maharashtra*. Mumbai: Government of Maharashtra. Available at http://www.mwrra .org/Document%203.pdf.

McCormack, Fiona. *Private Oceans: The Enclosure and Marketisation of the Seas*. London: Pluto Press, 2017.

McDougal, Topher. "The Political Economy of Rural-Urban Conflict: Lessons from West Africa and India." Ph.D. diss., Massachusetts Institute of Technology, 2007.

McGee, Terence. "The Emergence of Desakota Regions in Asia: Expanding a Hypothesis." In Norton Ginsburg, Bruce Koppel, and Terence McGee, eds., *The Extended Metropolis: Settlement Transition in Asia*. Honolulu: University of Hawaii Press, 1991: 3–26.

Mehta, Pratap Bhanu. "It's Land, Stupid." *Indian Express*, August 19, 2010.

Menon, Nivedita, and Aditya Nigam. *Power and Contestation: India Since 1989*. London: Zed Books, 2007.

Mhaskar, Sumeet. *Claiming Entitlements in Neo-Liberal India: Mumbai's Ex-Millworkers' Political Mobilisation on the Rehabilitation Question*. QEH Working Paper Series, QEHWPS200, November 2013. Available at www.qeh.ox.ac.uk/sites/www.odid.ox.ac.uk /files/www3_docs/qehwps200.pdf.

———. "The Roots of the Maratha Unrest Lie in Mumbai's Changing Political Economy." *Wire*, December 5, 2016.

Mishra, Deepak, and Barbara Harriss-White. "Mapping Regions of Agrarian Capitalism in India." In Barbara Harriss-White, Christine Lutringer, and Elisabetta Basile, eds., *Mapping India's Capitalism: Old and New Regions*. London: Palgrave Macmillan, 2015: 9–42.

Mitchell, Timothy. "The Properties of Markets." In Donald MacKenzie, Fabian Muniesa, and Lucia Siu, eds., *Do Economists Make Markets? On the Performativity of Economics*. Princeton, NJ: Princeton University Press, 2007: 244–75.

Mitra, Kushan. "Tata's Options." *Business Standard*, October 19, 2008.

Morse, Richard. "Trends and Patterns of Latin American Urbanization, 1750–1920." *Comparative Studies in Society and History* 16 (1974): 416–47.

Mukhopadhyay, Partha, and Kanhu Charan Pradhan. "Location of SEZs and Policy Benefits: What Does the Data Say?" In *Special Economic Zones: Promise, Performance and Pending Issues*. Delhi: Center for Policy Research, 2009.

Nadkarni, Mangesh. *Farmers' Movements in India*. New Delhi: Allied Publishers, 1987.

Nagaraj, R. "India's Dream Run, 2003–08." *Economic and Political Weekly* 48, no. 20 (2013): 39–51.

Nair, Janaki. "Indian Urbanism and the Terrain of the Law." *Economic and Political Weekly* 50, no. 36 (2015): 54–63.

Nair, Ranesh. "Magarpatta: Building a City with Rural-Urban Partnership." *Indian Express*, May 26, 2010.

National Rural Roads Development Agency. *Commemorative Issue on the National Conference on Rural Roads and Exposition*. New Delhi: Grameen Sampark, 2007.

Omvedt, Gail. "Shetkari Sanghatana's New Direction." *Economic and Political Weekly* (1991): 2287–91.

Ong, Aihwa. *Neoliberalism as Exception*. Durham, NC: Duke University Press, 2006.

Osborne, David, and Ted Gaebler. *Reinventing Government*. Reading, MA: Addison-Wesley, 1992.

Osborne, David, and Peter Plastrik. *Banishing Bureaucracy: The Five Strategies for Reinventing Government*. Reading, MA: Addison-Wesley, 1997.

Palshikar, Suhas. *Caste Politics Through the Prism of Region* (2006). Available at s3.amazonaws .com/academia.edu.documents/34764819/Suhas_Palshikar_Caste_Region.pdf.

———. "Limits of Dominant Caste Politics." Seminar No. 620 (April 2011).

Palshikar, Suhas, and Rajeshwari Deshpande. "Electoral Competition and Structures of Domination in Maharashtra." *Economic and Political Weekly* (1999): 2409–22.

Pani, Narendar. "Globalization, Group Autonomy, and Political Space: Negotiating Globalized Interests in an Indian City." Unpublished mimeo, 2013.

Pansare, Govind, Anirudh Deshpande, and Prabhat Patnaik. *Who Was Shivaji?* New Delhi: LeftWord Books, 2015.

Parikh, Anokhi. "The Private City: Planning, Property, and Protest in the Making of Lavasa New Town, India." Ph.D. diss., London School of Economics and Political Science, 2015.

Parnell, Susan, and Jennifer Robinson. "(Re)theorizing Cities from the Global South: Looking Beyond Neoliberalism." *Urban Geography* 33, no. 4 (2012): 593–617.

Parthasarathy, Ramya, and Vijayendra Rao. *Deliberative Democracy in India*. Policy Research Working Paper 7995. World Bank, March 2017.

Patel, Kalpesh, and S. J. Phansalkar. "Politics and Relationship with State in Commodity Cooperatives in Gujarat." Unpublished, 1992.

Patel, Shirish. "Regional Planning for Bombay." *Economic and Political Weekly* (1970): 1011–18.

Patel, Sujatha. "Co-operative Dairying and Rural Development: A Case Study of Amul." In Donald Attwood and B. S. Baviskar, eds., *Who Shares? Co-operatives and Rural Development*. Delhi: Oxford University Press, 1987.

Patnaik, Utsa. *Agrarian Relations and Accumulation*. Published for the Sameeksha Trust by Oxford University Press, 1990.

Pawar, Sharad. *Fast Forward: Reflections on Changing Economic and Social Scenario of India*. Pune: Rohan Prakashan, 2007.

Peck, Jamie, and Eric Sheppard. "Worlds Apart? Engaging with the World Development Report 2009: Reshaping Economic Geography." *Economic Geography* 86, no. 4 (2010): 331–40.

Phansalkar, S. J. "Political Economy of Irrigation Development in Vidarbha." *Journal of Indian School of Political Economy* 17, no. 4 (2005): 66–96.

Pistor, Katharina, and Olivier de Schutter. *Governing Access to Essential Resources*. New York: Columbia University Press, 2015.

Polanyi, Karl. *The Great Transformation: The Political and Economic Origins of Our Time*. Boston: Beacon Press, 2001. Originally published in 1944.

Pradhan, Kanhu. "Unacknowledged Urbanisation: New Census Towns of India." *Economic and Political Weekly* 48, no. 36 (2013): 43–51.

Prakash, Gyan. "From Red to Saffron." In *Mumbai Fables*. Princeton, NJ: Princeton University Press, 2010: 204–50.

Prashad, Vijay. *The Darker Nations: A People's History of the Third World*. New York: New Press, 2008.

Rattanani, Lekha. "Raiding Sugar Daddy." *Outlook*, November 24, 1997.

Ravindra, A., B. K. Chandrashekar, V. Govindraj, and P. S. S. Thomas. *The Committee on Urban Management of Bangalore City*. Submitted to the Government of Karnataka, Bangalore, Karnataka (1997).

Rodrik, Dani, and Arvind Subramanian. *From "Hindu Growth" to Productivity Surge: The Mystery of the Indian Growth Transition*. No. w10376. Cambridge, MA: National Bureau of Economic Research, 2004.

Rousseau, Jean-Jacques. *The Social Contract and Other Later Political Writings*. Cambridge: Cambridge University Press, 1997. Originally published in 1762.

Roy, Ananya. "What Is Urban About Critical Urban Theory?" *Urban Geography* 37, no. 6 (2016): 810–23.

———. "Why India Cannot Plan Its Cities: Informality, Insurgence and the Idiom of Urbanization." *Planning Theory* 8, no. 1 (2009): 76–87.

Roy, Ananya, and Aihwa Ong, eds. *Worlding Cities: Asian Experiments and the Art of Being Global*. Hoboken, NJ: John Wiley and Sons, 2011.

Rudolph, Lloyd, and Susanne Hoeber Rudolph. *In Pursuit of Lakshmi: The Political Economy of the Indian State*. Chicago: University of Chicago Press, 1987.

Sami, Neha. "From Farming to Development: Urban Coalitions in Pune, India." *International Journal of Urban and Regional Research* 37, no. 1 (2013): 151–64.

Sampat, Preeti, and Simi Sunny. "Dholera and the Myth of Voluntary Land Pooling." *Socio-Legal Review* 12, no. 2 (2016): 1–17.

Sanyal, Bishwapriya. "Antagonistic Cooperation: A Case Study of Nongovernmental Organizations, Government and Donors' Relationships in Income-Generating Projects in Bangladesh." *World Development* 19, no. 10 (1991): 1367–79.

Sassen, Saskia. *Territory, Authority, Rights: From Medieval to Global Assemblages.* Princeton, NJ: Princeton University Press, 2008.

Sastry, Trilochan. "How Commodity Cooperatives Differ from Milk or Sugar Cooperatives" (2011). Available at www.techsangam.com/2011/08/01/how-commodity-cooperatives-differ-from-milk-sugarcooperatives.

Scott, Allen J. *Regions and the World Economy: The Coming Shape of Global Production, Competition, and Political Order.* Oxford: Oxford University Press, 1999.

———. *The Urban Land Nexus and the State.* London: Pion, 1980.

Searle, Llerena. *Landscapes of Accumulation: Real Estate and the Neoliberal Imagination in Contemporary India.* Chicago: University of Chicago Press, 2016.

Sen, Amartya. *Poverty and Famines: An Essay on Entitlement and Deprivation.* Oxford: Oxford University Press, 1981.

Sennett, Richard. *Together: The Rituals, Pleasures and Politics of Cooperation.* New Haven, CT: Yale University Press, 2012.

Shiva, Vandana. *The Violence of the Green Revolution: Third World Agriculture, Ecology, and Politics.* Lexington: University Press of Kentucky, 2016.

Sivaramakrishnan, K. C. "Special Economic Zones: Issues of Urban Growth and Management." In *Special Economic Zones: Promise, Performance and Pending Issues.* New Delhi: Center for Policy Research, 2009: 93–114.

Slater, Tom. "Planetary Rent Gaps." *Antipode* 49, no. 1 (2017): 114–37.

Smith, Neil. *The New Urban Frontier: Gentrification and the Revanchist City.* London: Routledge, 1996.

———. *Uneven Development: Nature, Capital, and the Production of Space.* Athens: University of Georgia Press, 2010.

Srinivas, M. N. *The Dominant Caste and Other Essays.* New Delhi: Oxford University Press, 1987.

———. "The Dominant Caste in Rampura." *American Anthropologist* 61, no. 1 (1959): 1–16.

Starr, Paul. "The Meaning of Privatization." *Yale Law and Policy Review* 6, no. 1 (1988): 6–41.

Storper, Michael. *Keys to the City: How Economics, Institutions, Social Interaction, and Politics Shape Development.* Princeton, NJ: Princeton University Press, 2013.

Sud, Nikita. *Liberalization, Hindu Nationalism and the State: A Biography of Gujarat.* New Delhi: Oxford University Press, 2012.

Sukhtankar, Sandip. "Sweetening the Deal? Political Connections and Sugar Mills in India." *American Economic Journal: Applied Economics* (2012): 43–63.

Sweeney, Stuart. "Indian Railways and Famine 1875–1914: Magic Wheels and Empty Stomachs." *Essays in Economic and Business History* 26, no. 1 (2012): 147–57.

Teltumbde, Anand. "Behind the Ire of the Marathas." *Margin Speak* 51, no. 40 (2016): 10–11.

Tendler, Judith. *Good Government in the Tropics*. Baltimore: Johns Hopkins University Press, 1997.

Tendler, Judith, and Sara Freedheim. "Trust in a Rent-Seeking World: Health and Government Transformed in Northeast Brazil." *World Development* 22, no. 12 (1994): 1771–91.

Tewari, Meenu. "Successful Adjustment in Indian Industry: The Case of Ludhiana's Woolen Knitwear Cluster." *World Development* 27, no. 9 (1999): 1651–71.

Thorner, Daniel, ed. *Ecological and Agrarian Regions of South Asia Circa 1930*. Karachi: Oxford University Press, 1996.

———. *Investment in Empire: British Railways and Steam Shipping Enterprise in India, 1825–1949*. Philadelphia: University of Pennsylvania Press, 1977.

Tilly, Charles. "Processes and Mechanisms of Democratization." *Sociological Theory* 18, no. 1 (2000): 1–16.

———. "Trust and Rule." *Theory and Society* 33, no. 1 (2004): 1–30.

Varshney, Ashutosh. *Democracy, Development, and the Countryside: Urban-Rural Struggles in India*. Cambridge: Cambridge University Press, 1998.

———. "Is This India's Transformative Urban Moment?" *Indian Express*, August 25, 2011.

———. "Mass Politics or Elite Politics? India's Economic Reforms in Comparative Perspective." *Journal of Policy Reform* 2, no. 4 (1998): 301–35.

Vishnu, Uma. "Two Sides of an Expressway." *Indian Express*, May 15, 2011.

Visvanathan, Shiv. *From the Green Revolution to the Evergreen Revolution: Studies in Discourse Analysis*. IDS Seminar on Agriculture Biotechnology and the Developing World, 2003.

von Thünen, Johann Heinrich. *Isolated State*. Translated by Carla M. Wartenberg. Edited by Peter Hall. London: Pergamon, 1966.

Vora, Rajendra. "Shift of Power from Rural to Urban Sector." *Economic and Political Weekly* 31, nos. 2/3 (1996): 171–73.

———. *The World's First Anti-Dam Movement: The Mulshi Satyagraha, 1920–1924*. Delhi: Permanent Black, 2009.

Wadhwa, D. C. "Guaranteeing Title to Land: The Only Sensible Solution." World Bank, 2002. Available at siteresources.worldbank.org/INTINDIA/Resources/dc_wadhwa_paper.pdf.

Waghmare, Keshav. "Keshav Waghmare Writes About the Maratha Community." *Divya Marathi*, September 18, 2016.

Wagle, Subodh, Sachin Wargade, and Mandar Sathe. "Exploiting Policy Obscurity for Legalising Water Grabbing in the Era of Economic Reform: The Case of Maharashtra, India." *Water Alternatives* 5, no. 2 (2012): 412–30.

———. "Water Reallocation and Grabbing: Processes, Mechanisms, and Contributory Factors." Working Paper No. 2. Tata Institute of Social Studies, February 2013.

Weinstein, Liza. *The Durable Slum: Dharavi and the Right to Stay Put in Globalizing Mumbai*. Minneapolis: University of Minnesota Press, 2014.

White, Richard. *Railroaded: The Transcontinentals and the Making of Modern America*. New York: W. W. Norton, 2011.

Whyte, William Foote, and Kathleen King Whyte. *Making Mondragon: The Growth and Dynamics of the Worker Cooperative Complex*. Ithaca, NY: ILR Press, 1991.

Wolf, Eric R. *Peasant Wars of the Twentieth Century*. Norman: University of Oklahoma Press, 1969.

Wolford, Wendy. *This Land Is Ours Now: Social Mobilization and the Meanings of Land in Brazil*. Durham, NC: Duke University Press, 2010.

World Bank. *World Development Report 2009: Reshaping Economic Geography*. Washington, DC: World Bank, 2009.

Yadav, Yogendra. "Understanding the Second Democratic Upsurge: Trends of Bahujan Participation in Electoral Politics in the 1990s." In Francine R. Frankel, Zoya Hasan, Rajeeva Bhargava, and Balveer Arora, eds., *Transforming India: Social and Political Dynamics of Democracy*. Delhi: Oxford University Press, 2000: 120–45.

Yang, Anand. *Bazaar India: Markets, Society, and the Colonial State in Bihar*. Berkeley: University of California Press, 1999.

INDEX

ACKNOWLEDGMENTS

This book has been a few years in the making, and I have accrued numerous debts along the way. Susan Fainstein has been a role model in many ways, as an intellectual, as a woman mentor, and as a planner committed to spatial justice. Bish Sanyal and Jane Mansbridge have been unstintingly generous, both in scholarship and in mentorship. Narendar Pani made time for numerous conversations in our home city of Bengaluru, which helped ground me in the micro-politics of land in the raucous democracy that is India.

Research in India would not have been possible if not for the following scholars, activists, and bureaucrats: Suniti Suresh from the National Alliance for People's Movements, Suhas Palshikar at Pune University, Sachin Upadhye and Suvarna at Chaitanya, Shirish Kavadi and Amit Narkar at the National Center for Advocacy Studies, Ashish Kothari and Neema Pathak Broome at Kalpavriksh, Amitabh Kundu at JNU. Dr. Ravindra and Rajendra Kumar are a rare combination of bureaucrats who are also interested in research, and I learned much from them. My friend Anshuman Behera helped me check out library books, had spirited arguments with me on Marxism and Maoism in India, and in general, made it easier to settle into an intellectual life in Bengaluru. I was extremely fortunate to have had a few conversations with Prof. B. S. Baviskar in Delhi during the early phase of fieldwork. I met him, aware of how seminal his work on sugar cooperatives was for agrarian studies; little did I realize then how fundamental his work would continue to be for understanding contemporary urbanization. A major source of data in this book was the ready reckoner rate for agricultural land for 242 villages in western Maharashtra. At a time when media reports are rife with sordid stories of tahsildars and other bureaucrats involved in corrupt land deals, I am grateful that I came to know Mr. N. R. Kawale, Department of Registration and Stamps, Mumbai. Mr. Kawale not only helped me understand the challenges that bureaucrats face in regulating a liberalizing land market, but also called and set up appointments with various tahsildars both for data and for a ground-up view on the making of new real-estate markets. The interviews with bureaucrats were humbling, not least because many of them were genuinely public servants. Various residents in the corridor region (whose names are changed in this book) were in the throes of high-stakes, grave struggles, and yet they spared the time to talk to a researcher, and that too, over a span of many months; for their insights and time, I am beyond grateful.

In growing this project, I benefited immensely from the manuscript workshop supported by the Harvard Weatherhead Center for International Affairs, with Patrick Heller, Michael Goldman, Bish Sanyal, and Meenu Tewari offering incredibly helpful feedback on organizing the themes of the book. For giving me a chance to present parts of the manuscript at workshops and to gain invaluable feedback, I am thankful to Debjani Bhattacharya, Liza Bjorkman, Sanjoy Chakravorty, Mark Frazier, Ashok Gurung, Vicki Hattam, Marie-Hélène Zérah, Devesh Kapur, Sudhir Krishnaswamy, Laura Liu, Brian McGrath, Partha Mukhopadhyay, Balakrishnan Rajagopal, Champaka Rajagopal, Chella Rajan, Hashim Sarkis, Gavin Shatkin, Ajantha Subramanian, Vishnupad, and Namita Wahi.

Various colleagues in Cambridge, Massachusetts, supported this work in many ways. Neil Brenner and Arindam Dutta were the source of many inspiring conversations and ideas. Rahul Mehrotra and Jerold Kayden ensured that I had protected time for research and writing. Eve Blau, Diane Davis, Ann Forsyth, José Gómez-Ibáñez, and Rick Pieser created a collegial working environment. Sonja Dümpelmann and Mike Hooper helped me get through the vicissitudes of faculty life with humor and laughter. Brent Ryan, Tulasi Srinivas, Lakshmi Srinivas, and Lawrence Vale offered sage counsel on the publishing process. Scholars at previous institutions continued to be supportive interlocutors and mentors. Bob (Robert) Lake always found the time to engage patiently with my work and to situate even the most mundane planning practices in philosophical and ethical arguments. Exchanges with Bob on Polanyi opened up for me new ways of reading a seminal text. Katharina Pistor is a formidable mind and a wise and witty mentor, and the year spent at her center was filled with all sorts of learning, from how to do interdisciplinary research to how to navigate the U.S academy as a woman.

I am also fortunate to have found in Cambridge a community of scholars who double as good friends. The CAtS reading group with dear friends Ateya Khorakiwala and Chitra Venkatramani provided intellectual comradeship and nourishing camaraderie. I relied greatly on the razor-sharp critiques of Tijs Van Maasakkers, who made time to read various drafts of the manuscript. The summer writing group with Namita Dharia, Nick Smith, and Anand Vaidya was a warm, supportive space for exploring ideas. Other friends who read and helpfully commented on drafts were Gautam Bhan, Karthik Rao Cavale, Brian Goldstein, Atul Pokharel, Abby Spinak, Delia Wendel, and Raile Rocky Ziipao.

A special note of thanks to students in my "spatial politics of land" and "urbanization" seminars, who kept the classroom alive with critical argument. I draw immense hope from knowing that these are the people who are going to go out and plan and design our cities and staff our public-sector agencies. Thanks to Scott Walker and Mark Heller for preparing the GIS maps and to Aslam Saiyad for taking the cover photograph. At the University of Pennsylvania Press, I am grateful to Genie Birch and Susan Wachter, the series editors, for their support for the book, and to the two anonymous reviewers for their constructive feedback. I am also thankful to Peter Agree, the acquisitions editor, and his team for shepherding the manuscript smoothly from proposal to print.

It feels trite to even write a note of thanks to my family. My grandfathers lived through the Green Revolution: Sankaran thatha finished his PhD and started his entomology career as a Nehruvian bureaucrat in Delhi; Manne thatha dropped out of middle school and became involved in credit and politics in a Green Revolution village. Their lives could not have been more different and yet so connected by development politics. I miss them dearly. My father has been my bedrock of support. It was he who first came across the Khed SEZ in a newspaper article. I went to Khed on a hunch, and the case became the center of this book. To the women who are my anchors—my amma and paati—all my love and gratitude.